Blood Sweat and Teabags

K P Dee

Copyright © 2014 K P Dee
All Rights Reserved

The moral right of K P Dee to be identified as the author of this work has been asserted by him in accordance with Copyright, Designs and Patent Act 1988.

Take an exhilarating Ambulance ride through the 1970's Streets of Liverpool

This is a memoir of my time as an Ambulance man in Liverpool, which spans the years of 1969 to 1979.

From my nervous and apprehensive beginning, to becoming a seasoned and experienced Ambulance person. I attempt to let you, the reader, take that journey with me.

No two calls are ever the same; each has its own unique scenario and characters.

It's not just about 'blood and guts' Its about little old ladies, pompous doctors, violent drunks, sinister characters, tea and biscuits, impromptu parties, extra marital affairs, sudden death, spooky experiences, laughing, sadness and of course, those things that happen behind the scenes of a public Ambulance service..

Over those ten years I also had the personal experiences of my mother's death, getting married to a childhood sweetheart, then finding the marriage on a slippery slope that would end in divorce.

For my wonderful girls

1

"On the downside" said Vinny, "there might be the odd occasion when you'll have to go to road accidents, scrape up bodies with a shovel and put them in a sack but I should imagine it's only those who have been run over by a bus or a large truck, or maybe a steamroller."

I was sitting in the lounge bar of the Broadway pub with two of my friends who I went to school with, Vinny Stevens and Tony Hopkins.

Vinny had enrolled and was training to be a male nurse at Belmont General Hospital which was adjacent to the building that housed the Liverpool Ambulance Service headquarters.

He was the one who suggested that I apply for a job with the Ambulance service, claiming knowledge to the finer arts of what goes on in the Ambulance Service because he worked in the building next door and could see the Ambulance people through the windows.

The upside, he had said, was that the Ambulance drivers sat around all day with their feet up drinking tea and reading the newspaper, and it was this information that decided it was probably the right career path for me to follow

Tony had signed up to join the army and was just waiting for the Queen's shilling, or whatever it is they wait for, to come through the post.

It was that certain time in life that inevitably arrives and would see three teenage school friends go their separate ways into the big wide world.

Two weeks later, it was a dark, cold, damp and a drizzly morning at 7.45am on January 29th 1969. After an hour and a half bus journey I was finally standing outside the old combined courthouse and police station in Quarry Street, in the Woolton district of Liverpool.

Built of sandstone in the early 1800's, it was no longer used for its original purpose. It was now the training school for Liverpool Ambulance Service.

Day one of my new working life had arrived!

I was nervous and apprehensive, as anyone might be when starting a new job. I lingered outside for a moment, gathering my courage before entering, deliberating if I should, or shouldn't go ahead with this; after all, this wasn't the only job in the world and scraping people up with a shovel wasn't exactly an endearing prospect.

Two large heavy wooden doors painted green marked the entrance. Only one of the doors would open, the other was heavily bolted into place.

Deliberations complete, I took a deep breath and went in. I entered a neat vestibule; opened a glass-panelled interior door;

then stepped into a square foyer which had walls painted in a plain cream colour but was otherwise bare, no pictures or posters, no signs, nothing. The high ceiling sported lots of elaborate plasterwork and was painted white.

Ahead of me rose a wide, varnished but carpet less staircase leading towards the rear of the building. The floor was a mix of red, brown and black mosaic tiles and the room smelled strongly of soap and disinfectant. There were no seats but each sidewall housed a closed door, devoid of signs on them. I wondered if I had the correct entrance.

Just then I heard muted voices beyond the left door so I crossed to it; paused and listened for a moment, took another deep breath and knocked. The voices stopped and I heard footsteps padding towards the door. It opened to reveal a bloke of about my own age, dressed in jeans with blue shirt and red tie, he gave me a quick once over. I felt over dressed in my suit and overcoat.

"Are you starting today as well?"

I just nodded.

"You better come in and join the rest of us then."

The room I entered had a bay window that looked out onto Quarry Street, or would have if they hadn't had the frosted film over the glass. It was basically a classroom with ten separate desks, arranged in two horizontal rows of five. A large blackboard hung on the wall behind what looked to be a dining table trying its best to look like a teacher's desk.

The décor was two tones, white and grey with the same mosaic floor tiles as the foyer.

Opposite the entrance was another door which led through to a small lounge and separate kitchen area. In the lounge was an open fire which had been lit and was now settling with a new shovel load of coal.

I counted five others in the lounge as I entered, including the one who had opened the door for me. I would later learn that his name was Steve. They were all about my age and dressed in civilian clothes. These were my fellow cadets who were newbie's just like me.

"Alright?" I said. Not to anyone of them in particular.

"Grab yourself a cuppa, mate" said one of them.

"There's a pot just been made in the kitchen" said another.

"Cheers." I said, and went to help myself.

We all sat around a formica topped dining table that had seen better years, groping our mugs of tea around the sides to keep our hands warm.

General chit chat ensued, finding out who each of us was, where we lived, what we did before joining the Ambulance Service and who could drive and who couldn't.

It transpired that only Steve, who had opened the door for me and Terry, who had told me to grab a cuppa, had full driving licences. No one else did, including me. Out of those two, only Terry actually had a car, a baby Austin.

Our chattering was interrupted.

"OK lads" A uniformed officer peered through the doorway. "Into the classroom please."

We all shuffled into the room, some still carrying mugs of tea. A second but much shorter officer was standing by the blackboard and growled.

"You can lose those mugs for a start, we'll have no mugs in here if you don't mind." He smiled at his own little joke.

Those who didn't have to traipse back to the kitchen with their mugs, me being one of them, chose a desk to sit at. I selected the third desk on the left near the back row, a strategy reminiscent of my school days when I always sat as far back as possible, there being less chance of being picked on by the teacher, or at least that was the theory, but it wasn't fool proof by any means.

The taller of the two officers must have been in his forties, about six feet tall. He was smartly dressed but looked a little too thin for his uniform. There was a slight gap between his shirt collar and his neck. His thick dark hair was combed back and he had the thickest and blackest eyebrows I'd ever seen, I wondered if he was any relation to Dracula. He had piercing brown eyes that looked as if they could see right into your soul and a hooked nose that you could open a tin of beans with. His accent denoted that he was a Lancashire lad, and not indigenous to Liverpool.

The second officer who scowled at the tea drinkers was much shorter and much older. I am five foot nine and felt as though I could have towered over him. He had thick grey hair and a thick grey nicotine stained moustache to match. He must have been in his sixties but looked strong and muscular. His tunic sported several rows of multi coloured ribbons over his left breast pocket. I presumed military service. Although in full dress uniform, he somehow looked a little dishevelled.

"My name is Mr Potts." said the taller one; "And this is Mr Jones." Mr Jones nodded.

We all mumbled a " Morning" but not necessarily in unison.

Mr Jones now left the room.

Mr Potts continued. "You will all be collectively known as 'H' squad, which obviously means that you are the eighth squad of cadets since the cadet scheme was started."

Mr Potts advised us that we were to be paid weekly on a Thursday starting in two weeks time, the princely sum of eight pounds, fifteen shillings, weekly in arrears.

However, we were advised, we had to purchase a book called 'Anatomy and Physiology for Nurses' published by 'Bailliere and Tindall'; it cost one pound fifteen and six. Did anyone need a sub from their wages to purchase this?

My hand went up straight away, as did everyone else. It was going to cost me a small fortune for the bus fare to this place each day, never mind having to buy books. No one said we had to buy books!

As if by magic, Mr Jones opened the door and returned to the classroom with an arm full of books aptly entitled 'Anatomy and Physiology for Nurses.' A smirk was evident on his face as he placed one on each of our desks. With the task done he departed from the room again.

After this, Mr Potts spoke again.

"This book will be your property when you have paid for it, but until that time it remains the property of Liverpool Ambulance service, so don't lose or deface it until it's paid for."

We all flicked through the pages; there were lots of diagrams of body bits and lots of medical sounding words that I thought I would never be able to pronounce.

"Ob,ob,sir." Steve stuck his hand in the air.

Steve was lanky and skinny, looking as if he'd just crawled out of bed and quickly dressed in clothes that had been lying on the bedroom floor all night. He reminded me of a lad at my old school who was just the same, except the lad had had a permanent gravy stain down the front of his tie, where as Steve had a clean but creased tie.

We were later to find out that it was quite natural for Steve to look the way he did.

Everyone looked at each other as Steve spoke. What did the "Ob" mean before he said something?

"Yes." said Mr Potts

"Ob, can we sort of pay for this in two instalments instead of a one off payment?"

"What's your name son"?

"Ob, Steve Findlay, sir"

"Do you have a speech impediment Mr Findley"?

"Ob,ob, no sir, why sir"?

I felt a little embarrassed for him. He was sitting at the front and couldn't see the others sitting behind him mouthing ob, ob, ob to each other like a gold fish in a bowl, I suspected he could hear the sniggering though, and I have to admit that included me.

"Never mind" said Mr Potts, "You can pay it back over two weeks if that makes things easier for you."

"Thanks sir."

"And, Mr Findlay we're not at school now, you can address me as Mr Potts and I'll give you the same courtesy."

"Ob,Yes sir" said Steve.

Mr Potts raised his eyes momentarily and then looked back despairingly at Steve.

Most of that morning was spent filling out forms and being told what was expected of us in the coming months. I learned the names of the other cadets, who were Terry Clancy, Steve Findlay, (who was from now on to be nick named "Ob.") George Marley, John Jones and Gary Brough.

We found out later that Steve almost always said "Ob" before making any sort of statement, particularly if he was under any pressure. In his mind it came out as an 'Ahm', but to others it definitely came out as an 'Ob' He said he'd always done it and never even thought about it when speaking. I thought he probably had adenoid problems.

Lunch time arrived and we all spilled out of the building and walked to the chip shop just a little further up the street.

I just had enough money on me to get a bag of chips and ten cigarettes from the paper shop that was a few doors further up from the Chippy, leaving me with just enough bus fare to get home later.

I was last in the queue at the chip shop, so I decided to go and get the cigarettes first and give the queue time to thin out a bit.

The woman in the paper shop looked up from what she was doing and smiled as I walked in. I reckoned she must have been about thirty five, but I instantly found her quite attractive for her age. Being slim with dark shoulder length hair that curled under her chin, brown eyes and an attractive smile, she reminded me of Sandy Shaw. I'm not sure why I found her attractive, maybe it was the hairstyle or maybe because I had a bit of a crush on Sandy Shaw. She was wearing a pretty blue flowery mini dress that emphasised her shapely long legs

"Hello" she said.

"Hi."

I could feel myself getting those butterfly feelings in my tummy, which was stupid, and anyway she was much older than me. She wouldn't want anything to do with a bumbling teenager.

She continued to smile, but it wasn't a smile to welcome a customer who was about to make a purchase; there was something more to it, or was I imagining this?

"Er, can I have ten Number 6 please?"

She reached up to the cigarette shelf to get the packet, which had the effect of shortening the already short dress, I was mesmerised and she caught me looking.

"Are you working around here then?"

"Yes, at the Ambulance place down the street."

"I thought you might be" she put the packet on the counter top as I dug into my trouser pocket for the money.

"First day is it?" she enquired

I was stuck for words. Here was a really attractive woman making conversation, who had caught me looking at her legs and didn't scold me for it, and I was stuck for something clever and witty to say.

"Yes, does it show that much?"

"Just a guess." she smiled.

I paid for the cigarettes.

"What's your name then?" I blurted it out.

She took the money and rung it into the till. "Jane, she said, and what's yours?"

"Ken." I replied. Then there was that dreaded silence which seems to go on forever when you have no idea of what to say to continue the conversation.

"I suppose I'll see you again, next time I pop in?" It was all I could manage, but it broke the silence.

"You'll be in your uniform then?" she said with a smile turning up the corners of her very kissable lips.

"I suppose so, yes"

"I do like a bloke in uniform."

I felt my face go crimson, I was getting the come on and I was making a total mess of it. I could only smile.

"I'll see you soon then." I said as I opened the door, hoping I had appeared mature.

"I hope so." she replied and gave me a wink.

"Bloody hell." I said quietly to myself as I padded towards the chip shop. Girls my own age always wanted to play hard to get, but this was a mature woman and she didn't hang around.

I made the decision to keep my brief encounter in the paper shop to myself, I didn't know these lads well enough to trust them yet with such intimate secrets. I could see them walking back to the school, eating chips from the newspaper as they went. I was second in the queue now.

The afternoon was spent by having a tour of the building, visiting the old jail cells down in the cellar, and then the court yard at the back of the building which was enclosed by very high walls.

Mr Jones, who seemed to be in charge for the afternoon, told us this was where they used to hang prisoners, so we should all be on our best behaviour lest the same fate should befall us. The glint in his eye and smirk on his face as he told us the story belied the serious delivery of this information and gave way to the fact that he was pulling our legs! It was probably just an exercise yard for the unfortunates who inhabited the dank rooms down in the cellar. Nonetheless the place was creepy, and nobody doubted him when he told us the building was haunted.

Out of bounds were the crew rooms on the far side of the building, and out of bounds also was upstairs.

Later that afternoon, we followed him up the foyer staircase to the first floor landing. A sharp left turn took us along a passage towards the front of the building, where a large arched window gave the only view of the world outside. Near that, window another staircase swept back and up towards a second floor.

On the first floor landing, a wide oak panelled door opened into a large and high ceiling hall with arched wooden beams to support it, it reminded me of the interior of a church. A bay window larger than that downstairs, dominated at the front of the room, allowing the winter daylight to cast eerie shadows on what was evidently the old courtroom. Most of the fixtures had been removed, but there still remained fixed wooden bench seats along most of the far wall.

Floorboards creaked and echoed around the empty hall as we all shuffled in to take a closer look. Mr Jones explained that indeed this had been the old courtroom. He pointed to a smaller door at the back and described how prisoners, who had been found guilty of whatever charge, were sent through and down a flight of stairs to the cells below. Hence the saying "Sent down." The place gave me the creeps.

We continued further upstairs into a large attic room. The daylight filtered in through frosted glass windows set into the pitch of the roof. Along the far wall were rows and rows of black uniform tunics and trousers that hung from those chrome rails that you see in large department stores. Cardboard boxes were stacked against the opposite wall and some others lay opened on the floor, revealing new blue shirts in their plastic wrapping. This was obviously the store room.

We were each issued with a tunic that was a reasonable fit off the rail and two pairs of trousers, five collarless shirts, five collars and one set of studs. I had never worn a stud collar before, but I'd seen my dad wearing one, he'd have to help me out. All the shirts were long sleeved. Five pairs of black socks and one pair of black work shoes. Next, the peaked caps. After that the cap badge, which we would have to attach ourselves, a lilac coloured hat band and epaulettes of the same colour to wear on our tunics, to announce to the world that we were cadets, and last but not least, a black tie.

Mr Jones found some empty boxes in the corner and gave us one each, to place our kit into; then we all padded downstairs, back to the class room.

I put my new Anatomy and Physiology book in my box.

It was nearly three o'clock; the day had flown over and only a couple of hours to go.

Mr Jones, entered the classroom a few minutes later.

"Right then." he said. "That's your uniform issued and I want to see you wearing it when you arrive here tomorrow morning. When you're outside in public you'll wear your cap at all times. If you're seen without it, you'll be in serious shit."

He waited for a moment to see if he got any feedback on what he had just said. As no one said anything, he looked at his watch.

"Then, you can all get away early to give you time to sort out your uniform for tomorrow."

This was brilliant news as it take me a good hour and a half on the bus to get home. Then more good news, Terry asked me if I wanted a lift as he could drop me on Queens Drive, which was then just a ten minute bus ride to get home.

My first day had gone well; clutching my box of goodies on my knee in Terry's car on the way home, I wondered what Jane might think of me in my uniform tomorrow?.

I'm the youngest of three brothers, of which the eldest, Kevin, had died when I was six years old. He was just fifteen and had contracted rheumatic fever which eventually led to his demise.

My other brother, Bernard. Is five years older than me and had recently married and moved away to live in the Wirral. This left just me and my parents living in a three bedroom council house in the Norris Green area of Liverpool.

Being the youngest, I was familiar with the 'hand me down' method of clothing distribution between siblings, so arriving home with a box full of new uniform items was akin to having just received a birthday and Christmas present all rolled into one.

I could see the pride in my mothers face when I had first worn the uniform and inspected myself in the mirror on that first night. I think she was proud that I had a decent job with decent prospects and wouldn't end up working in a factory like my father, who we hardly ever saw. He was either at work or in the pub.

2

The following morning we all arrived at the training school in uniform.

I felt a little embarrassed being out in public wearing a uniform that was almost a carbon copy of a policeman's outfit and felt quite conspicuous as people stared at me on the bus, but I would soon get used to it.

George had arrived first on that morning and had busied himself by getting the coal fire started in the grate in the lounge. The dark mornings were bitter cold and we only had the fire as a means to provide heat. There was a back boiler to the fire which would heat up the radiators in the class room, so it was crucial to get the fire going in order that we didn't have to sit in a cold class room all day.

There was a small kitchen off the lounge, which had the usual sink, taps and draining board, along with an electric cooker which had seen better days, an electric kettle and a few cupboards screwed to the wall, and that was it.

There was a door that led into a small yard outside where a coal bunker could be accessed. We would learn that the service would provide one bag of coal per week; if we wanted more than that, we would either freeze or have to buy our own. Back in the kitchen and behind the door was a cardboard box that was half full with kindling wood; this too would be replenished each week.

The six of us devised a rota; George would make and light the fire each morning, he had been doing it for years at home and didn't mind continuing the tradition at work. Steve would be in charge of making the tea and toast. I volunteered to get the milk and whatever else we might need from the shop each morning, for obvious reasons, while Terry, John and Gary would keep the place clean.

It soon emerged that George was the practical joker in our group. We were all handed a folded piece of white card and asked by Mr Jones to write our names clearly in print and then place it on the front of our desks so he would know who was who, which we all dutiful did. After lunch, George swapped all the name cards around; I had now become Terry Clancy. It seemed to work as Mr Jones didn't appear to notice we had all suddenly changed names; that is until the end of the day when he quietly and calmly picked up all the name cards and put them back on the appropriate desks. "Tch tch, not very original." he said to no one in particular.

The classroom days were going well; for the first three weeks we had undertaken a first aid course, and we had all been issued, free of charge, a dog eared volume of a first aid manual according to St John. It was the basic requirement before we embarked on more academic matters like anatomy and physiology.

It emerged that John was the swat amongst us. He was about five foot nine, the same height as me. He also had the same black hair, but his hung straight, where as mine was almost curly. However, where his eyes were brown, mine are blue.

Steve was a 'come day go day' type of person with not a care in the world which showed in his dress sense; he still looked dishevelled even in uniform. He was about five foot ten; brown tight curly hair and his body shape could only be described as thin and straight.

Terry was a fidget and never seemed to be able to sit still. He had ginger hair, which was cut short. He was about the same height as John and me, but a little thinner.

George was cool, calm and collected in everything he did. He was the broadest of us all, not chubby, more thick set.

Gary was as quiet and as shy as a mouse. He was taller than any of us, probably six foot; his hair was straight and a mousey brown colour. As for me, I might have been regarded as a bit of a swat, like John, but I didn't think I was, I just enjoyed what I was doing.

The rota we had devised amongst ourselves on that second day was working well. I was getting into the shop each morning for a bottle of milk. Even after a few weeks I was still as nervous as hell when I walked through the door into the shop. I was finding Jane to be more attractive each time I saw her.

I was quite enjoying the learning. At first I thought anatomy and physiology would be difficult subjects to get my head around, but I found it interesting and I think that's what makes the learning process easier. If you enjoy it, you learn it.

Mr Potts, who we now knew to be Walter Potts, aka 'Wally' behind his back, was quite a good tutor when it came to the theory side of things. He could explain what appeared to be complicated subjects, like the nervous system, in simple terms, which made it easier to learn, whereas Mr Jones, now known as 'Harry' behind his back, was more at home with the practical aspects of things like resuscitation, bandaging and splints.

Four weeks had passed and I was really enjoying it, considering that I had been so apprehensive about starting in the Ambulance Service in the first place. I was elated when we were handed our first aid certificates. The only other certificate I ever had was for swimming six lengths of the pool when I was in junior school.

I felt as though I had achieved something worthwhile. I felt really proud and I couldn't wait to take it home and show my mother.

In the beginning I had known there would be classroom study and some sort of disciplined regime and this had put me off a little. I was eighteen, nearly nineteen, so why did I want to go back to a school type scenario?

My original plan was that I could always leave the Ambulance service and get another job if I didn't like it. There was plenty of work out there in the factories, but that would mean I was following in my father's footsteps and there was no way on this earth I was going to do that.

My father was a disciplinarian and had ruled the house with the constant threat of physical punishment. When I was a kid it wasn't uncommon to get a smack across the head for some minor misdemeanour; even my mother wasn't immune to physical abuse. However, these days it was just a constant atmosphere of tension whenever he was around the house. I was older and bigger and he must have known that I was more than able enough to retaliate.

I had received my second pay packet and now had a few quid in my pocket. I decided to pluck up the courage and ask Jane from the shop if she fancied going out for a drink one night.

I'd been going into the shop nearly every day to buy the milk and I felt as if Jane and I were getting on quite well.

I had started to relax and was now able to have a conversation or tell a few jokes without feeling like a fumbling teenager. It did get a bit awkward sometimes though, if another customer came in and I just stood there being quiet looking at my shoes waiting for them to be served and leave.

I finally plucked up the courage to ask her out for a drink. I thought she might laugh and tell me to sod off, that I was too young for her or that I should be going out with girls of my own age; but no, it was the opposite. She said she'd love to!

My heart leapt when she agreed. All sorts of things raced through my head. Most of all what do you do on a date with a woman who's practically old enough to be your mother?

This was on the Friday and we agreed to meet up in the Turk's Head pub just a few roads away in the main part of a local village at 8 o'clock the following night. We could get something to eat and have a few drinks.

All through Saturday my stomach was churning. What should I wear? Will I make an idiot of myself? Should I take a condom?

I stepped off the bus and took the short walk to the Turk's Head. I knew she wouldn't be in there yet, as we had agreed that I should get there first at around quarter to eight so she didn't have to be in the pub waiting on her own if I was a bit late, having to come so far and relying on the bus being on time.

I stood at the bar, ordered a pint and booked a table for a meal. This was going to cost, but what the heck, I wouldn't have missed it for the world!

It got to half past eight and I had just drained my pint and was about to cancel the table and go home feeling very rejected at being stood up, when she walked in. She looked flustered as if she had been in a hurry. She spotted me straight away and came to join me at the bar. A little flustered and slightly short of breath because of rushing, she apologised.

"I'm really sorry I'm late, the baby sitters didn't turn up till twenty minutes ago."

"That's alright, don't worry about it, you're here now," I said, with a hopefully convincing smile that hid my thoughts. Bloody hell, I didn't know she had kids! It hadn't crossed my mind to ask. I'd never been out with someone who had kids.

I ordered a couple more drinks and we sat down at the table. She took off her coat to reveal a black mini dress adorned with a gold belt around her waist; her legs were long and shapely and looked tanned. She was wearing shiny black shoes, almost high heels but not quite. There was a tantalising glimpse of cleavage beneath a v neckline. She excused herself to go to the ladies room.

I watched as she walked back to the table in a confident manner; I noticed heads turning as she past other tables. She looked stunning.

The evening passed quickly, it seemed like time had flown by. It all went well and we chatted about most things. I was very relaxed with her now and felt more comfortable in her company.
She must have seen the look on my face when I was handed the bill, and offered to pay half. I thought I had kept enough of a straight face when I saw the amount but obviously I hadn't. I declined her offer and made light of it. I would be broke until next pay day, but what the hell, I was enjoying myself.
It was then she asked if I wanted to go back to her house for a coffee.

The baby sitters, two young girls, had gone as soon as they had been paid and we were now alone in her house.

It was a modern, private house, nicely decorated and clean. It was on a new housing estate, about a twenty minute walk from Quarry Street where we both worked. She had two children; both boys aged seven and nine. They were upstairs fast asleep in bed.
We had coffee and she turned on the radio for some music; radio Caroline was playing Albatross by Fleetwood Mac, then she turned down the lights.

We both sat on the couch. I put my arm around her shoulder and she nestled her head into my neck. We sat like that for a while saying nothing, just listening to the music.

I decided to take a chance; I pulled away a little, raised her head and began to kiss her. I didn't know how she would react to this, but to my delight she was equally enthusiastic. The kissing began to get a little heated, more passionate. I slowly slid my hand from her waist up to her left breast and gently massaged her. I was certainly expecting to have my hand pushed away; it's what usually happened with girls my own age. But no, it had the opposite effect. Jane began to make groaning noises as we still kissed, she was quite happy to let me caress her boobs.

Then totally out of the blue, and completely unexpected, she started rubbing her hand over my crotch. There was no way of hiding my readiness for her now, she could feel it.

After a few minutes, she pulled away from kissing and whispered in my ear.

"Do you want to stay for the night?"

I couldn't believe what I was hearing, as we both knew what that meant. I told her that I'd love to, but what about the kids?

The only condition was that I was up and gone before the children woke up and saw me.

"What time do they usually get up?" I asked.

"About six."

I looked at my watch, it was just gone midnight. "Ok." It was a deal.

She got up, turned off the music and lights then took my hand, leading me out of the room. As she went upstairs ahead of me, still holding my hand, she placed the forefinger of her other hand over her lips, the gesture to keep quiet. My heart was pounding away inside my chest and I wondered if she could hear it, or if it might wake the kids.

On the landing, she opened a door quietly and guided me into the room beyond. A small bedside lamp barely illuminated the bedroom. Jane quickly slipped out of her clothes and tossed them onto the floor. She was naked and looked good. Her boobs probably weren't as pert as she would have liked them, but they looked good to me.

I was about to strip off my clothes, but she stopped me and took charge of the undressing. She had her back to the bed as I faced her and I let her remove my clothes until I was naked too.

She pulled me towards her and we kissed passionately. My hands were all over her and her's over me.

Then without warning, she sat down on the edge of the bed and took hold of me. I was still standing and my world was about to change forever as she pulled me closer and took me in her mouth. I had never had this done to me before. I'd heard stories about it, but didn't think any woman would ever want to do such a thing.

I had to grab hold of the headboard with my left hand as I felt my knees and legs beginning to buckle. The pleasure was so intense I hadn't noticed myself groaning. I had to place my other hand on her head; she had lovely silky smooth hair. I noticed that she was groaning quietly too as her head moved gently back and forth. Then it happened, I just couldn't hold out any longer and it felt as though my world had exploded. This seemed to encourage Jane; she stayed where she was and continued with increased vigour.

I was spent, but I was still enjoying what she was doing. Then I realised something, she would still want me to kiss her, I would have to kiss her knowing where her mouth had been and what she had taken in. I didn't relish the thought. Then, even worse, would she want me to reciprocate? The thoughts must have dampened my ardour and I could feel this was the case.

Jane pulled away and looked up at me, she smiled. "Was that nice, big boy?"
I crouched down to be eye level with her. "More than nice." Then I kissed her.
We climbed into the bed and kissed and cuddled for a while, and then I slid my hand down her thigh and explored her. I was ready again.
Jane was moaning quietly as I fondled and caressed her, she had her eyes closed as I lay on my side and watched her.
Then she whispered. "Make love to me." And I did.

It was four in the morning as I let myself out as quietly as possible through her front door. It was dark and cold, but at the time I didn't care. I had just spent four hours of pure ecstasy with a woman who had just taught me how to make love, and done things to me that I only ever fantasised about. Past fumbled teenage experiences faded into oblivion. She had been my Mrs Robinson, from the song by Simon and Garfunkel.

I walked along the bus route home for an hour before the first bus of the day came along, I'd forgotten that it was Sunday and buses were less frequent. I had to make a hundred yard dash to the bus stop to catch it. It was empty and cold on board, but I didn't mind, I was on cloud nine.

I arrived home around seven in the morning. It was still dark and I was looking forward to getting some sleep. Jane had exhausted me.

I had expected my parents to be in bed, but the downstairs lights were on as I walked down the path and opened the front door. I walked through to the kitchen to see my mother leaning over the sink. She was pale and wasn't looking well.
"What's wrong?"

She looked weary and explained that she hadn't slept much through the night; she had a persistent cough that stopped her sleeping, so she had come down stairs to make a cup of tea. The coughing had continued and now she was coughing up blood.
This worried me a little, but I knew that a persistent cough like she had could burst tiny little blood vessels which could result in blood streaked phlegm. The alternative reason for the blood didn't bear thinking about.

I told her to go and lie down on the couch and then I covered her with a couple of overcoats. I made her a cup of tea and lit the coal fire in the grate. She drank her tea and drifted off to sleep as the room got warmer. I headed off upstairs to bed for a few hours sleep.

I saw Jane a few times after that first night, always ending up at her place with me having to leave in the early hours of the morning. After a few weeks, she suddenly seemed to be hesitant about meeting me, claiming she couldn't get baby sitters, or her sister was staying with her for a while. She always had excuses. The relationship sort of drifted apart. We stayed friendly though and I still saw her in the shop now and again. I think she might have been a bit fed up with me not having a car or earning much money to go places and do things. I didn't know though, that was just my take on things.

As the weeks passed I saw less and less of Jane as 'H' squad were given individual time tables for training placements, each placement being of four weeks duration. Our attendance at Quarry Street was diluted to one day per month for refresher training and handing in our placement assignments.

It was early April of 1969 when my mother was diagnosed with cancer. After the episode in the kitchen when she was coughing up blood, she was reluctant but eventually had gone to see our GP who had sent her for tests at Broadgreen Hospital, where the tests had shown she had a tumour on her lung. It felt as if a dark cloud had descended over me on the day I got the news. I knew deep down that things had changed for ever.

We were told it was terminal, but there was just a slight chance of remission if she started a course of radiotherapy treatment.

I was relieved when she was admitted to Clatterbridge hospital in Cheshire, where they had the most up to date radiotherapy equipment for treating the illness. The only problem was the distance to travel for visiting; it was made difficult as we didn't own a car. Public transport was unreliable and haphazard with multiple changes. It would have taken several hours journey time, so by the time we could get there, visiting time would be almost over.

We were limited to weekend visits only, when my auntie could take my father and me in her car. On occasions my father couldn't make it because he would be at work.

Our visits would be spent mostly with mum walking around the hospital gardens, sitting in the café, even going out to local pubs for a meal. She enjoyed that. After the first week of her treatment she appeared to be improving, looking better and happier in herself, and I was glad to see it.

3

My first placement was with the transport officer at Walton Hospital, not the most exciting place to be as it meant being stuck in a cramped office and filing paperwork all day.

John Jones had the best placement, driving tuition. George was going to the Southern Hospital Casualty department, while Ob and Terry were seconded to the internal Ambulance at Walton Hospital where they would help transport patients from various hospital wards to remote outpatient departments within the hospital grounds. This was necessary because part of the hospital was newly built and part was still a Victorian building and not all corridors and passageways were interconnected, so certain stretcher patients needed to be transported by an internal ambulance through out the grounds to varying departments .

Terry and Ob already had driving licences, so this would be good experience for them to learn patient handling. It helped me too, as it meant I wouldn't be on my own at the hospital and we could meet up at lunch times. Gary was seconded to the transport officer at Broad Green hospital.

My placement at Walton Hospital seemed to last forever, as the hours seemed endless and the work mundane.

I was stuck in an office not much bigger than ten foot by ten foot, squeezed into a chair in a space next to the transport officer's desk and the wall. I wasn't particularly fond of Malcolm, the transport officer, either. Tall and thin with a narrow pencil type moustache, he must have been in his sixties. He was an arrogant character who didn't seem to have an ounce of humour in him, he reminded me of my father. His attitude towards cadets nearly had me walking out of that room on more than one occasion.

Rumour had it that he had been a sergeant in the marines and joined the ambulance service after being de-mobbed. He'd done his time on the road and was now seeing out his later years towards retirement as a rank 6 officer manning a desk job.

The room always seemed to be in a haze of fog from his chain smoking, but I gritted my teeth and stuck it out because I had come too far in my training to give up now. My next placement was in the control room, but after that it would be driving tuition and I wasn't going to miss that for anything.

I suppose I did get to learn the ins and outs of the Patient Transport System or PTS, which brings people into hospital for out patient appointments. It is a well honed logistical undertaking in terms of getting them all in for morning appointments, hopefully on time, then getting them all home again. The same procedure was repeated in the afternoon.

Depending on how many patients there were for any particular day, it would take five or six mini bus type ambulances to do the job for one hospital.

I also met many of the Ambulance crews who I would work with in the years to come. One of those crews was Stan Pratt and Phil Petch, also known as 'Snitch and Snatch.'

"The Gillmoss ambulance is over at the casualty department, they might give you a lift home" Malcolm said one evening when it was getting close to home time. "You better hurry before you miss them."

"Thanks." I didn't argue and put on my tunic and hat. It was always good to escape from his office and the blue haze of cigarette smoke. I left the room and scurried through the maze of hospital corridors to the casualty department which was situated on the far side of the building.

The ambulance was parked outside the departments' doors. I checked the cab; it was empty of driver and attendant.

I wandered into the casualty department in search of the crew and found them at the far end of the department, in a small room that served as a kitchen and staff rest room.

It was Phil and Stan, or Snitch and Snatch as everyone called them. If ever you need to find an ambulance crew at a hospital, the first place to look is in the kitchen or wherever there might be a brew on the go.

I had seen both of them around of course but had never actually spoken to either of them in any meaningful way until today.

A mug in one hand and a biscuit in the other, leaning against the sink unit, Phil looked at me as I entered the room.

"Ah, a guinea pig comes in search of a lift home?"

Some of the older crews called cadets 'Guinea pigs.'

Liverpool Ambulance Service was the first in the country to pioneer the concept of cadets within its service. By far the majority of older crews had joined direct from military service and had basic first aid training.

The chief ambulance officer who instigated the cadet scheme was Albert Guinney, hence the term guinea pigs.

"How did you know that?"

Stan, sitting on a stool with his head behind a newspaper, didn't look up from the page he was reading. "Malcolm's been on the phone."

"Where do you live?" asked Phil.

"Norris Green."

"Can we manage that, Stan?"

Stan, still with his head stuck in the newspaper, replied "I suppose so." Then he looked over the top of the page at Phil.

"Mind you, we have a patient to drop off on the way first, don't we?"

"Oh yes, forgot about that" said Stan. "You don't mind a little detour on the way do you?"

I shook my head. "Not at all."

It was the ambition of every cadet to ride with a crew whenever there was a chance. There was always the possibility they may get an emergency call and you would have to go with them.

"The patient is actually in the ambulance now waiting for us, why don't you go and get in the back and keep him company while we finish our brew, we won't be long."

"Ok." I was happy to sit in the ambulance and wait. I wandered off down the corridor and out to the ambulance.

The entrance doors to the casualty department at Walton hospital were sheltered by a large canopy; which protected patients from the elements as they were unloaded from the ambulance and wheeled into the hospital. It also had the effect of putting the entrance permanently in the shade. This, coupled with the dark tinted windows in the back doors and sides of the ambulance saloon, made it quite dark in the rear of the ambulance.

I opened the back door and launched myself into the rear of the vehicle. It took a moment for my eyes to adjust to the reduced light.

I could make out the man lying on the stretcher waiting to go home, but he wasn't moving and didn't react in any way to my entrance into the ambulance. I thought he'd fallen asleep waiting for Snitch and Snatch to finish their brew.

Then a thought crossed my mind; no ambulance crew would leave a patient alone on the ambulance while they had a cup of tea. I didn't think much of them as an ambulance crew at this point. It's not very considerate to leave a patient alone on the ambulance; it just wasn't right at all.

I took a closer look at the man, ready to make conversation. He was probably in his eighties, and as pale as I had ever seen anyone.

He was lying very still on the stretcher, the red woollen blanket pulled up as far as his chin, eyes closed. Only his head was visible. Not wanting to wake him up, I sat quietly on the bench seat opposite for several minutes. My mind drifted a bit and I wondered if I'd be lucky enough to go with the crew on a call before they could drop me off. It would be the talking point with other cadets if I did. And then it dawned. This patient wasn't breathing.

Just at that moment the back door opened and Stan poked his head inside. "Not very chatty is he?"

"Is he dead?" I hardly managed to get the words out as my heart was racing.

"Oh, sorry, didn't we mention that?" Stan's face was beaming.

"I've not seen a dead body before."

"Well, he won't be your last, mark my words."

In a sense, I had lost my ambulance virginity; I had seen my first dead body.

After taking the old man around to the hospital mortuary, I was taken home. I hadn't been lucky enough to get an emergency call with them, but I had seen my first dead body. Not as pleasurable, I will admit, but just like your first girlfriend or your first kiss, or that first night with Jane, It's something you will never forget, and to this day I will never forget seeing a dead body for the first time. Alas, I was to see many more in the years to come.

4

Liverpool Ambulance control room is situated behind a high wall at the eastern end of Lower Breck road in the Anfield district of Liverpool. The building was single story, and of a rectangular shape.

A continuous row of windows look out onto the large forecourt area that was also hidden behind the high wall.

The offices, occupied by the Chief Ambulance officer and the Deputy Chief were situated at the furthest end of the building.

Next was a reception area into which visitors could enter through a door from the forecourt. Once inside, there was a wall to the right with a sliding glass window set into it. This allowed the receptionist, who also doubled as the switchboard operator, to sit behind her desk and look busy whenever the boss came out of his office.

Beyond the reception was the control room proper. Two rows of five workstation desks were positioned side by side down the length of the building. Running between these workstations was a narrow, almost pencil thin, conveyer belt that led to the far end of the room where the controllers would sit.

Each workstation had a facia panel with a bank of switches and corresponding lights set into the facia that straddled the front of the workstation desk.

In total there were four rows of eight switches on the panel. The top row housed four 999 switches, and direct lines to the police and fire services, the two remaining switches were for overflow of the 999 calls.

The second row down was direct lines to the transport officers at eight hospitals. The third row down was direct lines to Ambulance stations, and the bottom row was for general incoming calls.

Each workstation had a red, bulbous light set into it. This flashed on and off, accompanied by a loud buzzer, whenever a 999 call was put through by the emergency operator.

Each call taker had a black plastic headset and combined microphone plugged into a jack socket in the side of the workstation.

Whenever a call came in, the light beneath the corresponding switch would flash on and off. The call taker would simply flick down the switch and speak to the caller.

Placed on the work station would be an A4 sized telephone pad, onto which all calls would be recorded.

If the call was a general request for an Ambulance by a GP or hospital and not too urgent, the information would be transferred from the telephone pad onto a carbonated form which was housed in a dispensing machine on the desktop. When completed, the form, now in duplicate, would be ejected from the machine by hand, and then placed onto the conveyer belt to be transported to the controller at the far end of the room.

Should a 999 call come through, once again the details were written onto the telephone pad, then transferred to a separate pink coloured form and, also placed on the conveyer belt to go to the controller.

The permanent control room staff consisted of the shift controller, assistant shift controller and one permanent call taker. During the day, the rest of the call takers were cadets on placement. Control room placements were the most common placement of all.

My placement in the control room was basically answering phone calls, including 999 calls. On occasion the controller would pick a cadet to operate the radio. This would mean sitting with the controller at the end of the room and taking instructions from him.

It was a little nerve-racking knowing that whatever you said on the radio could be heard by all the Ambulances in the city, and it wasn't uncommon to get things wrong at times while speaking into the radio microphone.

The pressure to speak in a manner dissimilar to normal conversation was, at times, disconcerting. The first time I was asked to man the radio was like a blow to the solar plexus, but I wasn't going to let my nerves get the better of me. I would be as professional as I could with my radio speak.

It is understood that in radio speak the word 'roger' means that a message has been heard and understood, and this much I knew.

I was doing fine until Ambulance 26 called in to clear at the Southern hospital.

"Stand by please 26" I said in my best radio voice.

I advised the controller that Ambulance 26 was clear at the Southern hospital.

"Send him back for his meal break." he said.

I nodded and pressed the radio button.

"26, return to station for your meal break, over."

"Roger", came the reply, but with an added sentence;

"Is it ok if we go back via Islington? There's something I need to collect, over."

I looked at the controller for advice and he nodded his head in agreement.

"26, the controller has roger'd you for that, over."

The controller spun around, eyes wide open. "What did you just say?"

The penny dropped. I knew only too well that the word "Roger'd" had different connotations.

The radio crackled into life and an effeminate voice came through the speaker.

"Oh no he hasn't." I could hear the laughter in the background of the Ambulance cab.

Thankfully the controller saw the funny side to my misuse of radio speak.

My placement in the control room also gave me a good overall picture on how the Ambulance service worked and how Ambulances were dispatched to calls all over the City.

It also gave me the opportunity to look through the none urgent calls that had been pre- booked by GP's, hospitals or other departments to take patients on inter-hospital transfers or none-urgent admissions.

On the odd occasion I would find pre-booked requests from GP's to take patients by Ambulance from the Liverpool area to Clatterbridge hospital.

I approached Arthur Kibby, who was the senior controller on the day shift and explained my mother's situation. I asked if I might go with the Ambulance crew so I could visit her.

Arthur was nearing retirement. He was quite tall with thinning grey hair that was swept back from his forehead and he wore thick black framed spectacles with lenses like jam jar bottoms.

He was like a granddad towards the cadets who were in his charge in the control room. He was firm, but fair. We all knew that underneath that austere exterior beat a heart of gold.

He gladly arranged for me to travel with the Ambulance crews who were taking patients to Clatterbridge, even if the visit was for just half an hour before the Ambulance had to return to Liverpool. Arthur arranged this for me on several occasions, for which I would always be grateful.

My placement on driving tuition had been put back for a month because a couple of the cadets from the previous squad had failed their driving tests and had to remain in place until they could take it again. This meant that I would do an extended placement in the control room. In a way I didn't mind too much. It meant that I didn't have to have that long bus journey to and from Woolton each day.

Getting to and from the control room at Anfield was just a fifteen minute bus ride each way, so I was home by half past five each night and there was the added bonus of being able to get the odd visit over to Clatterbridge.

"Hello, how are you?"

I was in the grocers shop near to where I lived; getting a few odd items we needed at home. My mother, who usually did the shopping, was in hospital and my father wouldn't know what the inside of a shop looked like, so it was down to me to keep the cupboards stocked.

I turned to see Beryl. We had gone to school together, and had had the odd date now and again. I hadn't recognised her at first; she had dyed her hair from auburn to blond, and it suited her.

"Hello" I said. "I'm sorry; I didn't recognise you for a moment."

She smiled. "It's the hair."

"Yes, it suits you."

She smiled again in appreciation.

For the next twenty minutes we talked about what each had been doing since we last saw each other, which must have been several years. Finally, I asked her if she would like to go out for a drink that night, and she said she would.

Beryl and I had got on quite well together in the past, but she was strict Catholic so hanky panky was never on the cards. I did like her company though and from that day onwards we re-kindled our past relationship. Over the next few weeks, Beryl came with me on three occasions to visit my mother in hospital.

It was the end of May, late at night and I was in bed. I'd heard my father downstairs when he came back from the pub, then I must have fallen asleep.

I was woken by loud rapping on the front door. I checked the time and it was just past midnight.

My father must have still been downstairs as I heard him muttering to himself about who the hell this could be at this time of night as he went to open the door. I heard mumbled voices, then a silence, then my father crying out "Oh no."

I quickly threw on a pair of jeans and an old jumper then scurried bare-footed down the stairs to see what had happened. My heart was racing and I feared the worst.

There were two uniformed policemen standing on the path, while my father was leaning against the door frame as if trying to steady himself.

"What's happened?" I asked.

My father turned to me. "It's your mother, she's died."

Beryl was in the funeral car with me and my father as we followed the hearse to the cemetery. I was looking out of the window as we travelled slowly along the road towards the cemetery, not yet taking in the gravity of it all. I was still emotionally numb.

I noticed an elderly man on the pavement. As we passed he stopped to look at the cortege. He removed his cap, held it to his chest and bowed his head in respect. I smiled, and in my mind I thanked him. He was a total stranger who understood.

It was now July, and 'Honky Tonk Woman was almost constantly on the radio, but that was ok, I liked the song.

Two months had passed since the funeral. Tension in the house between my father and me was on a gradual increase. If he hadn't been on shift work I shudder to think how things might have gone. I was willing to clean the house, but that was it. I cooked for myself, washed my own clothes and got my own shopping. My father was big enough to look after himself, but had been so used to everything being done for him, that he almost lapsed into total self neglect.

Beryl and I were still seeing each other, but I was only half committed to our relationship. I still had the need to explore my sexual feelings and felt it wouldn't be fair to cheat on Beryl if I was fully committed to her. I still found other girls attractive and the experience with Jane had opened up my need to gain more experience of a similar nature, which I knew wouldn't happen with Beryl. I did feel guilty because I knew Beryl was more committed than I was.

My time for driving tuition finally arrived in late August. My placements at Walton Hospital and the control room were over for the time being and I now had to travel to Quarry Street every morning; it was just like old times.

The driver training vehicle was a Morris J2 minibus. Painted cream, it had eight seats in the back and was somewhat battle weary from the onslaught of previous learner drivers, having sustained several scrapes on the paintwork and small bumps here and there as proof. The liver bird logo was stamped on each side of the vehicle.

I had applied for my provisional driving licence several weeks earlier, and had to keep this with me every time I was taken for a driving lesson. Wally and Harry shared what must have been interesting experiences in giving the cadets driving tuition.

John Jones hadn't passed his test first time, so he had a few more weeks of driving tuition to do, which entailed him tagging along with me until he took his test again.

John eventually passed his driving test in the September, so now Harry and Wally could concentrate their efforts on my driving.

We would drive all over the place, up the coast to Southport and Blackpool or across the Mersey to the Wirral and North Wales. We didn't go through the Mersey tunnel, I don't think learner drivers were allowed to go through. Instead we went over the Runcorn bridge.

It was during one of these trips that I plucked up the courage to ask Wally a question. It was something that had been niggling at me since I had started in the job and I needed to know the answer.

I was driving along a quiet, leafy, country lane and Wally was, as usual, giving his left arm a sun tan, head leaning back into the seat and eyes closed.

"Wally." I said. We were all on first name terms now.

Without changing position or opening his eyes. "Yes son."

"Can I ask you something?"

"Of course you can, son."

"It might sound a bit silly."

"No such thing as a silly question son."

"Is it true that you can get someone who has been run over by a bus or a steam roller and you have to shovel them up into a sack?"

There was silence for a moment, I wondered if he was going to confirm Vinny's story.

"No son, that sort of thing doesn't happen."

Then a smile came to his face. "However, they'll probably be a lot thinner and wider."

I considered Wally to be the better driving instructor. He had more patience than Harry and didn't shout "Oh shit" and slap his hands onto the dash board to ready himself every time I approached a road junction or red traffic light.

Driving every day from morning to night certainly gives you experience of driving in traffic, and the required confidence soon materialises.

I took my test at the Childwall driving centre. I was the first of that morning's appointments and I was nervous as hell, like all new drivers are.

I had made a few mistakes early in the test. A few minor things like forgetting to indicate at a junction and making a mess of reversing by being too far away from the kerb. More worryingly, I actually went through a red traffic light; (well it was amber really). I was going too fast to stop in time and it changed to red as I was half way across the junction. I was convinced that I had blown it.

After the traffic light incident, I didn't stress about passing as I was convinced I must have failed. For each mistake I had made, I could see from the corner of my eye that the examiner was making due note of it on his form, and he seemed to be making a lot of notes.

I just relaxed and did as he wanted to finish the test, knowing I could take it again.

We pulled over to the kerb near the test centre and I could see Wally a few hundred yards away lighting a cigarette, waiting for me to finish so we could get going back to Quarry Street for our lunch. I now just had the Highway Code questions to answer. I didn't see why he should bother; he was going to fail me even if I got them right.

I answered all the questions and a long silence prevailed as he completed his form, then from out of the blue he said "I see you live in Norris Green?"

"Yes." A curious question; I wondered why he wanted to know?

"That's where I live. Do you know an Ambulance driver called Stan Pratt?"

"Yes, I know Snatch"

He looked at me with a puzzled face. "Snatch?"

"He's crewed up with a bloke called Phil Petch; we call them Snitch and Snatch."

He looked down at his form and chuckled. "I've not heard that one before; he's my brother in law."

Oh bugger, I thought. I didn't even know if Snitch and Snatch knew they were called that. I had only heard others use the endearment.

The examiner looked over at me and beamed a smile. He tore off a pink slip from his pad and handed it to me. "I'm pleased to say you've passed your driving test."

I couldn't believe it, I was totally gob smacked. "But I made some lousy mistakes back there."

"Yes", he said, "but not lousy enough."

I wished my mother was alive to see me now.

I wasn't allowed to drive back to the training school after passing the test; I had to ride shotgun while Wally took us back via Barclays bank and a builder's yard for a bag of plaster. Finally we stopped outside Jane's shop. Wally got out and went into the store. I followed him inside. I was excited about passing my test and wanted to tell Jane, thinking and hoping she might be interested in seeing me again.

I was still seeing Beryl but I was tempted to stray at times. I knew it wasn't fair and was the wrong thing to do whilst I was in a relationship with her, but what could I do? I found some women to be attractive.

A different and older woman was serving Wally with his cigarettes. I looked around in case Jane was somewhere else behind the counter or in the back room. There was no sign of her anywhere.

"Can I help you?" said the woman after she had served Wally.

"I was just wondering where Jane was."

"She doesn't work here anymore."

It had been a while since I had last stepped into the shop: It had changed a bit. Things were stacked on different shelves and it had been given a lick of paint.

"We're the new owners now and Jane couldn't manage the hours we needed her to work because of the kids and school, so she left."

"I see. Can I have ten No 6 please?"

October came and once again I was placed into the control room, only this time there wouldn't be any trips to Clatterbridge hospital. This brought back sad memories and I tried desperately to brush them aside. It helped a little that George and Gary were also placed in the control room with me and sometimes, when we had finished work, we would call into the Claremont pub for a few beers which was just across the road from the control room.

There had been a new intake of cadets; 'I' squad and they were just starting on their placements out of Quarry Street. Being the more senior of the cadets, Gary, George and I sat at the back of the control room at our workstations and let the newbies do most of the call taking; it was the benefit of seniority.

I had saved up enough money to buy myself a second hand car. It was a Ford Anglia the type that had an inward sloping rear window and sported two tone green and cream paintwork. The car dealer must have seen the sign tattooed on my forehead that said in big capital letters 'MUG'

But as it was my first car I was proud of it. I know my mother would have been pleased too.

The fact that I had to get a new battery, a set of spark plugs and leads, then eventually give it to my mate to fix the cylinder head gasket and adjust the timing before it would run properly didn't really count. It was my very own and I could go anywhere I wanted. No more buses!

It was a Saturday afternoon, quite warm and pleasant for the time of year. I wouldn't be seeing Beryl until the next day so I had the bright idea of calling at Jane's house just to say hello and show off my car. It would be a pleasant drive on a Saturday afternoon.

I knocked at the front door, my face beaming and itching to present my new acquisition. I hadn't seen her for a while but I was sure she would be glad to see me, I hoped so anyway.

I could hear the kids shouting and playing inside the house and then the door opened.

A bloke the size of a brick shit house looked down at me from the doorway. He was casually dressed in string vest, jeans and hob nail boots. His bulging muscles and hairy arms were covered in a variety of tattoos. He had the individual letters of DEATH etched across the knuckles of his right hand, and an earring in his left ear. He glared down at me.

"Yes?"

My mouth must have dropped open and I know my heart rate practically shot through the roof. This I was not expecting.

I caught a glimpse of Jane behind him trying to control the kids further back down the hallway. Her eyes widened as she realised who I was and then, with fear on her face, she shook her head clearly, telling me not to ask for her.

"Er, er." I said, desperately trying to think of something to say that was convincing enough to keep me out of a hospital bed. My mouth was moving, a bit like Ob, but nothing was coming out; then finally. "I was just wondering if John was in?"

It was all I could think of in those heart pounding seconds, but it would give him a chance to tell me that there wasn't any John that lived there.

He gave me a very worrying look, and then he turned to look back down the hall at Jane and the two boys who were now standing there and probably wondering who this strange man was at the door. He returned his gaze back at me.

"And what the fuck do you want with my nine year old son?"

My legs nearly crumpled beneath me. I couldn't believe that I had just dropped myself even further into the mire.

"No, no. I don't mean that John. The John I'm talking about is twenty one years old. I think I must have the wrong address." I prayed that I had a way out of this. "Isn't this Hillside road"? I asked.

I knew damn well it wasn't Hillside road.

"No mate, it isn't."

"I'm sorry." I said. "I thought this was Hillside road, I'm not from around here. Anyway, I'll see him at work on Monday. Sorry to bother you."

I headed back down the path, hoping to look as if I didn't have a care in the world.

This must have been her husband and she had been cheating on him when she was with me. It was no wonder I had to leave before the kids saw me in the morning, but it was a good job that I had. I shuddered to think what could have happened if he had ever found us in his bed, in his house.

I walked to my car as quickly, but as calmly as I could. I didn't look back, but I was anticipating the sound of hurried footsteps behind me that would mean certain pain and blood loss. It never came and I never saw Jane again.

During the November I was sent to Broadgreen Hospital for my placement. I was to be with the transport officer, Billy, who was much nicer than Malcolm at Walton. It was the same work as I had done at Walton, but the office was next to the casualty department and we could often see when Ambulance crews brought in emergencies.

Billy wasn't as strict as Malcolm and would let me go and watch any interesting cases that came into the department, or wonder around the hospital to get a feel for the place. Billy didn't smoke either, so his office was pollutant free. However, I had to go outside if I wanted to smoke, which was fine by me.

November came and went without any memorable incident and I headed into December with the dreaded thought of Christmas without my mother being there.

My next placement was to the Southern Hospital casualty department. The brief was to watch and learn what happened in the department, and get involved if possible. Befitting my kind of luck; but good news for patients; nothing very interesting happened while I was on placement.

The only incident of note was the occasion when a man had been brought in by his workmate. He had been working on a building site and caught his right thigh on a nail that had been protruding from a wooden frame. He had lacerated his leg which would require three sutures. The sister on the department foolishly suggested that I should be the one to 'sew the wound' after it had been cleaned. After all, I had seen it done many times.

After a local anaesthetic had been injected around the wound, I was supervised by a very understanding staff nurse.

My hands were shaking a little as I took the forceps with the needle and thread attached and began to push the needle through the skin; so far so good. I pushed the needle through the skin on the opposite side of the wound to complete the process; now all I had to do was tie the knot and bring the folds of skin together. I had seen the technique used many times as the forceps are looped twice around the suture, pulled through and tied off.

I just couldn't get the hang of it at first but much explaining and hand waving from the staff nurse eventually saw me through the procedure. It wasn't a good job at all. The wound, now stitched, looked like a little smile on the patient's thigh. Big as the builder was, he just couldn't look at what I was doing.

"That'll do," said the staff nurse, and then proceeded with a marker pen to draw two dots to represent eyes and a small vertical line to represent a nose. I had to laugh, as she did. Now, somewhere out there, is a builder with a smiley face scar on his thigh.

There were no decorations, no Christmas tree and no presents ready wrapped to give out on Christmas day. The house was gloomy. It was a sad time and I just wanted to be somewhere else.

Beryl invited me to Christmas dinner at her house, she'd spoken to her parents who had agreed that I could. However, I was reluctant go. Maybe I just wanted to wallow in my own despair; feel sorry for myself and mourn my loss. I really didn't feel like being in company in what would be a happy time for others.

Eventually I relented and arrived on her doorstep on Christmas day at two in the afternoon. In a way, I think it was Beryl's way of letting her family look me over as a prospective future son in law.

The afternoon went quite well. I didn't manage to put my foot in anything I would later regret, but I did get the feeling her father was suspicious of me.

Beryl and I retreated to the kitchen while the rest of the family settled down in front of the telly to watch the inevitable Christmas film repeat.

I didn't stay long; I made the excuse that I wanted to get an early night. I left Beryl's house at seven and went straight to the pub for a few pints. I wanted to be alone, but not at home. I got drunk that night.

I was glad when Christmas was over and we were into the New Year, but the next bombshell was about to drop; my father was made redundant.

My father had worked a shift pattern at his factory which meant we saw little of each other in the house. I felt this was a good arrangement, however, this was to change drastically now.

He had been given a lump sum of redundancy money which helped as he looked for other work, but none ever came. He found solace in the pub every night, which eventually turned into daytime sessions too. The tension between us steadily mounted and heated arguments often erupted.

The house no longer felt like a home. When my mother was alive it was always neat and tidy, felt cosy and warm, and a place to feel safe in. Those feelings had now gone. The house was just a shell. Cold, unkempt and unloved. I knew I couldn't live there for much longer.

My placement in January was back in the control room and most of my squad were in there too. All of us had now passed our driving tests and were basically just treading water until we took our final exams and became fully fledged Ambulance drivers.

We weren't to be treading water for much longer as we were informed that we would be taking our exams at the end of January. We were six months short of what we were supposed to spend as cadets, but Harry and Wally had informed the boss that we were all ready to take the exams.

It was midway through January that we discovered Terry had resigned from the cadets. No reason was given to us, but it felt as if we had lost a friend. It was some years later that I would bump into Terry and find out the reason.

Terry had left the service after twelve months because the training and discipline, such as it was, didn't suit him. He had gone to work for his brother in his small bakery, and later he went into business on his own; opening a betting shop. He claimed leaving the service was the best thing he ever did, as he now had a string of six betting shops. I was happy for him; he was a decent bloke and I was happy to see that he was doing well.

The exams came and went and we all waited patiently for our results. It was reassuring to know that if any of us had failed, we might have been offered the option to drop down into the next squad and take them again. I felt sure that no one would lose their job if they failed; too much time and money had been spent on us to just throw it away.

The results came in early February and we had all passed. The Claremont pub was our destination when we finished in the control room that evening. At last I had a reason for celebrating.

Throughout my time as a cadet, I had passed my driving test, had been seconded to various hospital departments and had got to know the Ambulance system quite well.

I practically knew the Anatomy and Physiology book backwards, which was just as well; it helped me pass my final exams.

All the training was over and I was looking forward to putting it into practice and being a fully qualified Ambulance man.

During the graduation parade and ceremony we were awarded our certificates as 'Fellows of the Institute of Certified Ambulance Personnel', which is now more aptly named The Ambulance Service Institute.

My base station would be Anfield. Ob was to be based there too. George went to Stanhope Street in Toxteth,

John, although initially based at Anfield, would eventually transfer to Birkenhead, where he lived, when Liverpool Ambulance Service became Merseyside Metropolitan Ambulance Service.

Gary went home to Westmorland where his dad was a senior officer in their Ambulance Service and had a job waiting for him.

The decision was a spur of the moment thing, a rash thing to do maybe. When I look back at it now, it was probably more tactical than emotional, but I asked Beryl to marry me.

She said she would.

We decided that June might be the best time. We could each book holidays off work and it would give us time to plan for it

5

It was a sunny morning on that day in February of 1970, it was a little chilly but an azure sky and not a cloud in sight made it feel just right. It was a fitting start to my first day as a fully fledged ambulance man. I felt as though I had emerged into a brand new world.

Now that I had completed my training, Beryl and I agreed to get married in June. We would look for a flat to rent over the coming weeks and I could move into it before the wedding in June. Yes, things were looking a little better today.

I didn't need to be at the Ambulance station to sign on duty until 8am, but I was keen and arrived at 7.30. The night shift had gone home at 7am and the day crews had now taken over the emergency shift ambulances.

I was hoping and praying that one of the day shift crew members might have called in sick, and I would be seconded onto an emergency vehicle on my first day. Monday mornings were always the favourite time for staff to phone in sick.

Anfield station on Lower Breck Road was the HQ of Liverpool Ambulance Service. From the main road, I'd drive through the open gateway and turn right into a large courtyard.

The control room, chief Ambulance Officer and deputy chief Ambulance officer's offices were on my right. The single level red brick building housing these departments stretched along the whole length of the yard, some hundred feet or so.

To my left was another single level building which was used by the adjoining Belmont hospital to store hospital beds, mattresses, sheets and all kinds of other bulky hospital stuff. In later years this building would be demolished and rebuilt to become the new Ambulance crews mess room and shift leader's office.

Ahead of me and off set to the left of the court yard, a wide concrete ramp led the way up through a tall, wide doorway into the garage area that contained the mechanics workshops, stores, parking area for ambulances and, at the far end of the garage, the staff mess room and shift leaders office.

It was a large old spacious building with a high corrugated double, pitched roof held aloft by evenly spaced rows of green painted metal girders.

I would drive up the ramp in my newly purchased second hand Ford Cortina.

(The Ford Anglia now having departed this world to its final resting ground, aka, the scrap yard.)

At the far end of the garage I would turn left and out of the rear garage doors; past the petrol pumps and left again onto the gravelled surface which was the staff car park. This was behind the hospital storage building in the court yard.

The Ambulance fleet consisted of BMC vehicles, three emergency shift ambulances, along with three day shift Ambulances and six out patient ambulances.

The saloons of the outpatient Ambulances had been converted into a mini bus configuration for those patients who needed an ambulance to take them to hospital appointments, but who didn't need to be carried into the Ambulance. These vehicles were similar in size and shape to the emergency ambulances and had the same dark windows to the side and rear but no blue roof lights.

As new emergency ambulances were acquired, the older ones were converted to out patient vehicles. As out patient vehicles were thus replaced, they would go for sale; often being converted into mobile shops or motor homes.

I parked my car and walked back into the garage to enter the mess room, the entrance to which was down a couple of steps that took you directly into the kitchen area.

All the usual trappings of a kitchen were on hand; cooker, fridge, water boiler, pots, pans, sink, drain board and wall fitted cupboards.

On entering the kitchen, a door to the right, led to the outside toilets. There weren't any female toilets. Any female visitors would use those in the control room; not that there where many female visitors.

The only Ambulance women at that time were the girls who manned the Ambulance station at Liverpool Airport.

To the left of the kitchen the door led into the mess room. There, plastic topped tables stuck out along the length of the walls on each side at right angles, three along each wall, creating a passageway down the centre of the room, with four mettle framed chairs to each table.

The wall to the right had three rectangular windows set into it but they were high; too high to look out from when sitting down. I wondered how Vinny had claimed to see the Ambulance drivers sitting around and drinking tea all day.

At the far end of the room were a variety of well worn armchairs, none of them matching in either, shape, size or colour. A one armed bandit that only took silver sixpences stood in one corner and a television and radio in the other. A low wooden and stained coffee table nestled between the arm chairs.

I knew some of the crews, having had some placements here during my time as a cadet.

The shift rota covered a twenty four hour period. (A) Day shift, which was 7am to 3pm, (B) Afternoon shift, 3pm to11pm (C) Night shift, 11pm to 7am.

Every shift had three emergency Ambulances on standby, which meant there were six men on station at the start of any shift. In addition to the shift staff of six, there was the day staff, of which I was now one, who worked 8am to 4pm.

It was my brief to see the shift leader when I came in this morning and he would sort out what I would be doing for the rest of my first day on the road.

The none emergency day shift Ambulances, which were kitted out as much the same as the rotating shift ambulances, mainly took patients to and from out patient appointments at various hospitals around the city. These were for the patients who had to be carried out of the house and into the ambulance. They would also be the 'back up' Ambulances to attend at an emergency or take urgent admissions if the shift crews were busy and this was what I imagined I would be doing that first day.

I walked into the mess room and my heart skipped a beat, I could only see five ambulance men in there, one was missing. Maybe he had gone sick and I might have to cover for him? What a great start to my first day on the road that would be. The excitement was short lived however, when I heard the toilet flushing, and Martin Roberts emerged from the doorway.

I took off my cap and placed it on one of the tables that wasn't being used, and then unbuttoned my tunic like all the others had, with the aim of fitting in.

"Well then, it's the new lad. Piss the bed did you?" Alan, who I had met before, was looking at his watch. He was sitting at a table with his mug of coffee and the Daily Mirror spread out on the table in front of him. Probably in his early forty's, he had worked as a mechanic before joining the service.

"Get yourself a cuppa, there's some milk in the fridge courtesy of the Royal." said Jimmy, probably the oldest crew member of the shift, might even be close to retirement. The Royal, was pertaining to the Royal Liverpool Hospital. Milk wasn't bought when it could be scrounged from a hospital kitchen.

"Who's first out"? I asked to no one in particular as I went into the kitchen to make a brew.

"Me and Jimmy" said Martin. He was still in the kitchen drying his hands after washing them.

The system of deployment to emergency calls was a well established rotational system that had been adopted over the years. The first crew out would attend and deal with whatever they were called to. If they returned to station and the other two crews were still there, then the next call would automatically go to the first crew again. This would continue for the rest of the week. The following week, the crew who had been third crew out would now jump to the front and become the first crew out. This was a particularly useful system when on night shifts as the third crew out were almost guaranteed a full nights sleep each night while the other two crews did the work.

Martin seemed a decent bloke; he had been a cadet too. He was ahead of me by a couple of years and had been in 'E' squad. A happy- go- lucky type of person, but fastidious on being clean and tidy, you could eat your dinner off the floor of his Ambulance. But there was something about him that I just couldn't put my finger on; I would learn what it was in later years.

"Do you want one?" I said to Martin as I spooned tea leaves into the pot.

"No thanks, I've just had one."

"Been to anything interesting recently?" I enjoyed listening to the tales of the experienced hands, as Martin had now become.

"Had a BBA (Born Before Admission) yesterday, well, we almost delivered it. The baby was half way out when we got there."

"Wow, a BBA " I said.

" Two of them actually", he continued. "She was having twins and didn't bother telling us till she started with more contractions when she was in the back of the Ambulance.

"Bloody hell."

"That's just what it was. We had to stop on West Derby Road to deliver it, which went ok, until she started bleeding heavily. Good job we weren't too far away from the hospital."

"Was she OK?"

"We got all three of them into the admission room, dead quick like, problem was we didn't have time to warn them we were on our way in, so all hell let loose when we arrived. As far as I know she was ok, but I'll check next time we go there."

Maternity cases were the one thing I had a bit of a phobia about. We touched on obstetrics during training, but the subject was still a bit of an enigma to me. I hoped I would never be confronted with a BBA. There was to be no such luck!

"Ken."

I turned to see Charlie the shift leader in the doorway.

"Let's get you sorted out for today, pop into my office for a minute."

I put the teapot down and followed him into his office. There was a desk that stood beneath a metal framed window which looked out into the garage area. Along the back wall of the office were shelves stacked with folded and clean blankets, pillows and cases. On the middle shelves first aid bags were stacked in neat rows, full and ready to use, then on the bottom shelves were oxygen and entonox bottles, the latter of which were blue in colour and contained a 50/50 mixture of laughing gas (Nitrous Oxide) and Oxygen, to be given for pain relief.

His desk was cluttered with paperwork, but probably organised chaos. The shift leader didn't go out on emergencies, unless it was a major incident and he would bring out the extra equipment that may be needed. His job was to organise the crews, dish out overtime, find cover for staff sickness and holidays, oversee petrol deliveries and a host of other things that would keep him busy for the rest of the day shift.

Charlie had several bundles of A6 sized forms which I knew to be the out patient runs for the day. Each bundle contained around six sheets fixed together with a paperclip; each sheet with a name, address and destination hospital and department.

" Old Billy has gone off on the Pat- n- Mick again, so I'm going to need you to take over his work for the time being."

Charlie must have seen the disappointment in my face.

"Don't worry; I'll get you on a emergency Ambulance next week."

I was still disappointed even with that promise as it meant my first day, or first week even, was going to be ferrying around a load of old people to out patient departments, not very exciting or glamorous at all.

He handed me a bundle of papers. "Six from eleven into Broad Green. Take Billy's motor, its fleet number 32."

Six from eleven meant that I had six patients to collect from various addresses in the Liverpool 11 district and take them to Broad Green Hospital. Oh well. At least Old Billy's motor still had a blue light on top; it would at least look like I was driving a real Ambulance around the streets.

Chin on my chest, I padded back to the mess room to get that cuppa and sort out my route. Just as I sat down, the emergency bell rang out loud in the garage, a large wall mounted speaker crackled and clicked into life.

"Crash call. Crash call. Junction of Townsend Lane and Queens Drive. Townsend Lane and Queens Drive. (the voice repeated) An RTA (Road Traffic Accident) A motorbike and car. First and second crews to attend please"

Martin and Jimmy were out of their seats as they were first crew out, Alan and his mate, who I didn't know yet, hurriedly finished their drinks and followed. The Ambulances roared out of the station and I could hear their two tone horns blaring as they probably fought their way through the morning traffic, the sounds getting fainter as they faded into the distance. I wished I could be doing that, and then with a sigh got back to sorting out which route I would take for my own work.

I didn't need to consult the A-Z as I lived in the area and knew where the roads were.

It was ten to eight when Ob and John came in; they had been seconded to the internal Ambulance at Walton Hospital again and weren't best pleased. It was a duty we all became loath to do when we were cadets, it was so boring. At least I had the freedom of the streets to drive around and not be stuck in the hospital grounds all day.

After sorting out my route, I trundled over to the shift leader's office and collected a first aid bag and a couple of terylene blankets, standard issue for out patient vehicles. I knew there would be a small portable bottle of oxygen on the vehicle. A few log sheets and a clip board made up my kit.

Billy's Ambulance was tidy and well kept. He had a folded red woollen blanket on the driver's seat to make it more comfy to sit on. I wondered if he suffered from haemorrhoids? The engine cowling was between the driver's seat and the attendant's seat; I placed the blanket over it, feeling a little guilty about undoing Billy's normal configuration.

I checked in the saloon, there were two rows of seats; three on each side, facing forward just like a bus. Two people could sit in each seat. It was tidy and clean. I closed the back doors and got back into the drivers seat.

Just at that moment I heard the emergency bell going off in the garage, and something coming over the speaker. I couldn't quite make out what was being said, but soon after, the third crew were roaring down the ramp, across the court yard and into Lower Breck road, sirens blearing. I wondered where they were going to?

"Three two, thirty two radio check, over."

It was standard practise to do a radio check each morning before leaving the station. It was an old radio which took a minute or two to warm up. I pressed the hand mike again and repeated the check.

"That's received three two." The reply came eventually.

I pressed the hand mike again. "I have six from eleven for Broad Green, over,"

"That's received three two." The controller said again. "By the way, good luck on your first day."

It seemed as if everyone knew it was my first day on the road.

"Thank you." I replied, I tried to talk posh when on the radio.

There was a rapping on the door window, it made me jump a little as I was filling in the log sheet with the route I would be taking.

"Don't forget your cap." It was Charlie the shift leader.

Oh bugger! I had forgotten about it in the mess room. I dashed across the garage and into the mess. It wasn't on the table where I had left it. I hurriedly searched around, looking under cushions, tables and chairs, still no sight of it. It was nowhere to be found.

Oh shit, what was I going to do? Time was getting on and I should be on the road by now.

I had no choice; I would have to go without it.

I set off for my first pick up, it was just gone eight o'clock and all my patients had to be in the hospital by nine.

My first call was to Sandyville Road, which I realised was on the route to where the traffic accident had happened. I made my way towards the destination.

"Three two, thirty two, what's your location now?" The radio shouted.

I wasn't expecting the control to call me; usually they left you alone to get on with the work in hand. Maybe they had spotted me without my cap?

I pulled the hand mic from its holder. "I'm on Townsend Lane, approaching Clubmoore, over."

"Have you collected any patients yet?"

"Negative, just on my way to the first address." There was a moment's silence.

"Can you assist at an RTA, Townsend Lane and Queens Drive. Three crews are in attendance and are requesting a fourth vehicle."

My heart began to race. This was it, this was the real thing, I was in at the deep end on my first day, missing hat now forgotten.

The controller came back on the radio. "We have Gillmoss on route also, but if you can assist until they arrive please"

"Roger, will do." I said.

I switched on the headlights and put them on full beam, then reached for the blue light switch and flicked it on. I could see its reflections flashing in the shop windows as I passed them. My heart sank a little when I looked for the two tone horn switch, there wasn't one.

On the dashboard to the left of the steering wheel was a protruding round button, coloured brown and about the size of a milk bottle top. I was disappointed as I knew what it was, but I pressed down on it anyway as I overtook traffic that was now beginning to slow and queue as a result from the accident ahead.

It was a bell. Probably one of the last vehicles in the old fleet to have one. It worked by pressing down on the button and it would stop as soon as the pressure was released, why did I have to have a vehicle with a bell? It was so embarrassing.

I arrived at the scene just as Martin and Jimmy were leaving with a patient in the back of their Ambulance.

As is sometimes the case, the information given to the crews about a particular accident or emergency, isn't always what it seems. This was supposed to be a motorbike and a car; it turned out to be two cars, a motorbike and a bread van.

Martin and Jimmy had retrieved the motorcyclist from underneath the bread van and were now well on their way to hospital. The bread van, it was said, had jumped the traffic lights at the junction; hit the motorbike, dragging the rider underneath it, then two cars had piled into the van, one of them turning over onto its roof.

Alan and his mate and the third crew were dealing with the two people in the upturned car. There seemed to be a lot of blood about and both victims were unconscious. Alan looked over his shoulder to me for a moment. He was busy getting an oxygen mask onto one of the injured passengers.

"Ken, go and see to the bloke in the other car, there's a first aider keeping an eye on him for now."

"Ok." My adrenaline was flowing to the max now. The scene was utter carnage and a crowd had gathered to watch. I began to feel as though I was on a stage with the world looking on, watching everything I did.

There weren't any police or fire engines in attendance yet, but I knew they would be arriving soon.

I took my first aid bag, oxygen bottle and a blanket over to the car. The driver was in his seat, and his head slumped back. The first aider was an old guy who must have been in his late sixties or early seventies. He was sitting next to him in the front passenger seat and seemed to be having a conversation with the injured man.

I approached the driver's door and opened it. Instantly I could see that the driver was unconscious and struggling to breath; it was as if he was snoring.

"Are you a first aider? I asked the old guy.

"Yes, I did a bit in the army."

"Come round this side and give me a hand."

While the first aider eased himself out of the car, I dug into my first aid bag for an OP airway. (Oropharyngeal) This is a curved piece of bevelled rigid plastic tubing that can be slid over an unconscious patients tongue to help protect the airway. I spoke to the injured driver first, then squeezed one of his fingers; there wasn't any response to either of my actions. I opened his mouth to make sure there wasn't anything in there that was causing his noisy breathing. I couldn't see anything.

I took the airway out of its plastic wrapping and slipped it in, upside down at first, not wanting to push his tongue backwards, then midway through insertion turned the airway over so the curvature of the tube was over the top of his tongue and protecting his airway. Instantly his breathing became normal, nice easy breaths, in and out. Then I fitted the oxygen mask over his nose and mouth.

I needed a neck collar, which I knew I wouldn't find in my vehicle. The first aider was now at my side of the car. I told him to keep the patient in the same position and keep an eye on his breathing. He nodded at my instruction.

I'd never inserted an airway into anyone before. We had practised many times on a manikin at the training school, but this was my first real life attempt and it had worked brilliantly, I was so proud of myself. I realised all that training was now kicking into gear; I'd taken charge of my little scenario and was getting things organised.

Alan was now putting his patient into the back of their Ambulance and would be ready to go soon. I went over to him.
"Alan, can I have a neck collar from your kit?"
"You'll have to help yourself; I'm a little busy at the moment."
I took one from his bag which was still on the roadside by the upturned car. As I got back to my patient the first aider was once

again in conversation with the unconscious driver. He stopped talking to him when he saw me approaching.

I once more checked the patients breathing, it was ok. I climbed into the back of the car and positioned myself behind the driver. I slid the neck collar under his chin, and then fastened it at the back of his neck. I wasn't taking any chances; it was always possible that he had a fractured spine.

At this point I heard the distant sound of two tone horns. Gillmoss would soon be here to take over. Within a couple of minutes the fourth Ambulance pulled up at the scene, it was Snitch and Snatch.

I quickly gave them a run down of what had happened and what I had done for my patient. He was still unconscious as I helped them to lift him from the car and onto their now waiting stretcher on the roadway.

The police were arriving in droves now, some directing the traffic and keeping the large crowd that had gathered at comfortable distance, other police offices started drawing yellow chalk marks on the road and taking measurements.

Snitch and Snatch had loaded the patient into the Ambulance. Snatch was closing the back doors as I stood next to him.

"Where's your cap?" he said.

I'd forgotten all about it in the heat of excitement and adrenaline rush.

"It went missing from the mess room this morning; I don't know where it is."

"The boss doesn't live far from here" he said. "If he sees you without your cap, you're in big trouble."

"But I don't know where it is."

Snatch made sure the rear doors were securely shut, then started to walk around to the driver's door to get in. He turned, gave me a wink before getting into the Ambulance and driving away and said "Try the oven."

"Try the oven?" What the hell did he mean?

I gathered my bits and pieces from the scene. All patients had now been taken to hospital and it was now just a case of the fire service swilling away the petrol and oil that had spilled onto the road surface and the police waiting for the breakdown wagons to tow away the damaged vehicles.

I resumed my journey to Sandyville Road for my first pick up; it was just a few hundred yards further down Townsend Lane. It was a quarter to nine; they would all be late for their appointments.

As I turned into Sandyville Road I pulled over to the kerbside and parked the Ambulance. I had to light up a cigarette. My hands were shaking as the realisation of what I had just been through came flooding over me in waves. I kept going over and over in my mind if I had done everything right. Was there anything else I could have done? I couldn't think of anything that I might have done better.

I wasn't particularly surprised when I had eventually asked the first aider what he was talking to the patient about. It turned out that he was telling the patient all about his army days in Burma.

When I asked why, he told me that you should talk to people who are unconscious as they just might hear you. I could see his point, but at the time I was more concerned about keeping him alive. Still, it was something to remember for the next time.

I knocked at the door of the first pick up address. A woman opened it and scowled at me.

"You're a bit late aren't you"?

"I was delayed a bit."

"Well he had to get a lift from my brother; he couldn't wait around all day for you. Where's Billy anyway? He's never late"

"Billy's off sick."

"Mmmm; you'll have to bring him home though; my brother had to go into work after dropping him off at the hospital."

"Right." I said. Then turned on my heels and walked down the path. I heard the door shut as I went. What a come down this was. One minute I'm in the middle of carnage, then the next I'm being told off for being late.

Out of the six patients I had to collect, I only managed four of them. One had made his own way and the other was too ill to go. By the time we arrived at Broad Green hospital at ten fifteen that morning, the rear of the Ambulance was full of cigarette smoke.

All my patients were men, so there had been plenty of swearing and ogling of women on the pavements through the dark tinted windows as we drove by them. It was almost as if it was a social outing and we were on our way to Blackpool.

I opened the back doors when we arrived at the hospital and cigarette smoke billowed out from the saloon.

Three of them went to the fracture clinic to have the plaster casts on their legs checked out and the fourth patient was taken to the physiotherapy department. Once I had dropped them off, I drove around to the casualty department where the Ambulance transport officer was situated in his little office. Billy, the name sake of the man I was replacing, was a round portly man with a red face. He was a decent bloke, better than the one at Walton hospital.

"Morning Billy." I said as I walked into his office.
"Hello son, what run have you brought?"
I handed him the slips of paper. "Six from eleven, one made their own way and one was too sick, so I only got four of them."
"Sandyville Road; he's the one who made his own way in, and he is now in the waiting room ready to go home."

Billy took the slips of paper from me as he spoke and shuffled them into a neat pile with some others.
" The bugger can wait till the others are ready to go. First I get a phone call from his irate missus this morning, moaning down my ear that the Ambulance hadn't turned up for him and wanting to know how long it'll be before it does, then the next thing I know, he turns up here under his own steam. Do they think I run a taxi service here, or what?"
Then he looked up at me. "Why were you late anyway?"
"I was sent to help out at a bad RTA on Queens Drive before I'd picked anyone up."

"Ah" said Billy. "They brought the biker here, he's dead."

"I didn't get to see what he was like; the first Ambulance was just pulling away as I arrived."

"Twenty three, he was." said Billy

   Although I had never seen or known the biker, I felt a kind of sadness inside, he was only two years older than me. I could feel for his family; he must have had a family.

Billy changed the subject, for which I was glad.

"You go and get yourself a brew from the canteen; I've nothing for you right now."

"Cheers Billy." I was ready for a mug of tea and a piece of toast.

"Where's your cap?" he said just as I was about to leave the office.

"It went missing this morning, from the mess room."

"Oh" he said and just nodded his head a few times before getting stuck back into his paperwork.

   I sauntered down the main corridor of the hospital and found the staff canteen. I ordered a cup of tea and two rounds of toast.

I sat at a table on my own and people watched. At the other tables were nurses, doctors and a few people in civvies. After twenty minutes or so, I wandered back to Billy in his office.

   "They're all ready to go except the physio patient. I'm just waiting for them to phone through and tell me he's ready"

Just as Billy had finished speaking, the phone rang.

"Right, ok. The driver will be there shortly". He put the phone down.

"Talk of the devil. Your physio patient is ready to go."

Billy kept hold of the paper slips and I just copied the addresses onto my log board.

"Right then, I'll be on my way."

"Check inside the oven." said Billy

"Pardon?"

"I said check inside the oven for your cap when you get back to station"

"You're the second person who's told me to do that."

"It's a favourite place, last place you would think of when you're new."

"Cheers, I'll check, thanks Billy."

I rounded up my patients that I had brought in, plus the one who made his own way. It was the same rowdy and boisterous journey back as it had been on the way in. Each time I stopped to let someone out of the back door, a plume of cigarette smoke would erupt from the back of the Ambulance. At least it would allow for some fresh air to replace the smoke before the next stop.

I dropped the last patient off and pulled around the corner to park and have a cigarette myself. It was twenty past twelve. I made sure I had my mileages and times correct on my log sheet. I pulled the radio mike from its holder and called control to tell them I was clear of my work.

The message came back to return to station for lunch.

On the way back I called at a chip shop for fish and chips. I'd been there before when I was on placement with an Ambulance crew, so I knew what they would taste like.

Ambulance crews would try out all sorts of chip shops, cafes and pie shops and give regular updates to others as how good or bad they were. This particular Chinese 'Chippy' on Breck Road was ranked quite high in the ratings, plus the owner's daughter, who sometimes served behind the counter, was quite attractive. Not that that had any influence in my decision to call there for my fish and chips, oh no, and anyway, she wasn't there when I got served.

I parked the ambulance in the yard and walked over to the mess room. The first thing I did was go straight to the cooker in the kitchen and pull open the oven door, and there it was. My cap with another two; Ob's and John's I presumed.

I put it on my head then walked through into the mess room with my fish and chips. All three crews were back in now, and they clapped when they saw me wearing my cap.

"Who told you then?" asked Alan

"Snatch, and then Billy at Broadgreen."

6

During my lunch break that same first day, I had discovered that one of the car passengers in the accident had also died, It was the patient that Duggy and his mate had taken. The patient I had dealt with did indeed turn out to have a fractured neck, and he was now stable in intensive care at Walton.

I felt so pleased, not because the man had a broken neck and was still unconscious in intensive care, but more for the way that I had handled myself in the heat of the moment. Not that the others would have had time to watch me dealing with my first accident patient. To all intents and purposes, I was working on my own. I patted myself on the back and couldn't wait to tell Ob and John what they had missed. I might just tell them where to find their caps too.

Charlie the shift leader came into the room and sat at a table opposite to me to get his lunch. He'd brought sandwiches.

" I see you've been in the oven then," as he noticed I had my cap back

"Yes. Did you know it was in there, Charlie?"

"Course I did," he grinned

"So I was running around like a loose fart this morning trying to find my cap and you knew where it was all the time?"

"Got to have some fun with the newbie's" said Charlie.

"I thought all that had finished now that I'm not cadet."

" Your on the road now my lad, expect bigger and greater things" he smiled as he munched into his cheese and onion sandwich.

I didn't see John or Ob over the lunch break; they must have been busy with internal comings and goings at Walton hospital.

My afternoon shuttle service was 'five from six' into Walton hospital, all physiotherapy patients, which meant I had five patients to collect from the Anfield area.

I had to get my A to Z out for these addresses though; I discovered that they were all quite close together so it wouldn't take too long to pile them all into the vehicle and get them to their appointments on time.

What a difference from the crowd I had had in the morning. These were all women, the youngest must have been about eighty and not one of them could walk faster than a snail on crutches.

I walked a little old lady down her path towards the Ambulance. I had hooped my arm under her arm to steady her as she used her walking stick with her other hand as we went. We got to the rear doors of the Ambulance and I had to let go of her to open them. My back was turned to her and the next thing I knew, she's pinching my bum.

"Eeee," she said, "If I were sixty years younger!"

I couldn't believe it. "Now Nan, control yourself," I said.

I opened the doors and, before she hobbled up the few steps, she waved her stick in the air and shouted to those already sitting in the Ambulance, "I got him girls!"

"Hop on board, Nan"

There were howls of laughter and giggling, then clapping as granny grabbed my arm and eased herself up the steps and into the back of the Ambulance.

Twenty minutes later I dropped them off at the Physio department and then took the Ambulance around to where the Ambulance transport officer was located. It was a bit surreal for me. I had seen others do exactly the same all those months ago, only at that time I was a cadet trapped in a small office with a grumpy old man and I would be passing the time by, looking out of the window at the Ambulances. Now I could see a new cadet looking out at me as I parked the Ambulance. I felt sorry for him.

"Afternoon Malcolm, I've brought five from six into physio."

He didn't say anything, just took the slips of paper and looked through them, then handed them to the cadet to file away, just as he had done with me.

Then he looked at me and said, "Did Martha get you then?" His face beamed. It was the first time I think I had ever seen him smile.

"Would that be 'bum pinching' Martha?"

"So she got you then?"

"With a vengeance, a pound to a penny I'll have a bruise there by tomorrow."

He smiled and lit a cigarette. "Go and get yourself a brew, there isn't much on this afternoon so you'll just be getting the same run home."

"Ok, oh by the way, have you seen Ob and John knocking around anywhere? They were put on the internal this morning."

"Nope, not seen hide nor hair of them."

"Ok."

I left the office and began the search for my fellow ex cadets. It struck me that Malcolm was in a better mood than I seemed to remember. I wondered if it was, that he had a thing about cadets, just didn't like them? Now that I was a fully fledged Ambulance man, he had seemed to have altered his attitude, or maybe it was just me?

I found the internal Ambulance outside the old wards, but no sign of Ob and John. I checked in the back and could see that the stretcher and carry chair were in situ, which meant they weren't collecting anyone from a ward. I closed the doors and walked over to the casualty department to get a cup of tea from the WRVS counter. Tea and coffee was free to Ambulance crews.

I hadn't been standing there long, supping from my plastic cup, when Ob and John appeared through the doors.

"Well, well. If it isn't Batman and Robin," they spotted me and walked over.

"How's it going?" I asked.

John grunted

"Ob, ob, bloody awful" added Ob.

"Why? What's the matter?"

"We can't find our bloody caps anywhere!" John was serious. "They went missing in the mess room this morning."

I nearly choked as I swallowed a mouthful of coffee.

Ob continued the thread of conversation.

"Ob, we had to have our lunch here. Cost us a small fortune in that canteen."

"We couldn't go back to station without our caps in case the boss saw us. We've got sandwiches there," added John.

"Ob, we've had to keep out of the way of Malcolm because, as sure as eggs are eggs, he'd report us for not wearing our caps. You know what a miserable sod he's like."

I couldn't help chuckling as I regained composure from half choking myself.

"I don't see what's funny" said John. "We've finished here. No more patients to move but we can't go back to station yet."

"Why?"

"Because we haven't got our bloody caps have we! We're going to have to wait till gone five o'clock and hope the boss has gone home when we pull into the garage."

I changed the subject and told them all about the RTA I had been called to that morning and what I had done. The jealousy was almost tangible, so I kept on with telling them what a cracking day it had been up till now.

When I had finished my slightly exaggerated account of the morning's incident, I drained my coffee and looked at the time.

The clock behind the reception desk said it was five past three. "Well, I'll have to love you and leave you lads. It's time to take my grannies home."

As I walked away, I turned and smiled. "Look in the oven." I said. They looked at each other in bewilderment just as I turned the corner and disappeared down the corridor.

I loaded all my ladies into the Ambulance, taking extra special care to keep my bottom out of reach from Martha. I closed the doors and set off on the last journey of the day. It had been a good day, I had enjoyed it.

I'd got no further than a mile up the road from Walton hospital when I turned into Church Road West, then into Dunbar Street, heading for my first granny stop, as I now called them to myself.

I hadn't travelled more than twenty yards, when this man came running out from one of the terraced houses frantically waving his arms. He ran directly into my path and stood his ground in front of the Ambulance. It was a good thing that I wasn't going at any serious speed; as I'd have hit him for sure. I stopped the Ambulance with a bit more brake pressure than usual which had the old girls in the back cackling about Billy being a better driver.

The man hurried to my door and opened it.

"Quick, she's in the kitchen and she's having it now."

"Having what now?" I was puzzled.

"The baby! Are you stupid or something?"

"Have you called for an Ambulance?" I asked.

"Yes and you're here now, so come on, get move on. She's going to drop it on the kitchen floor in a minute."

My heart sank. It was my phobia come true and to top it all I was by myself.

"You say you've called for an Ambulance?" I wanted to make sure someone was on their way.

"Yes, and you're here, now come on, quick"

"But I'm not…….." I had actually forgotten that I was driving an Ambulance, which to him from the outside, looked just like an emergency Ambulance.

"Do I have to drag you out of there?"

I didn't even get the chance to call on the radio to control and confirm a vehicle was on its way. He almost dragged me from my seat. The last I heard, before being pushed towards the house, was a faint voice from the back of the Ambulance, shouting. "What's going on out there?"

I was herded into the kitchen, just a small room, not much space. His wife was sitting on the floor, legs wide akimbo clutching her tummy and rolling about in agony.

What the hell was I supposed to do? Here I was facing my biggest phobia on my first day as an Ambulance man and my mind had gone blank. I'd coped alright this morning, but this was out of the blue. I wasn't prepared. I had to think, yet there wasn't any time to think. This was really happening in front of me and they expected me to know what to do.

"How often are your contractions?" I hadn't even asked what her name was.

"All the fuckin' time, bastard, bastard, bastard. It fuckin' hurts. Have you got any gas-n-air?"

Why hadn't I thought of that? "Yes, I'll go and get it, I won't be a minute."

I hurried back to the Ambulance and flung the back door open. The entonox bottle which people often referred to as gas and air, was tucked away in the overhead locker.

"What's up son?" one of the grannies asked. I didn't know which one as I had my back to them.

"There's a woman about to give birth in the kitchen of her house."

There was a muttering between them as I was un-strapping the gas bottle from its harness.

"Do you need any help son? I was a midwife for forty years."

I looked down and around at the sitting grannies to see who had spoken. "Who has?"

Thankfully she was probably the youngest of them all, and the sprightliest. She held up her hand.

I helped Gladys, the retired midwife, down the steps of the ambulance and into the house. I entered the kitchen with a gas bottle in one hand and an old lady in the other.

"Who's this? The husband was still on edge. I couldn't blame him; I'd probably be the same in his shoes.

"This is Gladys, she's a midwife."

"Bloody ell love, no offence meant like, but shouldn't you be retired by now?"

I didn't think the husband meant any malice in what he had just said; it was a frantic scene as the mother to- be bawled, screamed and cursed all in Gods creation. Bastard seemed to be her favourite word.

"Have you got a cushion I could kneel on? My knees are really giving me jip lately." Gladys was serious, and I could understand, she must have been in her seventies.

I switched on the entonox and handed the mask to the woman.

"Do you know how to use this?" I asked between bastards and screams. The neighbours must have thought there was a murder taking place.

She nodded, and through grimaces she managed to get out a few sensible words.

"They showed us at the anti natal clinic."

"Ok, take nice long deep breaths."

Granny Gladys was now on her knees, on a cushion, and from somewhere below me she managed in her frail voice, "Do you feel like pushing, love?"

There was a hurried nodding of head by the woman.

"Ok," continued Gladys, "I have to take a look and see how much dilation there is, ok?"

More hurried nods.

"Shall I go and boil some water or something?" asked the husband.

"No, that won't be necessary. Is this your first?" asked Gladys from below.

"Yes, and the frigging last. I am not going through this ever again."

There was a quick retort from behind the mask. "And neither the fuck am I, you bastard."

"Come on Sally! It's not my fault."

At least we had a name now.

"The fuck it is."

"There's not much dilation going on down here," came the gentle voice of Gladys.

"What does that mean?" The husband was confused and feeling hopeless, a bit like me.

"It means that she's not having the baby just yet. No waters have broken I see, but that really doesn't mean anything," came the answer from ground level.

Sally was beginning to calm a little; it seemed the entonox was doing its job.

There was a loud 'rat tat' at the front door, and a man's voice shouted "Hello, Ambulance here."

Thank God, I thought. They can take over.

"In here," shouted the husband.

An Ambulance man that I had never seen before entered through the kitchen doorway. The small room was now full to capacity. I was explaining to him what had happened as I helped Gladys up from the floor.

"Right" he said, as he tried to take in the picture. "You're booked into Walton, is that right, Sally?" Sally nodded from behind the mask.

"Alright then, we'll get you aboard our proper Ambulance and take you down there."

Sally nodded in agreement again.

I disliked the remark of 'proper Ambulance.'

I leaned over to Sally. "I'll have to take that bottle from you in a minute, but the other crew will have another for you on their proper Ambulance. Ok?" I emphasised the word proper.

Another nod. She was much calmer now and less prone to expletives.

I was helping Gladys back into the Ambulance and I noticed the Ambulance man watching me as he removed the carry chair that was hooked on the inside of the rear door of his vehicle.

I closed the doors, and was about to go and retrieve my entonox bottle from Sally in the kitchen, when he came over to me.

"What station are you based at?"

"Anfield", I said.

"Was that your patient you had in the house with you?"

"Yes."

"Why?" he said.

"She said she was a retired midwife. This is my first day on the road, and to be honest with you, when that bloke dragged me into the house, I just bottled. I needed all the help I could get."

He burst into fits of laughter. "I don't believe this" he was sniggering.

My face was serious; I couldn't see anything funny at all. "What's funny?"

"She told you she was a midwife?"

"Yes."

"Hate to tell you mate, but she's a regular of ours. We'll get her down the town later; she'll be pissed as arse holes."

"You're joking?"

"Gladys from the Palace, regular as clockwork. She just lives around the corner. I thought she might have been a relative or something when first I saw her in the house."

"Shit, you're not going to report this are you?"

He laughed again. "No, don't worry about it; it's called a learning curve. Mind you, funny stories do have a tendency to get around."

He turned and headed for the house. I could see his shoulders bouncing up and down as he laughed to himself at my expense.

Gladys got the old finger wagging from me when I dropped her off at home. I couldn't shout at her, she was a canny old girl who had given me a bit of confidence in a stressful situation.

I dropped the rest of the grannies off and headed back to station with my tail between my legs.

What a day it had turned out to be. One minute I'm over the moon with my actions and treatment at a serious RTA, the next I'm making a bloody fool of myself. Would I ever learn, I wondered?

7

I was still working the day shifts at Anfield station when June arrived.

Beryl and I had agreed that we didn't want a lavish wedding, we couldn't afford it, but we did get married in church and had a small reception at the 'Lowlands', a mansion house with a room that was suitable for such a venue. The building was in the heart of West Derby village, and was a place once owned by Pete Best and used by the Beatles to practice before they hit the big time. The wedding went quite well without any serious hiccups.

Beryl and I didn't have any honeymoon as such; we were too busy moving into our rented one bed roomed flat just off Anfield road. This flat had one serious advantage to it, I could walk to work. The disadvantage, which we didn't really consider at the time of renting, was that it was only two hundred yards away from Liverpool FC. Traffic and parking was chaos every other Saturday. However, we were happy there, it was our own place and I had escaped from my father.

More than six months had ensued since my first day on the road and my encounter with Gladys from the Palace, not forgetting the pregnant lady. I often wondered if she had a boy or a girl.

At first I thought the Ambulance man, who I now knew to be Albert from Westminster station, was just adding a little rhyming slang to give Gladys the title she held, but I later found out that there really was a pub called the 'The Palace' tucked away in one of the labyrinth of side streets, and this was where you could find Gladys most nights of the week.

Over the past months I had collected Gladys several times, taking her to her hospital out patient appointments. She was as sharp as a pin during the day, although on occasion the smell of alcohol did linger from the night before. I got on quite well with her and it seems that she really was a midwife in the years before I was born.

Over a period of time I got to know a little more about her personal life. She had come from a 'well to do' family out in rural Lancashire.

She had married but never had any children of her own. She had trained as a Midwife in Liverpool, where she had met her future husband, Bert.

A problematic issue was that he was a Catholic and she was a Protestant, which had greatly upset her family. Mixed faith marriages were severely frowned upon in those days.

In order to marry, she had to forego her own faith and change her religion to that of Catholic. This was the last straw for her family. She was shunned and cut off from any inheritance that might have come her way.

Her husband Bert had been a docker at the Huskisson dock on the River Mersey, working all the hours he could get. Then in May 1941 there was a heavy and sustained air aid by the Luftwaffe on the doks and Bert never came home. Gladys never really got over her loss; she talked about Bert as if he was still out there somewhere. They never did find his body.

She had stayed in Liverpool, knowing that she couldn't go back to her family in Lancashire. She was alone and only had her work to keep her occupied. She retired in the early sixties, and that's when the drinking had started.

I found it amazing, sometimes heart warming and sometimes heartbreaking when talking to my old grannies on those journeys to and from hospital. Most of the life stories they told were of genuine hardship; of times that seemed so alien and cruel to me; in a world which I don't think I could have survived. Gladys's story was just one of them.

My troubled and total display of inexperience with Gladys and the pregnant lady had now just about done the rounds of all the Ambulance stations in the City. It was fast becoming a tired story to be talked about over cups of tea and coffee in the mess rooms and ward kitchens.

Everything comes to those who wait as the expression goes. So I was glad to hear about Albert who was the other Ambulance man on that day and who had been the one to spill the beans on my little escapade. He himself had now become the butt of gossip around the stations.

It was over the last weekend of October. There had been a torrential downpour of rain on the Saturday night. The following day, Albert and his mate were called to Clubmoore playing fields.

A footballer from one of the Sunday league games had been involved in a heavy tackle and broken his leg. Albert, who was driving the Ambulance at the time, had taken the decision to drive the Ambulance across the pitch to get as close as possible to the patient who was lying in the middle of the field. In the majority of cases, this would have been the right thing to do, Albert didn't take into account that the ground was soaked from the night before and the inevitable happened.

They had treated and loaded the footballer into the Ambulance and were about to drive away when the rear wheels began to spin furiously, spraying showers of mud and grass over most of the people who had gathered around at the time. There wasn't any way he was going to drive that Ambulance off the field. The more he tried, the deeper the wheels sank into the mud. He had tried driving backwards and forwards, in an attempt to rock the ambulance out of the mire. The more he did this, the more the howls of pain came from the footballer clutching at his broken leg in the back of the Ambulance.

Eventually he had to admit defeat. Another Ambulance was called which wisely parked at the edge of the pitch on hard standing ground. The patient was duly stretchered from the stricken Ambulance to the second Ambulance.

Apparently it took several hours before a tractor could be commandeered from a small farm several miles away to pull the stricken vehicle out of its muddy trench.

This was a new story to do the rounds of the station mess rooms and it took the pressure off my episode, putting it into the history books of service anecdotes. It was ironic that it had to be Albert who had made it happen; revenge is sweet.

Charlie, the shift leader, called me into his office; it was a Friday morning, last day of the week for the day staff like me. I was looking forward to the weekend as I was going to meet Tony, an old school friend of mine who had joined the army. He had a couple of weeks of leave and we had arranged to meet up and have a few beers, it was going to be a boozy weekend.

I strolled into the office wondering if I had done anything wrong. It was usually the way of things when summoned by the boss to join him in his office.

"What have I done now Charlie"?

Charlie smiled. He was a kindly man, well over six feet tall with fair wavy hair and built like the Michelin man. He wasn't slim.

"How do you fancy going onto the relief shift rota, starting next week"?

It was the news I had been waiting for, for months. The next step up the rung of the ladder that would eventually lead to a permanent shift rota.

I think my face beamed. "Yes, I'd love to."

This meant that I would be working to a regular shift pattern, but the downside was I would be working at different stations all over the city; filling in for absences and holidays.

For the last six months I had been working on the single crew out patient Ambulances, and every so often on the double crew day Ambulances. This was usually with a permanent shift worker who was working a day shift as overtime on his day off.

I never did get called to anything more interesting than that on my first day on the road. Whilst I was crewed up on a day Ambulance, it was mainly what was categorised as urgent calls. These were patients who had been visited by their GP and required hospital admission within one or two hours after the GP had left the house. Mostly it was chest infections, back pain or abdominal pain. Nothing that required the blue light to be used and in the majority of cases the patient would walk out to the Ambulance.

Of course, there were those who were bed ridden and needed to be carried downstairs. There were also those with what we dubbed 'P J syndrome' This was when a patient had seen a GP, either at home or at the Doctors surgery, and were then told they would be going to hospital for admission by Ambulance. Most of the time this was because they couldn't get anyone to give them a lift to hospital or a taxi would be too expensive.

The 'syndrome' was that they would go upstairs, put on a pair of pyjamas, get into bed and stay there until the Ambulance arrived. There was absolutely no need for them to go to bed before the Ambulance arrived. They just thought it was the right thing to do, to look right for the part as it were.

Ob and I were taken in by this during our first few weeks on the road when we had worked together on the day Ambulance. We were under the impression that if anyone was in bed they were in need of being carried downstairs and into the Ambulance.

After being crewed with more experienced ambulance men a few times, I discovered the Pyjama syndrome and how to handle it.

It wasn't that we were lazy; it was more a case of self preservation. I was told by a more experienced ambulance man that if we carried every patient we went for, we too, would soon end up being carried into an Ambulance with chronic back problems. This was a major hazard of the job.

The way to handle this was by careful questioning. First, we would ask what the problem was? Why were they going to hospital? If that passed the test and it wasn't a serious problem, the next question was where had they seen the GP? If it was at the surgery, we knew we were onto a winner; in other words they could walk. If that didn't work out, it was determined whether they were in bed at the time the GP came to visit, or downstairs? If they were in bed when the GP came to visit, it narrowed the options. The final question would be. "Do you think you could walk out to the Ambulance?"

If the answer was, "No", then they were carried. If the answer was, "I'll try," then almost all of the time they could manage with just a little under arm support. At the end of the day, if we, as the crew, were unsure, then the patient was always carried.

This approach wheedled out many patients who didn't need to be carried and it was good for our backs too.

Charlie handed me a sheet of paper which had three rows of squares, seven squares in each row. Each row of squares represented one week. Across the top row of squares were the days of the week, starting with Monday on the left, and down the side of the squares were the shift patterns to be worked for that week. Basically the rota worked out as seven days on a shift then two days off. After three weeks there would be four days off, then the cycle would start again.

Now I knew what shifts I would be working, but not at what station. According to my newly acquired rota, Charlie wanted me to start on the Wednesday, which would be an afternoon shift. Then he told me it would be at Westminster station.

I would find out where I would be working a week of night shifts, which followed on after afternoon shifts, probably sometime in the middle of next week. Charlie always tried to let you know where you would be working as soon as he could, and that was always appreciated. This now meant that I would have next Monday and Tuesday as days off as well as the Saturday and Sunday, which was fine by me.

"I'll have to put you on the outpatient Ambulance on your own today, though." Charlie was shuffling through some patient address cards as he said it. "It's just four from thirteen into Broadgreen this morning."

"Cheers, Charlie." I took the address cards from him and wondered out to my Ambulance. I was thrilled to bits! I'd be a proper shift worker as from Monday, no more outpatients. All calls would be mainly emergency calls, and better wages came with the shift allowance. I now loved this job!

The morning passed without any problems and after lunch I was still on a high with my relief rota position.

Ob was still working the day shifts, but it would happen for him too, as a new squad of cadets would graduate in a few weeks and they would start were we had, on the bottom rung. We looked forward to hiding their caps, but it wouldn't be in the oven. We would think of more devious places.

It was a lovely afternoon as I drove through the avenues and roads of West Derby, warm and sunny. Tunic draped over the back of my seat and shirt sleeves rolled up, life couldn't be better with just another three outpatients into Broadgreen again this afternoon. I'd be finished well before five today and that would be it. My days as a day shift worker would be over.

Billy the transport officer gave me an extra patient to add to my take home list. It was only just past three o'clock when I had them all loaded aboard and set off for what I thought would be the final journey of the day. I'd drop off the last patient in West Derby village at around half past four and then it was just a fifteen minute ride back to the station to finish for the weekend.

I was early; it was only five minutes to four when I dropped my last patient at their front door. I drove off to find a quiet place to park, finish my log sheet and have a relaxing cigarette before calling in on the radio that I was clear and available in West Derby.

I was parked in a narrow leafy lane where there was very little passing traffic and all the large detached houses were set well back behind tall, well manicured hedgerows. Although I couldn't see them, I knew there were large well trimmed lawns behind these hedges, some with full sized tennis courts. This was a well to do area of the city.

With window rolled down and enjoying the sunshine that filtered through the leafy rows of trees, I counted my blessings. It had been a good day. Good news regarding the relief rota and I'd be seeing my old school mate in Preston tomorrow. I checked the time, it was nearly a quarter past four; time to clear and head back to station.

There was a long silence after I had radioed control and told them where I was. Then came the reply.

"We have a VP (Voluntary Patient) with escort, a walking patient for admission to Rainhill. Can you manage this before you finish?"

I wasn't expecting this; usually it's just a curt "Return to station," but not this time. I had been in the wrong place at the right time to fall for a late call. Rainhill is a psychiatric hospital on the outskirts of Liverpool, heading towards St Helens. At best I would be an hour late getting back to station. However, it would be an hour's overtime and after all; it had been a good day.

I accepted the call to an address which was just a few hundred yards from where I was parked. It would be a large house in this up market area.

I flicked my cigarette out of the window and started the engine.

Two minutes later I was driving down the wide, grass verged and tree lined avenue looking at the name plates on the gateway entrances. It didn't take long to find the one I was looking for and, to my delight; the gateway and drive were wide enough to drive the Ambulance through and along to the turning circle outside the front door. This was going to be a cushy job; I'd soon be on my way to Rainhill.

There was a wooden porch over the front door, almost like church entrance, with ivy climbing each side. Inside the porch I rang the door bell.

I heard the barking first, then footsteps across a tiled floor. At least the dog was somewhere off in the distance and it wouldn't be accompanying its owner to the door.

I was confronted by a woman in her mid-forties, well dressed, and rather attractive. She looked a little distraught and seemed to sigh with relief when she saw me and the Ambulance parked outside her door on the driveway.

"Thank goodness you brought your van to the door." She didn't have a Liverpool accent. "The last time they came they parked in the avenue and we had to crawl all the way down the path. Thank God none of the neighbours saw anything."

"I'm sorry?" I didn't have a clue what she was talking about.

"My father."

"Yes." I said, "I've come to take him for admission to Rainhill."

"I'd take him myself in the car, but he would only be jumping around the seats and making a thorough nuisance of himself."

"That's ok, we have seat belts in the back of the Ambulance."

"Oh, he won't wear a seat belt."

I shrugged my shoulders. It wasn't mandatory to wear them in the back. That would be their choice.

"Can I come in?"

"Yes, yes. He's in the kitchen. I've got his case upstairs, packed and ready to go."

The hall was huge. A high ceiling with ornate plastering and a sparkling chandelier on a solid chain dangled like the sword of Damocles over my head. The hall was so big it even had its own furniture.

What looked like polished oak antique dressing tables and chairs were placed against the walls. The floor had large black and white tiles and these too were polished. A wide and carpeted central staircase ascended directly in front of us, to a landing that divided at the top to the right and left. There were four doors that led from the hallway. She directed me through the second door on the right.

"Just go through there into the kitchen, I'll get his case."

She scurried off up the stairs and I did as I was told and opened the second door. I entered what I thought must be the dining room. A table that could seat at least twenty people was in the middle, but there were no chairs. The table had a vase of flowers at its centre and two laced runners down the length, one on each side of the vase. There was a grandfather clock at the far end of the room, its pendulum swinging behind the glass door. There was another door off this room which was ajar. I headed towards it. Then I heard the growling. I'd forgotten about the dog.

"Hello"? I thought I had better make my presence known to whatever was behind the door.

"Hello, it's the Ambulance." No response. The growling had stopped.

How stupid is that? I thought, telling a dog that I'm an Ambulance.

I opened the door and entered the kitchen. A large farmhouse table sat sturdily in the middle of the room. An array of pots and pans hanging from a wooden beam were the first things that took my eye. Then I noticed him. To my left and lying on the floor was an older man, maybe in his seventies, it was hard to tell. Tweed jacket and grey flannel trousers. He didn't move, but just kept still and stared right at me. It was a little un-nerving to say the least.

I crouched down to get a better look at him and make sure he was conscious. I put out my hand to squeeze his shoulder and he moved. His head turned and he started to lick my hand. I pulled away.

"Are you ok?"

He came back at me with a whimpering sound.

And then it dawned.

I remember Harry at the training school telling us of an experience he once had with a psychiatric patient who thought he was the invisible man. He had refused to go to hospital unless he could make himself invisible by taking all his clothes off. Harry played along with him, but insisted that he left his socks on so he could see where he was. So there was Harry, walking with this bloke from his house and into the street to get to the Ambulance, totally naked except for his socks. But it had worked. 'The moral of the story', he had said, "is to go along with what the patient wants, play the same game and they're as quiet as lambs."

The man's, or the dog's, daughter, whichever way you want to look at it, now entered the kitchen, suitcase in hand.

"I'm sorry about this" she said. "Every time he has one of these turns it's so embarrassing."

"Don't worry." I said. "It's an illness just like any other illness."

"Oh, I don't mean for me, I meant for you."

"Me, why me"?

"Because he won't move unless you pretend to be another dog, then you go out to the van and he will follow."

"What?"

"That's the only way we can get him to move. I've tried putting a lead on him or coaxing him with the dog dish, but the only thing he'll move for is if the Ambulance driver pretends to be another dog. Didn't they tell you before you came"?

My shoulders drooped. "No, they didn't." I'd been well and truly had by control. How they must be laughing their heads off now. I've never been so truly embarrassed in my life.

I had to crawl through some strange house on my hands and knees, out to the Ambulance with a mentally challenged elderly man crawling along behind me, sniffing my bum as we went. I was so grateful that he didn't think I was a bitch!

He followed up me the steps and into the rear of the Ambulance, with the woman tagging along behind.

I got up from my doggy position and sat on the bench seat which ran along the offside wall of the saloon. The patient remained on all fours while the woman placed a collar and leash around his neck. She sat next to me holding onto the leash.

"I'm awfully sorry about this, but it's the only way we can get him into the van."

"Ambulance." I corrected her.

The patient now lay down on his side on the floor of the Ambulance between where we were sitting and the stretcher. He was almost in the foetal position. I was sorely tempted to rub his tummy with my foot.

"He'll be fine now" she said.

At the hospital end, I flatly refused to do the same thing to get him out of the Ambulance and into the ward.

It took two strapping male nurses to carry him out of the Ambulance.

I would remember that address for a long time and make sure if I was ever called again, I would send in whoever I was working with first and let them have the pleasure.

They say that the truth can be stranger than fiction and this was certainly a case that supported that theory. If there is anyone at all who knows about this theory, it will be the Ambulance crews all over the world who deal with different people and different situations day after day.

When I called Control to inform them that I was clear at the hospital it was quarter past five. It would still take me at least half an hour to get back to station. They couldn't give me any more calls; it was now well past my finishing time.

I now knew that the controller must have known what I was about to face with that patient, but I supposed if he had warned me, I would have turned it down, claiming that it would take me past my finishing time.

The rule was, if it wasn't an emergency then it was reasonable for the crew or person to decline the assignment if it would take them past their finishing time. However, if it was an emergency, then it had to be responded to, no questions asked.

There was a brief pause before the controller came back to me on the radio.

"Four seven" (which was my call sign on that day) "Did you have any problems with that last patient"?

I could tell he was suppressing a giggle as he spoke.

"Negative." I replied

Another pause. They must have been scratching their heads in the control room, wandering why I hadn't ranted on about the embarrassment that others must have endured with that patient.

"Thank you, return to station."

"Will do" was my reply.

I lied, but it felt good. More importantly I wouldn't be the butt of another joke to do the rounds of the mess rooms.

8

Westminster station is aptly situated just off Westminster Road in the Kirkdale district of Liverpool.

A number of Ambulance stations took their names from the name of the road or street in which they were situated, not necessarily the district of the city.

Kirkdale, is a large populated area and behind the main roads that dissect the district is a maze of back streets, each crammed like sardines with rows of small Victorian terraced housing. Many of the streets are still cobbled and are a nightmare to drive over in wet or icy conditions. Some street lighting is afforded by the old gas lamp posts which had been converted to electric lamps, giving a somewhat false illusion of being stuck in the time of Queen Victoria, particularly on dark, foggy nights.

My first afternoon shift was due to start at 3pm. Westminster was a busy station and I knew afternoon shifts were generally the busiest. This was going to be valuable learning experience for me. I was apprehensive, but looking forward to it at the same time.

The station itself is at the end of a row of terraced houses. A ten foot high wall enclosed the forecourt, garage and mess room on three sides, the fourth side being the gable end of a house. A wide gateway, minus the gates, led onto Westminster road. It was an old building, probably built in the 1920's or 30's

There is only one emergency Ambulance stationed here, along with three day shift out patient vehicles.

I arrived early for my shift. It was half past two and the place was empty. No Ambulance and no out patient vehicles to be seen. I didn't have a key to let myself inside the station building, so I had to wait in my car until someone came, which was just ten minutes later. It was the morning shift returning, to go off duty at 3pm.

I didn't know either of the morning crew, so I introduced myself and explained this was my first shift on relief duties.

The taller of the two must have been in his thirties, dark haired and athletic looking. His mate, probably in his fifties, had greying hair and was a little overweight.

"I'm John and this is Harry" said the taller one as he took a bunch of keys from his belt and fed one into the door lock.

"You're early" said Harry.

"It's my first relief shift and I didn't want to be late."

"Early is always good, son."

John pushed open the door. "I'll get the kettle on; you'll be gasping for cuppa."

"Not really thanks" I said. "I had one just before I left home."

"Tch, tch." Harry frowned. "First rule of Ambo work is that you're always in need of a cuppa."

I nodded, lesson learned.

"I take it you were a cadet then?" John was filling the kettle from the tap

"Yes."

"I was in 'A' squad, the first batch, loved every minute of it. How are Harry and Wally these days?"

"All right I suppose, I haven't seen either of them myself for a while. I did hear that Harry had gone off on the sick. I don't know what for though."

"I liked Harry, he said, he had a wicked sense of humour."

I had to agree.

After starting in the cadets, we got to know our trainers quite well and Harry was a typical born comedian. That was why I wasn't sure if he had been telling us the truth about the patient who insisted on being invisible by taking his clothes off. After the dog incident, I had decided that it was probably true.

"Who'll I be working with to day?"

"It'll be Frank, his mate is on holiday this week. He's an experienced bloke, you'll be ok."

I was glad to hear it.

"Talk –o- the devil; he's just pulling into the yard now."

I looked through the mess room window into the court yard and saw Frank getting out of his car. He was tallish, maybe in his fifties with a moustache. He slung the strap of a khaki bag over his shoulder and headed towards us. My first relief shift was about to start

The clock on the mess room wall ticked away the minutes and then the hours. I discovered Frank was married with three teenage kids and was looking forward to next week when he'd have two weeks leave and would be going on holiday to Cornwall, just him and his wife. He was a keen caravan'er and enjoyed getting away in the summer, but this would be the first time he'd be going without the children in tow, but he was a little apprehensive about leaving three teenagers behind to take care of the house. I couldn't say I blamed him.

"I don't believe this" he said, as he looked up at the clock on the wall, and then, as if not trusting what time it was displaying, he checked his watch.

"What's that"?

"It's seven o'clock and we haven't turned a wheel."

We had been on station for four hours and not a single call had come in. I was getting a bit bored with watching the telly in the corner.

As if by providence, the telephone rang just as he had said it. I could feel my heart begin to race; this could be my first emergency call as a proper shift crew.

"I'm sure they've got hidden microphones in here," he said. Frank took the call as I stood and readied myself to go out to the Ambulance, picking up my cap and psyching up to whatever emergency lay ahead.

"Ok," he replied to whatever message he had been given by control, and replaced the receiver.

He turned to me. "Get your meal break."

We ate our respective sandwiches, and then watched Star Trek without any interruptions. When that had finished, the draughts board came out of the cupboard and the kettle went on for more tea.

I began to like Frank. He was quietly spoken, but confident in his manner. I also learned that he'd been in the Ambulance Service for fifteen years. He had been a prison officer before joining and had never regretted the move. I got the impression that his character was too soft hearted to be ordering prisoners about. He wasn't pushy or of a mind to feel superior to me because I was inexperienced, unlike some I had worked with on the day shift Ambulance.

He told me a story about the time when he was working a night shift at Walton prison; it was actually the catalyst that made him decide to apply to join the Ambulance service.

There had been a prisoner who had been on what they call 'suicide watch.' He didn't go into the reason why this was the case, but it meant he had to check on the prisoner at regular intervals through the night.

It was around three in the morning when he slid the door hatch back to look inside the cell. It was dark and he had to use his torch to peer inside and check that all was fine. The prisoner was in solitary, so there was only one single bed in the cell, unlike other cells where there were bunk beds.

The light from his torch showed him that the bed was empty. He beamed it around the cell looking for the prisoner. His initial first thought was that the prisoner was using the bucket in the corner, but then the beam found him hanging from the bars of the cell window.

He couldn't take it in at first, and then realisation flooded over him. He called to his colleague further along the landing as he rummaged for the cell door key.

Somehow the prisoner had managed to obtain an extra pillowcase from somewhere, and had painstakingly managed to tear it into narrow strips. When he had torn enough, he had then plaited them together to make enough rope to hang himself.

His colleague had now arrived and together they managed to unfasten the makeshift rope and lay him on the floor.

Frank had been given some rudimentary first aid training when he first joined the prison service and began to try and resuscitate the prisoner, while his colleague went to raise the alarm and call for the Ambulance. He was there for fifteen minutes trying to resuscitate before the Ambulance crew arrived and took over.

"The thing was" Frank said "I had managed to get him breathing again before the Ambulance arrived, but in the end he died in hospital. He was pronounced 'brain dead' a few days later and they switched off the resuscitation equipment."

"It made me realise, he continued, that I had actually done something that gave me so much satisfaction. It felt good, you know? I was proud of myself, which wasn't the feel good factor I was getting in my job at the time. I'm not saying that a screws job isn't worthwhile, but at that moment I knew I was in the wrong job."

I could understand what he meant about the feel good factor, it was the feeling I had had on that first day at the traffic accident.

Frank was smiling to himself as thoughts must have been drifting through his mind.

"The irony of it is, not long after I'd started in this job I had an emergency call back to the prison. The night shift had been called there in the early hours as two prisoners were having a go at each other in the cell after lights out, and one of them had his front teeth knocked out. Later on in that day, when we had come on shift, we got a call, prisoner attempted suicide, that's all the information we got from Control. It seemed strange going back in there, but with a different hat on, if you see what mean? Anyway, it turns out that the prisoner who had his teeth knocked out in the early hours had been discharged from hospital that same night and unknown to the warders, he had somehow managed to smuggle a small suture needle from the hospital, probably hid it in his mouth. He'd used the sharp tip of the needle to try cut away at his wrists. He managed to cut through his skin alright, but it wasn't very deep; some bleeding but not life threatening."

"What happened then?"

"We took him back to casualty where they put a couple of stitches in the wound and then they sent him back to prison later that day.

"I bet he was thoroughly searched the second time."

"Strip searched I would think."

"What a waste of space these people are."

"Aye you're not wrong there, but it worked in his favour though."

"Why was that?"

"I heard he was put in the hospital wing when he got back. It's a cushy number for a prisoner being on the hospital wing."

"Is that why he did it?"

"It would seem that way."

"Another brew? Frank said, abruptly changing the subject.

"At this rate, I'll be piddling tea till the cows come home."

"Ah, but you have to learn to get brew whenever you can, you never know when your next chance for a cuppa might be."

"Go on then, if you insist." I said.

Frank picked up our mugs and teapot from the coffee table that was parked between the two arm chairs and disappeared out to the kitchen area.

Frank took his tea seriously; he was the only one I had met so far who used tea leaves instead of bags. He took great store in letting it brew for the correct amount of time in the pot before pouring through a sieve. I had to admit, it was a nice brew that he served, even if the odd tea leaf did end up at the bottom of the mug.

Frank was still in the kitchen when the phone rang. I nearly jumped with the noise. I heard a voice from the kitchen. "Bloody typical, just when I'm in the middle of making a pot. Can you get that, Ken?"

This was it I thought, our first job of the night. My hand was actually trembling as I reached for the phone and note pad.

"Hello, Westminster." I said.

A thick scouse accent came into the earpiece, which I recognised as being Stan, the controller.

"Alright Frank?"

"It's not Frank." I said. "It's Ken."

"Oh, hello son, having a quiet night then, eh."

"Yes, it's boring."

"Boring? Make the most of it lad, you don't get many slow shifts, especially at Westminster."

"Have you got a job for us now?" I almost pleaded.

"Nah, just wanted to know if Frank managed to cover the night shift with overtime, can you ask him for me?"

I shouted the question to Frank who was still in the kitchen.

"Yes, George is doing it," came back the reply, which I duly passed on to the controller.

"Ok, thank you" he said, and then cut the connection.

I was still leaning over the table with pen poised, ready to write the job down on the pad when Frank stuck his head through the doorway. "Is that a job?"

"No, just wanted to know about the shift cover."

"Good," I heard him mumble.

I checked the time on the wall clock, it was just after ten. An hour to go before the night shift took over. Although I had been on the station for seven hours, it hadn't seemed like it. Frank's stories, watching telly and a few games of draughts had seemed to pass the time reasonably quickly. Frank returned from the kitchen with a fresh pot of tea. We had to let it brew for a few minutes before he poured.

"So, how long have you been on the road now, Ken?"

"Nearly a year, but it's only been on the day Ambulance at Lower Breck. This is my first proper shift."

"Some shift, eh? Still, it isn't over till the fat lady sings at eleven."

"I thought we might have got at least one job."

"There's time yet. So enjoy the peace and quiet while you can."

"That's what Stan said on the phone."

"He's right. In fact I can't remember the last shift we did without turning a wheel. Must be months ago."

"I must be a jinx." I said.

"Hey, I;m not knocking it. You can come again if you're that sort of jinx."

"Looks like we'll be having a quiet week then, I'm here till Sunday."

Frank smiled and took a sip of hot tea. "You'll understand after you've been on the road for a few years. It's called experience."

Then the phone rang again.

   Frank answered this time, and started to scribble on the pad. At last we were getting a job.

Frank put the phone down. "Damn, this means were going to be late back."

It was now half past ten, and we should have been finishing in half an hour. I made similar moans and groans to keep up an appearance of disappointment at the late time, but inside I was excited at the thought of my first emergency call on shifts.

"What's the job?" I asked as I put on my tunic and cap.

"Possible drowning. There's someone in the river Mersey down at the Pier Head."

My heart started to race at the thought. This could be a serious incident, a drowning.

I hurried out of the mess room and headed for the garage where the Ambulance was parked. I was desperately trying to remember the differences between fresh water drowning and salt water drowning; a person would drown slower in salt water.

Frank was locking the station door as I reached the garage.

"Who's driving?" I shouted back to him.

"You can, so long as you don't go mad and get us killed."

I hopped into the driver's seat and fired the engine, full of excitement and eager to go.

Frank climbed into the attendant's seat and reached for the radio to tell control that we were mobile.

I switched the headlights and blue emergency lights on. The beam of the blue lights swirled around the dark station yard walls like a revolving search light.

"Four three, forty three is mobile to the Pier Head, over." Frank spoke our call sign number into the mic.

There was a moment's silence, and then Stan the controller came back through the speakers.

"Four three, stand down, stand down, we have a closer vehicle. Stand down on station."

"Roger, will do." Frank replaced the mic back into its holder and turned towards me. "Wow! that was close. We'd probably have been out till gone midnight with that job."

I was bitterly disappointed, but dared not show it.

I switched the lights and engine off. We hadn't moved the Ambulance at all; it was still in its parking bay inside the garage and it remained there until I went home for the night.

My first emergency callout with Frank was the next day. Only twenty minutes had passed since signing on duty at Westminster station, quite a contrast to the previous day.

The call was to a high rise block of flats in the Everton district. They were recently built on the sloping incline of Everton Valley, which gave the residents a panoramic view down to the River Mersey and beyond to the Wirral peninsular.

The emergency call had come via the Police, who said they would be attending. Apparently the occupant was an elderly man who lived on his own and hadn't been seen for a few days by the neighbours. This in itself wasn't all that unusual; the concern was about the smell that was evident when a neighbour had pushed open the letter box to call through to the man and there had been no answer.

Frank drove quickly, but safely with blue lights flashing. It was Frank's turn to drive and my turn to attend.

We came to a halt at the entrance to the block of flats and parking outside the main doors. As per usual, the police hadn't arrived yet.

A crowd of kids had begun to gather; it wasn't every day that Ambulances came into your street.

"What's up Mister?"

Frank and I had hardly stepped down from the cab before we were inundated with a barrage of questions.

"Is someone dead?"

"Who's dead Mr?"

"Is there loads of blood?"

An older and taller lad, wearing jeans, white trainers, brown jumper and looking as if he had come dressed straight from a jumble sale, pushed through to the front of the gathering crowd of kids and asked if we wanted him to 'mind the Ambulance'. This was apparently the normal sort of question on a Saturday afternoon close to Anfield or Goodison.

The streets around the football grounds would be flooded with parked cars on match days and fans heading to the football games would be asked the same question by small gangs of young kids.

Each gang would have its own patch of several streets. This was in the hope that the driver of the parked car would drop them a tip when they returned from the game. It was always wise to agree to the terms as a rejection almost always caused scratched paintwork, missing hub caps or snapped aerials or a flat tyre on return to the parked car.

"Good idea son, make sure no one touches or goes inside." Frank patted the lad on his head. The contract agreed.

We gathered the carry chair, blanket and first aid bag and headed through the entrance doors for the lift.

The lift doors swished open and we entered what was almost a silver corrugated metal box. I pressed the button for the fourteenth floor and the doors swished closed.

"You're not going to pay him anything are you?"

"Nah." Frank said. "Just keeping on the right side of them until we leave, anyway, the coppers will be along soon, and that'll take their minds off our motor."

The lift doors swished open and we walked out onto the fourteenth floor landing. It was just a large vestibule. Two front doors belonging to two separate flats were on the opposite side to the lift and two other doors on either side of the lift. A fifth door on the landing, half open, was in the far left hand corner that led the way to the staircase. Large, sealed windows to the right and left of the vestibule allowed daylight into the concrete space.

A man in just a pair of jeans and sleeveless vest was talking to a woman by the furthest door on the right. She was wearing a pale blue rain coat and tartan scarf which covered the curlers in her hair, the handles of a large brown handbag were hooked over her left arm at the elbow.

"Took your bloody time didn't you? We've been waiting twenty friggin minutes. There could be a man dying in there for all we know."

The woman was looking at Frank as she spoke. He was taller and older than me, and so must be the more senior. She wasn't wrong there.

Frank ignored her comments. "What's going on then?"

The man was about to answer, but the woman beat him to it and told us the story of not seeing the old guy for a while and the milk bottles on the door step which had accumulated over the past few days. They had knocked and got no answer, shouted through the letter box with the same result, and the smell emanating from the letterbox when it was opened was disgusting.

"When did you last see him?" asked Frank.

"Been a few days, hasn't it Arthur?" Arthur in the vest nodded.

"Has anyone got a spare key?" Frank said to no one in particular and stooped down to push open the letter box to look through. His nose crinkled as the smell wafted through the small opening.

"The council should have one." proffered the vest man.

"I meant relatives or neighbours." said Frank

Both shook their head. "I've never seen him have any visitors." The woman probably came out of her door every time the lift stopped at their landing to see who it was.

"Do you know his name?" I said, thinking I should ask something to justify my presence.

"Think it's Dan." said the woman. "He keeps himself to himself, don't really see much of him."

Frank nodded, pushed back his cap and shouted through the letter box.

"Dan, it's the Ambulance service. Can you get to the door?"

We all fell silent as we listened for a reply. There wasn't any.

He tried again.

"Dan, can you hear me? Can you get to the door?"

No reply.

Frank straightened up, and then pushed his boot against the bottom of the door where it closed against the frame; it gave a little movement. He then reached up and pushed on the top of the door with his hand, and that gave a little movement too.

"Nothing else for it then, we'll have to break in."

"Are you allowed to do that?" said vest man.

Frank gave his reply to the woman; she was obviously the dominant one in the relationship.

"Well we could wait for the police to arrive and let them do it, or we could take the chance of being prosecuted for breaking and entering trying to save someone's life. Either way, this door needs to be opened."

The woman and vest man looked at each other. "Oh dear, we don't want any trouble" she said

Frank took a couple of paces back from the door, then brought up his right foot and lunged at the door just beneath the Yale lock which was about waist height. There was a splintering sound that echoed around the vestibule as the lock failed to hold its grip on the wooden frame, and the door burst open.

The smell from inside the flat wafted out into the vestibule, quickly followed by half a dozen cats that squealed and made directly for the open door to the staircase.

"Jeez" The woman almost jumped as the cats flashed by our feet. It gave me a bit of a start too.

Frank pushed the door inwards from where it had bounced back off the hallway wall and entered the flat. I followed him through and along the hall.

"Hello, Dan." Frank shouted as he opened the first door on the right off the hallway, it was the kitchen.

Newspapers, yellowing with age, were spread out across a kitchen table as a makeshift cloth. Used empty plates, cups and bottles were scattered across the table; some had fallen to the floor and broken, probably with the help of the cats. The sink was piled high with unwashed pans and crockery. The room was empty and we moved on to the next door in the hallway. It was the living room. This too was in a dishevelled state. Finally we reached the bedroom. The heavy, thick curtains were drawn which allowed little daylight to enter through the window.

"Hello, Dan. Are you in here?"

Frank swished his hand over the wall next to him looking for the light switch. He flicked the switch when he had found it, but nothing happened.

I gingerly trod over to the windows, not knowing what I might stand in, and pulled back the curtains so we had light to see by

We could hear some commotion and hurried talking out in the hallway. The police had arrived and were getting a full appraisal from the woman about the Ambulance men breaking down the door and entering into the flat, but it had nothing to do with her and she wasn't responsible, she was the one who dialled 999, nothing else.

The curtains fully open now, we could see Dan lying in his bed. He was beneath the sheets, with just his head and shoulders visible, propped up slightly by a couple of stained pillows. He was wearing a blue striped pyjama top. He must have been in his eighties or nineties, frail looking, unshaven with a thinning crop of silver hair. His eyes were open and he stared directly ahead. I looked in the direction of his gaze. On the wall opposite was a large black and white picture in a glass frame of a woman in a 1940's style floral summer dress, with sand dunes as the backdrop, and her hair blowing in the wind. It must have been the last thing he had looked at before he died.

I wondered if it was his wife in the picture, who had probably died some time ago.

A policeman entered the room. "Evening." Even though it was still afternoon.

Frank turned away from examining Dan and looked at the policeman.

"DOA I'm afraid." Meaning that the patient was Dead on Arrival.

"Anything suspicious?" asked the Policeman.

"Nothing that I can see" said Frank. "No pill bottles, no injuries, no suicide notes that I can see. Probably just passed away quietly while he was in bed."

The Policeman surveyed the room, taking in the general untidiness. an old wardrobe with a couple of suitcases resting on top, a dressing table, a bedside table with an overflowing ashtray, clothes on the floor and strewn over chairs. He grunted, then turned and left the room.

I got closer to Frank and whispered "What's he grunting for?"

"Because he'll have to organise someone from the council to come and secure the flat, and he'll have to stay here until the door's fixed. That could mean hours of waiting around."

"Can he charge us for breaking in?"

"In theory yes, breaking and entering, criminal damage, you name it, we just did it."

"So if that copper charges us for breaking down the door, we both take the rap?"

Frank smiled and sat on the edge of the bed. "That's not going to happen."

"Why?"

Just at that point the policeman came back into the room with his note book in hand.

"Can I have your names and station, lads?"

I stared at Frank as he told him who we were and from which station. I was convinced we would be spending the rest of the night in a cell.

"We'll take him down to the Royal to be certified," added Frank.

The policeman nodded and left the room.

Frank chuckled. "Did you think we were being arrested?"

He continued. "Sometimes you will have to break into places to get to a patient that needs your help. In theory it's illegal, but in reality no copper or court in this land will prosecute you for trying to save someone's life. In fact the reverse could see you land up in trouble for doing nothing."

"So what did he want our names for?"

Just for his own report, he'll need to send it to the coroner."

Frank stood up, hands on hips and straightened his back. "Well then, let's get demised Dan here down to the Ambulance shall we?"

I took the carry chair from Frank and un- folded it.

"That's not going to be any good, he's as stiff as a board, and he'll just keep sliding off."

I could see the problem. The lift wasn't big enough to get our trolley in, so we would have to improvise.

Frank sent me down to the Ambulance to get the 'Neil Robertson' stretcher. This was a specialised stretcher that was more commonly used in extracting people from the likes of a ships hold or from heights. Search and rescue helicopters used them to winch injured people from ships. Basically it was long strips of bamboo, woven side by side into a strong canvas material. The patient would be laid onto the stretcher and the bamboo canvas wrapped around them and fastened with straps. The feet would be placed into webbing to stop the patient from sliding out as the stretcher was hauled into an upright position.

The kids had long gone since the police had arrived, so I wasn't pestered by them as I hooked the carry chair onto the inside of the back door of the Ambulance, then retrieved the Neil Robertson from the overhead locker. I had only used this type of stretcher in training school, but now I would see it in action for real.

Back in the bedroom we laid the Neil Robertson open on the floor next to the bed and placed a blanket over it. Frank took hold under Dan's arm pits and I took his legs. It was helpful that he stayed rigid throughout the lifting process as we moved him from the bed and placed him onto the blanket that covered the stretcher on the floor.

We wrapped the blanket around him first, just leaving his face visible. It wasn't considered good etiquette to cover his face before he had been certified. Next, we folded the bamboo canvas over the blanket and around him, finally fastening all the straps, ensuring his feet, on which Frank had clad a pair of slippers he had found, were secure in the foot webbing.

The stretcher had four strong handles, two at the top and two at the bottom. This allowed four people to carry it and distribute the weight of the patient evenly. However, as it was just Frank and me to do the carrying. I took the feet end while Frank took the head end and we hoisted Dan up to waist height and manoeuvred out of the bedroom. It was just like carrying a rolled up carpet. We continued down the hall and out of the front door onto the landing, and then just a few paces took us to the lift doors.

The policeman had been rummaging about rooms in the flat as we had been seeing to Dan.

"I've got some details if you want them?" said the policeman as he now appeared at the front door. Scarf woman and vest man were nowhere to be seen.

Frank nodded to me to get the details; it was my task as I was the attendant. We propped Dan up against the wall next to the lift doors. I took a pen from my breast pocket and went back into the flat. I found a scrap of paper on the living room table and wrote down Dan's full name, date of birth and Doctors surgery address as recited by the policeman from an old prescription he had found.

"Can I take that prescription?" The policeman handed it over. It also had a list of medications Dan had been taking; it could be useful for the hospital or coroner.

The lift doors swished open and we heaved Dan into the corner of the corrugated box , still in the upright position, we propped him up in the corner and at an angle so he wouldn't fall over, and pressed the button for the ground floor.

The lift stopped at the sixth floor and the doors opened. An old couple entered the lift and pressed the ground floor button and the doors swished closed.

Frank looked at me with a broad smile as the couple turned and stood facing the doors, their backs to Dan propped up in the corner, as we continued down.

We loaded Dan into the back of the Ambulance and released him from the Neil Robertson, placing him onto the trolley. Ten minutes later we arrived outside the Royal casualty department. Frank went inside to find a doctor who would come out to the Ambulance and certify death. I stayed in the back of the Ambulance with Dan as I completed my paperwork.

The Royal hospital was a busy place. Located in the centre of the city, they tended to get the bulk of the accidents and emergencies from the city area.

Although all hospitals have their own mortuary, DOA's that were brought in by Ambulance and then certified at the Royal casualty department, were taken to the City mortuary, just a short distance away in Pembroke Place.

Outside office hours, the City mortuary was locked. This meant that we had to take Dan on a short detour, to Copperas Hill police station to collect the key, then around to the mortuary itself.

Someone with a macabre sense of humour at the police station had carved a wooden shaped coffin with a small drill hole, through which was looped a piece of string tied to the key that opened the mortuary doors.

The City as we affectionately called the public mortuary, was something straight out of a Hammer horror movie. A narrow cobbled street poorly lit and always deserted. You could just imagine a Jack the Ripper character, stepping out of a darkened doorway to greet you.

It was always the driver's job to open up the doors and switch on the lights. The problem with this little task, was that the bank of light switches were well inside the building, through a couple of interior doorways, and not situated near the entrance doors as you might expect.

In the middle of the night, when it was pitch dark, it meant getting out a torch, opening up and going in search of the light switches through two dark rooms; always knowing that you were very close to the rows of fridges that held all sorts of bodies that had arrived at the City through fair means or foul. It wasn't only that, but the place always reeked of coal tar soap and dead meat, not the best combination of smells.

We eventually delivered Dan to the City and completed the admission form so the mortician would know who he was when he opened up the next day.

Control sent us back to station for our meal break.

9

The following night at Westminster station, lunch lasted for fifteen minutes before we were called out again, this time to a ship in Canada branch dock. It was a report of a sailor with abdominal pains.

We entered through the dock gates off Regent Road and were flagged down by the police officer who manned the entrance. His official duties included the protection of the docks, and to readily stop any Dockers who might have something on their person that had 'fallen off the back of a ship', or had 'accidentally on purpose' spilt from a damaged crate of imported clothes. 'Diesel Fitters' were rife in the Dockers profession. The name comes from the phrase. "Diesel fit the wife, or diesel fit the kids."

The policeman had been forewarned of our arrival at the docks and directed us to where the ship was berthed.

It's an eerie feeling driving around the dock quays at night. Very little in the way of street lighting exists. The only meagre lighting to hand is either from the odd spotlight hanging from the high wall of a warehouse, which tends to cast long shadows, or the light emanating from the ships gangways and port holes.

It was almost an obstacle course driving slowly along the quayside avoiding wooden pallets, coiled ropes and other dockside paraphernalia. We had to turn right half way along the dock and drive through the large open doors of a warehouse and out the other side, turning left onto another quay. Our ship was berthed at the end of this quay.

As we approached, the name of the ship was painted in white Cyrillic letters. I didn't have a clue as to what it said.

Frank expertly manoeuvred the ambulance into a very tight space, avoided dropping off the edge of the quayside into the water, and brought the ambulance to a halt at the bottom of the ship's gangway facing in the direction we had just come.

The ship wasn't an ocean going liner, more like an old coastal steam tramp that you might see in a Humphrey Bogart movie, and we weren't going to be disappointed with that image when we climbed aboard.

The water was calm in the dock and the lights of the ship reflected across the inky black water. There was a pungent smell of oil and sea water, as you might expect in such a place.

I opened the back doors of the ambulance to get the carry chair and blanket as it was almost certain this sailor would have to be carried ashore and into the ambulance.

Somewhere in the distance from another ship, Arabic music was playing and drifting across the dock.

Frank carried the first aid bag and bottle of entonox and headed up the wooden stepped gangway. I followed close behind.

We were halfway up the steep incline when a figure appeared at the top. It was difficult to make out who it was as a bright spotlight shone down on us from behind the figure.

It was difficult to recognise the accent at first, but it sounded Russian to me, which would fit with the Cyrillic name painted on the side.

"Ah, Ambulance gentlemen's, welcome aboard, you have come very quicklys I see."

We reached the top of the gangway to be greeted by the captain. True to form as with our Bogart movie theory, he was probably in his forties, needing a shave and wearing the obligatory black polo neck jumper with sleeves rolled up. He sported black trousers and the cursory, grubby white topped cap with a squiggly line of gold braid across its peak. His face was weather worn and tanned like leather.

"I am captain, welcome, welcome."

He shook each of our hands as though we were long lost ship mates suddenly reunited.

"You have a crew member who's unwell?" Frank asked.

"Yes, yes, is unwell as you say through his stomach." The captain rubbed his own stomach as if to emphasise the problem.

"The doctor, he say, must go the hospital."

Although I was attending and in theory I was the one to take charge of the job in hand, I decided to let Frank be the lead on this one. Frank had been to this type of call before; this was my first time in dealing with foreign sailors from the docks.

"Please, come this way, I would like to talk." The captain gestured for us to follow, which we did, struggling along behind him with equipment in tow.

The ship seemed to be a labyrinth of corridors as we clanked along metal gangways beneath bare light bulbs housed in metal cages. We eventually climbed a steep metal stairwell into a part of the ship that immediately transformed into what was probably the accommodation area. There was an aroma of food and smoke in the air.

True to form, as in the movies, the walls were no longer painted sheets of metal, but had now given way to dark wooden cladding and threadbare carpet, which had replaced the metal gangways, and the lighting was from shaded wall lights.

Like lambs, we followed the captain to a door at the far end of a short corridor. Without knocking he turned the handle and walked in, beckoning us to follow.

We fully expected to see a sailor rolling about in agony with abdominal pain but instead we were inside what quickly became obvious as the captain's cabin.

It was a spacious room and continued the theme of wood panelled walls, wall lights and carpeted floor. Rectangular windows on one side of the cabin looked out over the quayside below where we could see our vehicle, and on the back bulkhead were two larger rectangular windows that looked out to the water in the dock at the stern end of the ship.

There was a bed, neatly made, to the right of the cabin and on the left beneath the dockside windows, was a large desk that was cluttered with maps and charts. Beneath the stern windows was a three seat sofa, accompanied by a long and low coffee table.

Where space allowed, there were wall cabinets on each of the walls. A door had been removed from one of the wall cabinets over the desk, which housed a television set and radio.

"Please sit gentlemen's" the captain motioned to the sofa.

"Where's the patient?" asked Frank.

"Please, my crew getting him ready as we speak. I wanted to talk to you first."

The captain opened a cupboard next to the desk which seemed to be full to the brim with bottles of alcohol. He took one of the bottles out of the cupboard.

"I wanted to ask about your hospital systems here, we have to know what will be happening to Vlad."

As Frank answered, the captain placed three shot glasses on the table and filled each one with a clear liquid from the bottle.

"We'll take him to the Northern hospital, which isn't far from here, and then he'll be examined in the casualty department. Depending on what the problem is, depends on what happens next."

"Please, best Russian Vodka, you are a guest on my ship, please drink." he gestured towards the drinks on the coffee table.

I looked at Frank and he looked back at me. He shrugged his shoulders and picked up a glass.

"Nostrovia" the captain sank the shot in one go.

Not wanting to be left out, I followed suit. "Cheers".

This call was turning into something of a pleasure, it's not often you get to drink vodka while waiting for a patient.

The captain made to pour another into our glasses but we both declined; one was enough; we had the rest of the shift to get through.

"So, are we saying that Vlad could be in the hospitals for couple days?" the captain took out a packet of Camel cigarettes and offered one to Frank.

"No thanks, I'm a pipe man myself."

He offered me the cigarette and I accepted it.

"That all depends on what the problem is" answered Frank.

"Mmm" murmured the captain as he offered me a light for the cigarette.

"We sail tomorrow and I worry that we leave Vlad behind. He is good engineer."

The captain sauntered across the cabin and peered from the window onto the quayside, taking a long draw on the cigarette.

"Vlad does not speak English, I have to send someone with him who can."

"I'm sure the hospital will have an interpreter. Are you Russian?"

The captain turned from looking out of the window.

"Russians, no not Russians, Latvian; the only good about Russia is the vodka yes."

He turned to look back out of the window again.

"Ah, Vlad is ready to go; they are putting him in your van now".

"Ambulance, you mean?" I was not pleased at an ambulance being called a van, although to all intent and purposes, that's exactly what it was. It was just the principle of the matter.

"Yes, ambulance van."

Frank and I padded over to the window. Down below we could see a man being helped between two others, up the steps and into the back of the ambulance.

There was something not quite right about this job. I sensed that Frank could feel it too.

"Come on then." Frank picked up the first aid bag and entonox bottle and I collected the chair and blanket.

"I shall walk with you" said the captain. Once again we followed him down the twists and turns of corridors and out to the open deck and gangway.

The captain remained at the top of the gangway where we had first met him.

"Take good care of Vlad gentlemen's. Thank you's."

We didn't answer. We scurried down the steps of the gangway. It wasn't good to have people sitting in your ambulance when you weren't there.

Vlad was sitting between the other two sailors on the bench seat opposite the stretcher. He was holding his stomach and giving the odd groan now and again.

"Where's the pain, Vlad?" He leant forward slightly and shook his head.

"No English" said the man next to him, "his pain in belly."

Frank closed the back doors to the ambulance ready to drive the short journey to the Northern Hospital.

I sat on the edge of the stretcher facing Vlad. I wanted to get a better look at him as I had to make some sort of report out about this. I leaned closer to take a look at his face and at the same time felt for a pulse in his wrist.

Vlad must have been in his thirties. His hands were those of an engineer, large with thick stubby fingers. Years of working on engines had left the tell-tale sign of grime under the finger nails.

His face was weather worn, making him look older than he really was. His mate sitting next to him handed me a sealed envelope containing a letter from the doctor who had seen him earlier. I opened the envelope and read the contents. As per usual, and I was getting used to this, the writing was hardly legible.

I could just make out that the doctor was suspecting appendicitis, high temperature, onset over last two days, etc, etc, and would be grateful if the casualty officer would consider admitting him to the surgical ward.

It struck me as being odd. Firstly, since being on the road I had been to many calls with patients complaining of abdominal pains, some more severe than others. Of those that were severe, there was a distinct paleness and clammy skin about the person and signs of shock, such as the pulse rate being increased considerably. Vlad, on the other hand, was quite flushed in the face, sweaty rather than clammy and his pulse beat at a strong and steady eighty beats a minute. He certainly wasn't in shock. There was also a strong aroma of peppers and garlic about him. This was not right somehow, but what the heck, who was I to argue about it.

Frank had the blue lights flashing as we emerged from the dock gates. The dock's policeman had stood in the middle of the road to stop any traffic that might come along and impede our progress. A few minutes later we arrived outside the doors of the Northern Hospital casualty department.

This was an old red bricked hospital, originally opened in 1902 and I don't think it had seen any modernisation since that time, well not much anyway. The problem for us as an ambulance crew was that we had to park on the main road outside and carry patients across the pavement, sometime past pedestrians, then up the three steps to the entrance doors. However, on this occasion, we were spared that effort.

Frank opened the back doors and lowered the steps. At that moment Vlad was hoisted between his crew mates and trundled out of the ambulance.

"Wait, I'll get you a wheel chair." I said.

"No need, no need." Said Vlad's crew mate

Frank and I stood at the back of the ambulance and watched as they helped Vlad up the steps and in through the doors.

"Something strange about that job, it didn't feel quite right somehow."

Frank nodded in agreement and closed the back doors to the ambulance.

"I know what you mean, and I have a feeling I know what it is." He said.

"What do you reckon then?"

"Come on, get in the cab and we'll park in that road opposite and out of line of sight. I just want to test a theory."

Frank spun the ambulance away from the kerb and headed for the side street were we could remain hidden, but still see the hospital entrance. Engine and lights were turned off and we sat in silence in the dark for several minutes.

"What's happening, Frank?"

"I think we just helped those sailors smuggle something off that ship."

"Like drugs or something?"

"I don't know, just let's see what happens."

Frank took out his pipe and opened his window, stuck his arm out and tapped it gently on the door to dislodge any old tobacco.

I lit a cigarette. This really was turning out to be like a Bogart movie.

Only a few minutes had passed, when a black Vauxhall zephyr came around the corner and stopped outside the hospital doors. Sure enough Frank's theory seemed to be proved correct. Out of the hospital came Vlad, walking upright and with purpose, followed by his two crew mates. The three of them made straight for the Vauxhall and got inside. It then sped off down Old Hall Street and towards the city centre.

" Thought so." Frank said, but just as he said it, a car that had been parked a little further down the road roared into life, headlights on and quickly moved off in the same direction as the Vauxhall.

"Bloody hell, what was all that about?"

"Definitely something fishy going on there." Frank puffed at his pipe, satisfied that he was right.

"How did you know they were smuggling something?" I asked.

"Think about it, what would be the best way to get something past the coppers on the dock gates?"

No way in this world would they have got passed that copper in a taxi or private car, they would have been searched, without a doubt.

The penny dropped, we had been used for criminal purposes.

"Shouldn't we inform the police?"

Frank looked at his watch.

"Nah, too much paperwork and I don't want to be late home tonight.

10

1970 soon rolled into 1971 and I was beginning to gather some experience.

I had worked at several stations across the city by now, with varying characters for crew mates.

Stanhope street station was considered, unofficially that is, to be the punishment station. Nobody on relief shifts particularly liked working there, so when I was given my weeks shift rota to work nights at Stanhope, I asked Charlie what I had done wrong?

He assured me that I hadn't done anything wrong, it was just the same old problem they always had there, long term sickness. They were desperate to cover the vacant shifts.

Stanhope station is just off Upper Parliament Street in the Toxteth area of Liverpool.

It would be reasonable to describe Toxteth as one of the run down and deprived areas of the City. However, in times gone by, it was probably one of the most affluent.

Shipping merchants, philanthropists, Bankers, Architects, Doctors, Surgeons and generally those who were wealthy, had once lived in tall elegant terraced Georgian houses, along wide and leafy streets that eventually spread out to form the district of Toxteth.

The main Street running from South to North is called Parliament Street, becoming Upper Parliament Street as it nears the city centre and the Anglican Cathedral.

In the main, it is now an Afro Caribbean community, and a bit further along Upper parliament Street, a Chinese community thrived.

There is no doubting that Liverpool is a multicultural city and proud of it.

Stanhope station is an old building and had possibly been some kind of warehouse in the 1920's era. I don't think much transformation had ever taken place to convert it into an Ambulance station.

A network of rust coloured metal frames and girders supported a high double-pitched corrugated asbestos roof. The frontage was two large wooden doors, painted green, which had faded over the years. Inside the building and to the left of the garage area, was an open wooden stairway leading up to a mezzanine which stretched above the station doors from one side of the building to the other; this was the mess room.

The mess room was typical of any other station, threadbare carpet, old dusty arm chairs, a few tables and a TV in the corner. There was a small kitchen at the far end of the room. The mezzanine was enclosed from the interior of the garage by a shoulder high wood panelled wall and glass windows that looked down into the station area.

I never felt comfortable at this station, particularly as the floor of the mezzanine seemed to bounce as people walked around on it, I always had the feeling that it would collapse at any moment sending us all crashing down to the garage floor below. It never did.

It was the rule that when all out patient ambulances had finished for the day, they would park their vehicles inside the garage in such a way that the afternoon and night shifts could park their private cars inside the station; it was that kind of area. During the day there was a station officer on duty who would keep an eye on the staff cars parked outside.

I parked my car and went upstairs to sign on duty. I would be working with Phil for the rest of the week.

I had met Phil a few times in passing at the Southern and Royal casualty departments. It was the usual thing to hang around, have a smoke, a cup of tea and a chat with other crews after delivering a patient to a department. This was how the grapevine worked and how you learned what was going on around the rest of the service. It was at these gatherings that we learned of the horror stories about Stanhope station. Most of the Ambulance staff at Stanhope were older hands who had been on the job for years, and to be honest, some of them shouldn't have been doing the job according to some of the stories.

There was a story about one of the older hands at Stanhope. He and his mate were called to a routine maternity call, and when they arrived at the house, the woman was about to give birth. Instead of standing his ground, calling out a midwife and being prepared to deliver the baby if needed, it was alleged that he put the lady in the ambulance and tied her legs together, working on the theory that if her legs weren't open, then the baby couldn't be born. I had met the man and I have to honest , I could well imagine that would be a true story.

Another story about someone else at the station was just as bad. It seems that he was called to a traffic accident, an elderly woman knocked down by a car. He had quickly decided at the scene that the woman was fatally injured. He and his mate, who must have been just as bad, put the elderly woman into the Ambulance and took her along to the casualty department where they parked the Ambulance. They wondered inside the casualty department looking for a doctor to come out and certify the death of the woman who was still lying prostrate in the rear of the Ambulance. It was about ten minutes later when the doctor appeared and stepped into the Ambulance. Within a few minutes, the woman was rushed from the Ambulance and into the resuscitation room. She wasn't dead.

I found it really difficult to believe these men were still driving emergency Ambulances around the city, but then again, they were just stories.

It was these stories that made Stanhope the feared place that it was. It was the dread of being teamed up with one of these blokes that made me so apprehensive prior to that night shift at Stanhope.

Phil seemed like a decent bloke, so I wasn't too apprehensive about working the week of night shifts with him. He was in his mid thirties, over six foot and looked as though he kept fit. Phil had several years of service under his belt, which made me feel better.

There were two crews on night shift at Stanhope, and we were first call out. It didn't take long before we were on our way to an assault at a pub in the city centre.

It was the usual thing, something I was getting very used to. Too much beer, heated words and then fists starting to fly. A lad of about my age, early twenties, cut lip, missing a front tooth and sporting a red and bruised eye that would in time become a nice big black one.

He was still inside the pub and hardly able to stand, so I told him to sit down so I could examine him, which he did like an obedient child. It was his mate that we were about to have some problems with.

Phil was standing close by as I crouched down to shine the pen torch into the patient's eyes, normal procedure to check pupil reaction for someone with head injuries.

Then it started.

"Stop fucking about and get him to hospital now." came the voice from somewhere in the crowd.

Phil must have seen who it was. I saw from the corner of my eye as he pointed somewhere into the crowd.

"Less of that language, mate" he said

"I'm not your fuckin mate, and he needs to go to hospital now."

Phil took no notice.

I asked the patient the usual questions. Was he knocked out? Could he remember everything that happened? Did he have any other pain besides the obvious? Was he on any medication? Did he have any blurred vision?

"I'm not going to hospital, I'll be all right" he said before I could finish my questions.

"I think you should, you've had a fair old smack about your head."

"Should see the other fucker." He managed a tooth missing smile.

"I can't force you to go, but I think you should."

"I'll be all right mate; you've got more urgent calls to deal with than me."

"If you're sure you don't want go?"

"I'm sure."

I stood and told Phil he wasn't going to go to hospital.

"You're not fucking leaving him here. He's going to the hospital and that's all there is to it."

I could now see who was doing the shouting and swearing as he came close to where the patient was sitting. He put his arm under his mates' shoulder and tried to lift him up.

"Come on, you're going to hospital."

The patient shrugged his arm away.

"Just leave it Tommy, I'm all right."

"You're going."

Tommy turned to Phil.

"Get him in the van will you." This was an order, not a request.

"He doesn't want to go, and we can't force him" said Phil

"I don't care what he said, he's going and that's that."

Phil turned to the patient. "Do you want to go to hospital mate?"

"Na" said the patient.

Phil turned back to Tommy. "He isn't going but we are, do you have a problem with that?"

"Yes I fucking do."

"Tough shit." said Phil. He took my arm and began to walk out of the pub doors. I heard a commotion behind us and turned. Tommy was coming at us, face ablaze with anger. Phil had seen this too. Tommy threw a punch at Phil, who side stepped it and returned a solid blow to Tommy's abdomen; he went down like a sack of potatoes. A cheer went around the pub as Phil crouched down to speak to Tommy.

"You're only winded, you'll be all right in a few minutes."

Tommy didn't say anything; he lay on the floor on his side, knees drawn and holding his belly.

Outside in the Ambulance, we drove around the corner just to be out of the way. I lit a cigarette; my hands were shaking a little.

"Bloody hell Phil, where did you learn to do that?"

"I teach boxing at our youth club, and would you mind not smoking in the cab?"

I looked at the cigarette. "Sorry." I stepped out of the vehicle to finish it, now feeling guilty about smoking around someone who took his fitness quite seriously.

One vomiting drunk with a cut hand, a psychiatric case and a child with whooping cough saw us through to two in the morning and back to station for a meal break. After eating, the sleeping arrangements at the station were a stretcher in the rear of an out-patient ambulance. The same as it was at Anfield.

It was around four o'clock when the emergency bell went off; it was loud enough to wake the neighbourhood.

It was a call to a woman having a baby.

My stomach churned, I was attending and I still had this fear about having to deliver a baby.

The streets were dark and empty at this time in the morning and Phil drove with the blue lights flashing, there being no need for sirens. I didn't know the area and was reliant on Phil's local knowledge, not that there wasn't a well thumbed A to Z available on the dash board.

We turned from the main street into a side street, then turned again into another street, and yet another. I was completely lost at this point. The housing in the area was small Victorian terraces; most of the street lighting was out.

We came to a halt outside the house. Phil doused the blue lights and switched off the engine. There was an eerie silence, not even distant traffic noise disturbing the night. However, there was a problem. The house was in darkness, nothing stirred. It's usual to have someone meet you on arrival at these types of calls, usually the panicking husband, but not tonight.

I unhooked the radio handset and asked control to confirm the address they had given us. A few moments later the voice from the speaker did indeed confirm we were at the correct address. There was nothing else for it, we had to knock at the door, break the early morning silence and risk waking the neighbours.

As I was attending, it was my job to climb out of the vehicle first and do the knocking. My earlier adrenaline rush began to subside as this was obviously going to be a false call and I wouldn't be faced with my trepidation of having to deliver a baby.

That all changed quite rapidly as I was still approaching the front door. It opened and out stepped an Asian man dressed in a shalwar kameez. He had a long, thick black beard and moustache.

"Please, quick quick!" He beckoned me to hurry.

He turned and went back into the dark house. My adrenaline rush kicked in again.

I followed him into and along the dark hallway. My eyes were only just now beginning to adjust to the darkness. The house smelled of damp and spices. I could make out a staircase just in front of him, and then he stopped.

"Please, quick quick!" He pointed up the stairs and ushered me to take the lead.

"Can you switch the lights on" I said as I took the first couple of steps on the stairs.

"Please, quick quick!" It seemed this was all I was going to get out of him.

I tentatively climbed the stairs, hoping someone would turn on the lights. The man remained at the bottom of the stairs as if there was an invisible barrier that prevented him from going any further. I wished I'd brought the torch, I didn't know what I was going to come face to face with in this darkness.

I reached the landing, and then called out. "Hello, Ambulance." I listened for any reply to give me a clue to what direction I should go, but there was nothing.

Ahead of me there was a plain wallpapered wall, I held on to the banister rail and followed that. It took me back along a landing now heading towards the front of the house. At the far end was a bedroom door that was half open allowing a little light to seep onto the landing from the only illuminated street lamp outside. I headed towards it.

Rhythmic moaning sounds came from inside the room. I knocked lightly on the door and pushed it open. I couldn't see too much, there were too many dark shadows. The curtains were almost fully drawn. The street lamp was on the opposite side of the street to the house and a little further along, so it wasn't shining directly into the room.

I felt around the wall for a light switch and eventually found it. I flicked it up and down, but nothing happened, the room was still in darkness. The moaning sounds were coming from my right hand side as I entered the room. "Hello, Ambulance." I said again. Still no reply and the moaning continued.

I made my way to the window to open the curtains fully and hopefully allow a little more light into the room. I just caught a glimpse of Phil down in the street as he headed to the front door with torch in hand.

The room was a little brighter and I could now see the figure of a woman sitting on the edge of a double bed holding something in her arms, rhythmically rocking backwards and forwards. She was the source of the moaning sounds.

"Hello love," I said as I picked my way towards her. It was if I didn't exist. She continued rocking backwards and forwards as if in some kind of trance.

As I got closer, it was then I noticed the small new born baby in her arms. My heart sank, I could see, even in this dim light, that the baby was dead.

I approached her full on so as not to surprise her, I still didn't know if she knew I was in the room or not. I carefully crouched down in front of her and took the tiny body from her arms. It was only now that she looked up. Tears were streaming from her eyes.

Her sari was hoisted up to her knees, which at first struck me as very unusual, until I saw the umbilical chord disappearing underneath it.

Oh shit, was my first thought. She hadn't yet delivered the placenta. The baby was white, almost like a porcelain doll, floppy and lifeless. I knew it was probably still born, but that didn't exclude the need to try and resuscitate it.

The baby was still covered in slimy mucus as I lay it on the bed next to her. I couldn't do anything else as the chord was taught even at this position. I wiped around its face as best I could with the bed sheet and began blowing into the baby's nose and mouth. It was probably the most unpalatable thing I had ever done in my life, but my adrenaline high had taken over and the unpleasantness of it didn't register with me at the time.

I heard Phil's size 10 boots enter the room and a beam of torch light hit on the bed, the woman, and me trying to resuscitate the baby.

"We need to cut this chord." I said between inflations.

The woman said something in her own language, but neither of us knew what she was saying. Phil asked her if she could speak English, she shook her head and said something else in a foreign tongue.

It was going to be a case of doing what we had to do and hope she would understand that we were trying to do our best for her and her baby.

Phil delved into the first aid bag and retrieved two pairs of artery clamps. The first clamp was attached to the chord, just a couple of inches away from the baby's abdomen, and then the second pair was attached a couple more inches from the first. Finally, the baby was detached as Phil cut the chord between the clamps.

With the torchlight and the assistance of the street lamp, we had some clearer vision in the room.

There was a dressing table against the wall near to the light switch. I held the baby in one arm and with the other I swiped the dressing table clear of its contents, which duly clattered and crashed to the floor. I now had the space I needed and a hard surface to continue resuscitation and cardiac compressions.

I knew there was a resuscitation bag and mask in the first aid bag, but I didn't think we had a mask small enough to do the job, so it was going to be mouth to nose and mouth all the way with this one.

Phil had now put the woman fully back onto the bed. She was still crying and moaning. It was understandable.

Lets face it, she was in a country where she couldn't speak the language, with two strange men in uniform in her bedroom who were now dictating what was going to happen to her and her baby in what was a traumatic moment in her life.

The baby was cold to touch and not responsive. I knew this resuscitation wasn't going to have a happy outcome, but I had to try.

"Ok, we have two choices" said Phil. "We can call for another Ambulance to look after the mother, then we make a dash to the Children's hospital with the baby, or we can call for the maternity flying squad and get a team out here to deal with it."

Phil was right; we couldn't deal with both mother and baby on our own. It would be easy enough to take the baby down to the Ambulance, but then one of us would have stay with the baby to continue resuscitation in the back of the vehicle, the mother wouldn't be able to walk downstairs, she needed to be carried.

"Flying squad" I said, knowing they would have more expertise to deal with this situation.

Phil nodded in agreement and left the room to go down stairs to the ambulance and ask control to send them out to us.

I knew what the procedure would be. The other night shift crew at Stanhope station would be sent to the LMH (Liverpool Maternity Hospital) to collect a team of nurses, an obstetrician and a whole pile of equipment and deliver them to where we were.

Phil returned to the bedroom. "They're on the way."

I didn't acknowledge, I was still resuscitating the baby.

"That bloke who opened the door is nowhere to be seen downstairs and the front door's wide open," continued Phil.

I still didn't acknowledge, I was too busy.

"Come on" said Phil. "Let me take over, you can have a rest."

I didn't argue with him, I was beginning to feel the strain. It's amazing how exhausting performing CPR can be, even on a baby.

Phil took over and I went across the room to check on the woman. She was fully on the bed now and leaning forward with her head in her hands. I wasn't sure what to do, so I did what came naturally, I put my arm around her shoulder and patted her, as if to comfort her. She shrugged as if she wasn't comfortable with my gesture. I moved my hand away, not knowing if I had committed some sort of religious misdemeanour.

There were sounds downstairs, people entering the house. At last I thought, the flying squad was here.

The bedroom door swung open and three Asian women came into the room. The looks that Phil and I got were not of the friendly kind. They rushed over to the bed and began talking to the woman in her own language. No one had bothered about the baby that Phil was resuscitating in the corner.

"You go now," said one of the women.

"You what?" I said.

"You can go; she will be fine with us."

I looked over at Phil, then back to the woman.

"I'm sorry, but that's not going to happen. We're waiting for a medical team, and if you haven't noticed we have a very sick baby here."

She turned to the others and said something I didn't understand, and then turned back to me.

"You take baby, we look after her now."

I wasn't sure what was happening, this was very strange. I could understand that they were concerned over the woman, but there seemed to be no love lost regarding the baby.

The noise of an Ambulance engine came into the street and I could see the blue lights reflecting against the bedroom window. Thank goodness, the flying squad was here.

The obstetrician officially pronounced the baby dead and halted resuscitation. Phil and I packed up our equipment and went downstairs to join the other crew who had brought the squad. Two

Ambulances outside the house brought on a twitching of curtains in the street, even at that time of the morning.

An hour later the team came out of the house. The woman was fine but would still need to be admitted to hospital; the baby would need to be taken to hospital for certification and eventually a post mortem.

Phil and I took the baby to the children's hospital where it was pronounced deceased once again, this time by a paediatrician, then we took it over to the city mortuary for the pathologist to deal with the following morning.

The other crew took the flying squad and the mother back to the LMH.

We never did find out why there seemed to be no concern for the baby from the other Asian women who had arrived at the house. I guessed we never would.

11

It was Thursday night and my last shift with Phil at Stanhope station. I would finish at seven the following morning, a Friday, which was counted as a working day, so Saturday and Sunday would be my days off for that week.

The following week I knew I would be working day shifts, but as yet I didn't know where. I had hoped Charlie would have let me know by now. It was looking like I would have to ring him in the morning to find out.

Our first call of the night was to the city centre, usual thing; a drunk had fallen over and was too inebriated to get up from the pavement.

For some reason, and don't ask me why, this usually happens in the back streets more so than on the main roads. However, wherever they do happen I have come to the conclusion that there are three phases to these events.

Phase one is someone getting drunk.

Phase two is being drunk and not caring what they act or look like.

Phase three is someone being drunk, not caring what they act or look like, but falling over and saying to themselves, "Sod it, I'll sleep here for the night."

There are also several other equations that can be taken into consideration with this type of call. Joe public sees the said prone figure lying in the street, has a look and decides serious illness is happening, calls the Ambulance and waits around in order demonstrate what a good Samaritan he/she is to a fellow human being in distress.

The other is Joe public sees the said prone figure lying in the street, notices that said figure has been throwing up and crotch of trousers looks damp and stained with a strong smell of urine and assumes figure is possibly of the homeless species. Decides to call Ambulance and then bugger off, doesn't want to get involved. Our first call was of the latter type.

The old guy was a regular in the city; Phil had been called to him many times and always for the same reason. Harold was his name. He was harmless enough and with a little encouragement we managed to get him to his feet and support him as we walked him into the back of the Ambulance. We sat him on the bench seat and both Phil and I sat on the edge of the stretcher opposite him.

"What do we do with him then?" I asked Phil. "We can't really take him into casualty, just because he's pissed."

"Well, we have three choices." As Phil spoke we both caught the old guy as he tried to flop down on the seat and go asleep. We sat him upright again.

"We can get the police out and they can do him for D&I (Drunk and Incapable) and lock him up for the night, or we can leave him on the street, or we can take him to casualty. It's your call" said Phil. "You're the attendant."

For starters we couldn't leave him on the street. It wasn't the thing to do and we'd only be called out for him again at some point. I wasn't happy with calling the police; the poor guy hadn't done anything wrong. There was only one option.

"Casualty," I said. "They have a 'drunk tank' at the Royal. He can sleep it off there for the night."

We were half way to the hospital when control called us on the radio, enquiring as to our location and whether we were available for an emergency call.

I was sitting in the back with the old guy and I heard Phil telling them what our situation was.

I heard the control reply. "Roger, clear as soon as you can, we have a serious incident in Toxteth."

Phil shouted back into the saloon. "Did you hear that?"

"Yes, I wonder what's going on?"

We didn't have to wait long before we found out.

Control made an open call broadcast so all Ambulances could hear and take notice.

"Live Amb Base." (Which was the call sign of Liverpool Ambulance service.) "Live Amb base to all vehicles, House fire in progress, Toxteth area, persons reported, any available vehicles?"

Here we were, an Ambulance based in Toxteth and we were dealing with a drunk. We were needed elsewhere at this very moment and there was nothing we could do.

"Hold on." Phil shouted through to me. "Pedal to the metal."

Phil gunned the accelerator and switched on the klaxons, we reached the hospital in half the time it would normally have taken. Harold was none the wiser as he swayed about in the rear of the Ambulance, a short time later we frog marched him into the casualty department.

It was a little unfortunate that old 'cement face' was on duty. The sister in charge of the casualty department was witness to our arrival with sirens and blue lights, and then she saw us walk the drunken Harold into the department.

"What on earth?"

"I know it looks over the top" I said "but we have another emergency to go to."

"I bet you do." Sarcasm was one of her better traits.

She looked at our old man, barely able to stand. If we had stepped away from supporting him, he would have taken a nose dive.

"And what is wrong with this man?"

"Overdose" I said it without thinking too much about the consequences.

"Of what?"

"Alcohol."

"Don't be audacious with me young man." Sister Jones, AKA concrete face. It would crack if she smiled. She was old school. She must have been ready for retirement any day now. She was skinny and tall, taller than me, but then that wasn't difficult. She wore the old fashioned dark blue uniform with starched white cuffs and collar. She was the only one I knew that still wore the old fashioned uniform hat that seemed to rise above her head in a convoluted tangle of lace material, which in turn appeared to make her a foot or so taller than she really was. I always thought that it looked like a chef's hat, only more feminine.

"Sister, we're needed to go to a house fire and we can't do that while we have this gentleman in our care."

I think the word gentleman might have hit a chord somewhere inside her. Even the dregs of the earth needed a little TLC at some time, and she was old school after all.

"Put him in the drunk room," she snapped. "I'll have someone look at him."

No way was she going to examine the man, some underling would do that.

The drunk room at the Royal casualty was just a rectangular room with old mattress's placed on the floor down each side of the room. There were two high windows at one end, still with the original lead light glass in place harking back to a distant era when the hospital was built. Each wall was covered from floor to shoulder height in shining plain white tiles. The room gave me the impression of a gent's public toilet without the urinals.

It was here that most of the down and outs who arrived by Ambulance would spend the night to sleep off the alcoholic oblivion of the night before.

We put Harold down on a mattress and gave a quick history of what had happened to the staff nurse who had followed us in.

Once in the Ambulance cab, control gave us the location of the house fire. It was a side street off Princes Avenue.

Phil gunned the Ambulance like I had never seen him do before. It's scarier when you're not driving and you just have to hold on and put your life in your partner's hands.

We arrived in the street four minutes later. There were crowds of neighbours held back by policemen, watching as the event unfolded.

Two Ambulances were already at the scene.

I counted four fire engines. Hosepipes criss-crossed the street. There were no flames, but thick, black smoke billowed out of each broken window on all three floors. Phil parked the Ambulance as close as he could to the scene without driving over the hose pipes, but we still had several yards to run until we reached the other Ambulance crews.

To me it all seemed like chaos. Where were we supposed to begin? Phil ran to the nearest Ambulance and threw open the rear doors. He shouted to me to go to the other Ambulance and see if they needed assistance. I diverted to my left and was just about to open the rear doors, when the Ambulance took off like a bat out of hell. I was left standing.

I looked over to see what Phil was doing; but he was still at the back of the other Ambulance. I was just about to go and join him when a fireman took hold of my arm.

"They're bringing another one out, a child. They'll be down in a minute." I froze for a moment. What was I supposed to do? I had no equipment with me and our Ambulance was parked several yards away.

I ran back to the Ambulance and drove it closer to the scene, bumping over hosepipes and parking it where the other Ambulance had been just a few moments ago.

"Always get the Ambulance as friggin close as possible to the patient" Harry Jones had drilled into us.

I raced to the rear of the Ambulance and flung open the doors. I leapt inside and switched on the interior lights, then grabbed the minute man resuscitator.

The street stunk of acrid smoke and burning plastic as I headed towards the front of the house. There was a low wall, and a small grassed front garden with a path leading to the front door. I stood on the path in readiness for the patient to be brought out. It was at this point I noticed a green tarpaulin to my right which was covering something. Phil now joined me as the other Ambulance sped away.

"They're bringing another one out" I told him.

"Ok, I'll go get the stretcher out" and he disappeared back to the Ambulance.

I crouched down and gingerly lifted the tarpaulin to see what it was covering. To this day I wish I never had.

Several contorted burned and charred bodies lay motionless beneath it. It was impossible to tell if they were male or female. It was the horrific image that belonged in horror movies and not real life.

I dropped the canvass as a fireman in breathing apparatus emerged from the front door. He was carrying a child wearing a flannelette nighty, but limp and lifeless, arms spayed out and legs dangling. She must have been eight or nine years old. Her face was covered in soot; but thankfully I could see no burns. I took her from him in one arm and ran to the Ambulance, trying desperately to inflate her lungs with oxygen from the resuscitator as I ran. Phil hadn't yet had time to remove the stretcher. I climbed into the Ambulance and placed her on to it, and now I had better lighting to see with.

Her nostrils were black with soot, and so too was the inside of her mouth. She was breathing, but only just. My heart was racing. I set the minuteman to resuscitation mode and placed the mask over her nose and mouth. This had the effect of forcing oxygen into her lungs and assisting her poor respirations.

"Let's go now, Phil." I didn't even look at him, I just barked the order.

We were about five minutes away from the Children's hospital. I knew I could keep the respirations going for that length of time, but I didn't know how badly her lungs and air passages had been damaged. She had all the signs of having inhaled hot poisoned gasses, which would literally burn all the air passages as she had breathed. The danger now was swelling, and that could kill her.

I heard Phil on the radio asking control to warn the hospital of our impending arrival.

Doctors and nurses were at the hospital entrance waiting for us. We pulled to a halt and the back doors flew open. The trolley was wheeled out of the Ambulance and rushed to the resuscitation room. We never saw the child again.

My adrenaline kick began to subside as we waited for our trolley to be returned from the resus room. Phil tidied the back of the Ambulance, while I had a very shaky cigarette. I hoped the kid was going to make it.

It was about twenty minutes later that we finally got our trolley back. The news was that the child was still alive, but had severely damaged lungs.

Control sent us back to station for a break. The other night shift were back on station when we got back. They had also been to the fire and told us that there had been eight people in the fire. Five had died and three, including our young girl, were serious. There had been some kind of explosion on the ground floor which had killed four of them instantly. They were the ones beneath the tarpaulin, and the fifth had died in hospital.

We all spent the next half hour talking about what could have happened to cause the explosion and how we all dealt with the job. Could we have done this? Could we have done that? Could we have done better? The eventual answer was that we all did the best that we could. I didn't realise it at the time, but this was post traumatic therapy.

The other night shift crew had been out on a call and returned to the station sometime around two thirty, and they brought sad news.

They had heard from another crew that had recently been to the children's hospital, that our young patient from the house fire had died.

I felt an overwhelming sadness, almost as if it was a personal loss. I had been with the child while she was alive, and now she wasn't.

My mind was thankfully distracted by the emergency phone. We were going out to another call, a stabbing at a local night club.

I had been called to numerous stabbing victims before and all of them had been fairly minor incidents consisting of a cut to the arm or hand, maybe a leg or two, but never really life threatening, so I wasn't too concerned about what might be facing me when I got this call.

We arrived outside this so called 'night club'. It was in a small back street off Upper Parliament Street. The 'night club' was basically the basement of a tall, three story Georgian terrace house. A low level sandstone wall, topped with wrought iron fencing separated the pavement from the building.

Several concrete steps led up to the large wooden front door on the left of the facade, and to the right, another set of concrete steps lead down from the pavement to what appeared to be the cellar. There was no indication of it being a night club. No bright lights or thud thud of music, but the hurried exit of people up the steps from the cellar told us we probably had the right place.

"It must be kicking out time," said Phil as we both descended the steps against the flow of people.

"Have you been here before?" I asked

"No, it's new to me."

I carried the first aid bag and Phil carried the chair and blanket, just in case. We pushed through a metal covered door and descended more concrete steps. The exiting crowd had thinned a bit now, with just the stragglers passing us on the stairs. There was very little light to show the way down, and no hand rails to hold onto, so each step was carefully taken.

At the bottom, the steps opened out into a low ceiling room. To the left, in the dim light were tables and stools, all empty; and to the right, at the far wall was a small bar, next to which was a small area of smooth wooden flooring that had been laid as a dance area. The size of the cellar must have coincided with the flooring area of the house above, and it was surprisingly large.

The room was dimly lit with a string of red and green fairy lights fixed to the ceiling over the dance floor area. Only one small white light over the bar gave us enough light to see what we were dealing with.

Lying face down on the dance floor with his head turned to one side was the patient. He was Afro Caribbean, as were the few people that remained in the club. I knelt down beside him to see if I could get a response. It was only then that I realised the man was unconscious and I had knelt in a pool of blood.

"The minute man and the police, Phil." Once again I was barking orders to someone who had several more years of experience than me.

Phil disappeared and I pulled the man onto his back to get a better look at him. He was floppy and lifeless as I pulled him over. He was wearing what I thought at first to be a dark coloured shirt and leather waistcoat; but it was difficult to tell in the poor lighting. Then the realisation hit. The shirt was stained by copious blood loss which spread across his chest and now pooled on the floor.

He wasn't breathing and his eyes were glazed.

I snatched the bag and mask from the first aid bag and began to try and ventilate his lungs. It was like trying to inflate an inner tube with holes in it; not much was happening. I started with chest compressions, which just seemed to make things worse as blood oozed from his chest and mouth with each compression.

I looked over to the few people that were just standing and watching. "What happened here?"

They looked at each, and then one answered.

"Dunno, man. All we know is that there was boogying on the floor, then a scream, the crowd parted, and this guy was lying there."

"So you don't know him then?"

"Uh, uh." The speaker shook his head.

I carried on trying to resuscitate the man, who looked to be in his late twenties, but I knew that it was useless.

Phil arrived back with the minuteman resuscitator. He switched it on and took over the ventilations.

This gave me time to pull the man's shirt apart to see what we were dealing with. I grabbed a couple of dressing pads from the bag and wiped his chest. There were three obvious stab wounds, two to the right of his chest, just below the nipple and one on the left of his chest but a little lower down. As the resuscitator blew oxygen into his lungs, blood bubbled up through the stab wounds. It was decision time.

We could continue to attempt resuscitation, which we both knew would be futile and would probably disturb any forensic evidence there might be, or we could stop and protect the scene until the police arrived. We chose the second option. We didn't have to wait long until the boys in blue arrived on scene. We were ushered out of the club and told to wait in the Ambulance until the detectives arrived.

We informed control of the situation and that we wouldn't be available for a while. Not only that, but I needed to change my trousers, as my left trouser leg was soaked in blood.

We waited inside the vehicle for what seemed to be an age before a civilian clothed policeman approached the Ambulance. He asked us for a quick description of our actions and what we had noticed, and then suggested that we drive to Copperas Hill Police station to give a full written statement.

Ten minutes later, It made a nice change to enter Copperas Hill police station and not be handed the coffin key to the city mortuary. Phil and I were lead into separate rooms were we each re-countered what had happened as a police officer wrote it down.

We finished our shift after giving our statements to the detectives. I had managed to clean myself up a bit, but even more welcome were the hot cups of tea they gave us.

We timed it to perfection; finishing at the Police station at 0640 and driving back to the Ambulance station by 0650, just in time to sign off and go home at 7 oclock.

I was looking forward to getting out of my uniform, getting a hot bath and climbing into bed. It had been a long night. I would have to phone Charlie later too, and find out where I would be working next week.

Although I had just been at a murder scene, my thoughts drifted to that poor girl from the house fire. A young life lost before it had properly begun.

12

We had been married and living in our one bed roomed flat for more than a year when Beryl told me that she was pregnant. It wasn't something we had planned for or thought about, but the news was almost mind blowing. I was elated. There was so much we had to consider now; the main one being, finding a bigger place to live.

We decided to drive to Beryl,s parents at the weekend and give them the good news. It wasn't the sort of life changing news to be announced by telephone, particularly when you had to traipse half a mile to the nearest phone box.

While we were in the area, I'd reluctantly agreed to drop into my old house and tell my father the news also, after all, he had the right to know he was going to be a granddad. I hadn't seen him since the wedding, and to be honest I wasn't in any rush to see him again.

It was a Saturday afternoon, it was warm but the sky was overcast and looked as though it might rain.

We left Beryl's parents house in a happy go lucky mood and drove the short journey to my old house. As we walked down the front path I noticed the living room curtains were drawn, which was an unusual thing to see during the day.

I still had my key but knocked on the front door, more out of respect for privacy than anything else. After several knocks without an answer I used my key to open the front door. Once inside, we found the living room empty. A table lamp was switched on in the corner by the television.

I drew the curtains back to let the daylight flood the room. The first thing Beryl and I noticed was how clean and tidy it was, I was expecting it to look like a doss house. It smelt clean and fresh too. I shouted out to announce our presence, but there wasn't any response. I checked the kitchen, then upstairs and each bedroom. The house was empty, but it was spotless.

I decided to leave him a note to let him know we had been to visit and I'd be in touch with him in the next week or so.

As we left the house it was noticeable that the garden had had a makeover too. The grass was neatly cut and short, not overgrown as I last remembered it, and the flower beds were neatly tended to. My father was a keen gardener, but things had gone to wreck and ruin after my mother had died. Now the garden was back to the way it used to be. I wondered what had brought about this change of heart.

I had now worked at almost every station there was in the city, except Hatton Garden.

Charlie had scheduled me to work at the 'Garden', as we called it, and I looked forward to my week long shift there starting on

Monday; not just because I would be working with Brian, who I knew and got on well with, but because it was a nine to five station, which meant I wouldn't have to get up at stupid o'clock in the morning to get into work.

Hatton Garden Ambulance station was a one vehicle Ambulance station, and was there, to all intents and purposes to cover the City centre stores and office buildings during the day time.

When on station, the Ambulance was parked in its own designated bay beneath the health authority office building which was an underground car park for employees. The ceiling and overhead pipes only just skimmed a few inches above the blue light on the roof of the Ambulance.

The entrance was to the rear of the office block, but the exit was to the front, directly opposite the fire station. The car park had a one way in and one way out system.

The so called Ambulance staff room was a pokey little box room, no larger than twelve foot by eight foot and with no windows because it was also below street level. It had probably been some kind of storage room in years gone by, but now it was the repository for the cleaners mops and buckets and the Ambulance crew between call outs.

I arrived at the Garden at 0840 on the Monday morning. It was a sunny day, but chilly.

Brian was there before me and had the kettle on the boil. I was glad to be working with him as I thought we did get on well together, as was the case when he had worked an overtime shift or two with me at Anfield station.

After the obligatory cup of tea, it was time to go and check the Ambulance and make sure that all that was supposed to be there, was there.

Brian was three years older, and had been in the cadets just two years ahead of me. He had been on permanent shifts at Anfield, but had opted for the job at Hatton Garden when it became available. His usual mate, Tom, who I was covering for was on holiday for the week.

Brian wasn't much of a fan of shift work; he liked his weekends off and the easy start times. Hatton Garden was ideal for him, emergency calls and no shift work.

Brian was a good looking lad, slightly taller than me at six foot. He was certainly one for the ladies and would flirt whenever he got the chance. We chatted and reminisced about our time as cadets as we checked out the Ambulance.

"Did you ever meet Jane from the paper shop?" he asked.

"Yes, nice looking woman."

"Did you ever manage get it on with her?"

"Get it on with her?"

"You know, get your leg over?"

"That's for me to know and you to find out." I said with a vivid memory flashing through my mind

He laughed. "You did, didn't you?"

"What if I did?" It seemed so long ago now, I'd forgotten about her, particularly after the encounter at her front door.

"I was just curious who it had been out of your squad."

"Out of our squad, what are you on about?"

"Didn't you know she had a thing for younger blokes? She always had at least one new cadet from each squad."

"What?" I'd thought I had been the only one. "So did you then?" I asked.

"Yes, then the squad after me it was Dave Price, and obviously it was yourself from your squad. Horny bitch! I wonder who she's shagging now?"

"No one I don't think, she's not at the shop anymore."

"Not surprised," mused Brian. "Probably had her wings clipped by now. Last I heard her old man kicked the Merchant navy into touch and got a job at Fords." I kept my mouth shut about meeting that very man on his front door step.

The office phone rang and Brian jumped from the rear of the Ambulance to go and answer it. I remained in the vehicle and finished off the check list. I thought of Jane and was disappointed. I felt used, even if it had been almost two years ago.

I was closing the rear doors of the Ambulance as Brian came out of the box and locked the door. This meant we had a job. Not being too familiar with the City centre streets and one way systems, I climbed into the attendant's seat and switched on the radio.

"This could be interesting" Brian said as he hauled himself into the driver's seat.

"What is it?"

"Man on a roof with a back injury."

"Where?"

"India Buildings. Water Street."

I knew the India Buildings. It was where the passport office was.

We came out of the underground car park, lights and sirens blearing; more to reminded the water fairies over the road that we didn't sit on our bums all day like they did. We turned left and down towards Dale Street, took a right along Dale Street, then a left into Castle Street. A few hundred yards further and we turned right into Brunswick Street. We had arrived, no more that three minutes from getting the call.

I got out of the cab and looked up to the roof.

"Jeez, I never realised how high this place is."

I grabbed the first aid bag and Brian took the chair and blanket. There wasn't anyone there to meet us; maybe we had been too fast for them?

We went up the steps and under one of the three large archways that adorned the entrance to the building, pushed open a huge glass door and made our way to the lifts which were half way along the wide lobby.

India buildings is quite an old building, but very well kept. High arched and intricate plaster work ceilings towered over us as we made our way to the lifts. It was a building with kudos for those who could afford the office space

We took the lift to the top floor. The plush silent lift came to a halt on the top floor and we stepped out into a thick carpeted corridor. There was no welcoming committee.
"Ok" said Brian. "Let's see if we can find a stairwell to the roof"
Three minutes later we found the stairwell door and then climbed two flights of concrete steps.

As we neared the top, we could feel the cool air from the outside brushing our faces. The steps ended on a landing. There was a heavy wooden door that stood ajar from which the breeze had come. Brian pushed it open, went through and I followed into what was a narrow passageway. There was an absence of windows, but the several fluorescent strip lights fixed to the ceiling were bright and led us down the narrow passageway for about thirty feet. The passageway was too narrow to walk side by side so it was single file only. We could feel the cool air a bit more now. At the end of the passageway there was a sharp turn to the left. This part of the passageway was bathed in daylight. Ahead of us was a dead end, but a steel ladder fixed to the wall led vertically up to a hatchway, approximately four feet square.
Brian looked at me. "Are you thinking what I'm thinking?"
I nodded.
If this bloke had really injured his back, there was no way we could get him to the Ambulance by the way we had just come.

Brian propped the chair against the wall, put the blanket over his shoulder and began to climb the ladder. I watched as he climbed through the hatch and disappeared from sight, and then I followed.

There was a strong breeze as I climbed out through the hatch and onto a flat roof. I had to admire the view over to the Liver buildings and River Mersey.

There were several tall air vents dotted around the roof, along with other metal structures, which I didn't have any clue to what they were for. Brian had already made his way to a group of workmen who were standing around a man lying on the floor.

He was conscious and told us that he was carrying out routine maintenance to the ventilation systems and had slipped, lost his balance and fallen about five feet onto his back.

The man had considerable pain in his lower back, but he had full movement of all his limbs.

There was no way this bloke was going to walk, never mind climbing through that hatch and down the steel ladder. He needed to go in the Neil Robertson and although we could get it up here, there was no way on this earth we were going to get him down through that hatch.

Brian unfolded the blanket and placed it over the workman to protect him from the wind; I could see he was pondering on what to do. It wasn't a life threatening injury, but there could be a spinal fracture which we couldn't rule it out.

"Is there any other exit from the roof other than through that hatch?" I asked the group of workers standing around the injured man.

They all shook their heads.

"So it's the only way up and down?"

They all nodded

I tapped Brian on the shoulder, as he was still crouched down next to the patient.

"I'll go and get the Robertson and entonox."

Brian nodded in agreement, although it really should have been me who stayed with the patient and him doing the fetching and carrying. I was the attendant and in theory in charge of the situation. However, Brian was the more senior through experience. It's what's called passing the buck.

I went down to the Ambulance and collected the equipment, then trudged back up towards the roof. On the way back I studied the route and considered the manoeuvres we might have to take to get him through the hatch and down to the Ambulance. We certainly wouldn't be able to do this on our own, but with the help of the workmen, it just might be possible. The problem was going to be the sharp corner in that narrow passageway. I pushed the Neil Robertson stretcher ahead of me and out through the hatch, then climbed the steel ladder to follow it.

Brian was still kneeling down next to the patient as I carried the equipment over to them. A few of the workmen were now at the roof's edge, leaning over and fiddling with some mechanical equipment, I didn't take much notice of them at first and began to open up the stretcher. Brian turned on the gas bottle and explained to the patient how to administer the gas to him self.

"We just might get him down the hatch an around that passageway corner if these guys give us a hand." I said.

Brian smiled and gave me a wink. "No need, we've got it sorted."

"There's another exit?" I was glad to hear it.

"In a manner of speaking." he replied.

I didn't understand what he was getting at until the workman at the roof's edge called over to us.

"Ok, It's ready."

I looked over and saw a window cleaning cradle attached by two ropes to a winching mechanism. It looked flimsy, just two planks wide with a meagre wire handrail. The ropes didn't look too healthy either, too thin for my liking.

I looked at Brian. "You're joking?"

"It's the only way mate."

It took just a few minutes to place the patient into the Neil Robertson and strap him in securely. It was now just a case of lifting and carrying him over to the cradle. Two workmen helped us carry him to the roof's edge.

I looked over the edge and felt a little nauseous. I wasn't good with heights at the best of times. We were a long way up; traffic and people below seemed so small.

Brian had a wide grin on his face. He knew it was my responsibility as the attendant to be with the patient. It was the unwritten rule. Someone had to go with him.

"Get in and we'll pass him over to you," he said, still with a wide grin. He was enjoying every moment. I turned from the workmen and the patient so they couldn't hear me, and whispered to Brian.

"Not for fucking big clock am I getting in that cradle."

"You're the attendant." The grin was wider. The trouble being, he was right.

"Maybe, but I don't get paid enough for this sort of thing, you can go if you want?"

I tried to pass the buck again, but it didn't work this time.

"No way Hosé, I'm strictly a stairs-n-lift man."

I had to think of something quick; the poor man was immobilised in the cold wind and trussed up like a turkey, waiting to be placed on the cradle.

I turned to the workmen. "Anyone here got a first aid certificate?"

Two of them nodded.

"Would one of you mind going in the cradle with him?"

The older man of the two nodded. "No problem" he said. "I'll go."

"Are you sure?" I said, thanking the lord that I was getting out of this.

"No problem mate, we do it all the time. Just thought you might want go with him for the ride, that's all"

"I'll give it a miss this time."

We loaded him onto the cradle and let the workmen take charge of getting him down the side of the building.

Brian punched the ground floor button in the lift.

"You Jammy sod."

I smiled. "Improvisation, Brian."

The rest of that morning and most of the afternoon we were kept busy with the usual trips and falls in the street, and anything from headaches to tummy upsets in the office buildings. As usual, none of them really required an emergency Ambulance to attend, but it was par for the course. What was most annoying was the phrase we seemed to meet every time. "You'll need a wheelchair." Or, "You'll need your stretcher." This was before we had chance to see the patient and make the decision for ourselves. As usual, ninety nine times out of a hundred, the patient could walk without any detrimental effect to their condition.

Unlike other Ambulance stations, the Garden station didn't seem to get many false calls. But wasteful calls to office workers were in abundance.

It was getting late in the afternoon on my first day at the Garden. It had been a run of the mill day, except for that bloke on the roof of India Buildings. It turned out that he was just badly bruised, no fractures of the spine.

We had just finished a cup of tea when the phone rang. Brian answered. It was a call to a large department store in London Road, an epileptic seizure. It took just a few minutes before we arrived and parked outside the store.

Over the past eighteen months I had been to many calls for someone who was having an epileptic seizure, and every time, the patient was either coming to the end of the seizure or was in the passive stage where they just felt sleepy and exhausted. In reality there wasn't much that could be done for these people, except keep an eye on them and make sure they didn't injure themselves. The thing to be aware of with these patients is the possibility of multiple seizures, one after another, or a seizure that continued for more than just a few minutes.

Brian and I walked into the store together. Usually there would be someone to meet us and point the way to the patient, but not on this occasion it seemed.

I went over to the nearest staff member I could find and asked if she knew about someone calling for an Ambulance. She had no knowledge.

"What's supposed to have happened?" she asked.

"It's supposed to be someone having an epileptic seizure," I replied.

She shook her head; then shouted across the busy shop floor.

"Hey, Mary, do you know anything about someone having a fit in the store?"

I could now see Mary, another staff member, on the far side of the perfume counter, and now too could everyone else in the store.

As we waited for Mary to reply, she seemed to be pondering on the question for a moment. A little old lady tugged at my arm.

"I'd have a fit too if I had to pay the prices in this shop."

I smiled as she wandered away to the exit.

Mary shouted back in a manner that befitted a fisher woman. Twice as loud as the woman who had shouted over to her.

"Maybe the manager knows, Liz. Mr Brown, he's a heppy-lectic isn't he?"

All heads turned to see what might be shouted back in return.

"Is he in to day? I haven't seen him about," shouted Liz

"Ok, it must be a false call," I said, more to myself than anyone else.

Brian was almost at the exit when I turned to follow him.

"Excuse me, excuse me," another member of staff came scurrying along the aisle.

"Mr Brown's in the stockroom, I saw him in there just a few minutes ago."

"Where's the stockroom?" I thought we might as well see this through just in case, I called Brian back.

"It's on the top floor, well it's the attic really."

We left Mary and Liz behind on the ground floor and followed the woman to the lifts. We pulled open the black metal concertina lift doors with a screech.

"Just press the top button; it opens out directly to the stockroom," she said.

It was a large goods lift. With the outer door closed, and now the inner spring door firmly in place, Brian pressed the top of a row of four buttons. The lift was slow and we stood watching the brickwork move past as we ascended.

Opening the doors we found ourselves in a large room filled with dozens and dozens of boxes, some piled almost to the ceiling. There were quite a few windows, covered by metal bars. This allowed a good amount of daylight in.

"Over here lads." We heard the man's voice from behind a stack of cardboard boxes.

Brian followed me as we negotiated our way around the boxes in the direction from which the voice had come.

The store manager was dressed in shirt, tie and dark suit trousers but no jacket. He was in his mid forties, and sitting on the floor with his back to a wall. Surrounding him were dozens of empty cardboard boxes.

"Did you call for an Ambulance mate?" Brian was the first to speak.

"Yes, sorry to drag you up here lads, I'm sure you have better things to do."

"That's ok." I said. "So what's the problem? Are you epileptic?"

"Yes I am and it's so bloody inconvenient when this happens."

"Well you don't look as though you've sustained any injuries." I said

"Do you want to go and get checked over at the hospital?" interjected Brian.

"No, no. I was just hoping that you lads would look after me as I go through the seizure."

"Go through the seizure? I thought you'd been through it already?"

"No. That's what I tried to explain when I rang, I haven't had it yet, but it's coming anytime soon."

Brian and I looked at each other.

"So you're saying you're going to have a seizure, rather than you've had a seizure?"

"That's right. I just wanted someone here to look after me when it happens."

This was a new situation for both Brian and me.

I had been to many epileptic seizures over the past eighteen months, but never before had I been there before a seizure had started.

The majority of people who suffer from epilepsy do get some sort of warning that a seizure is about to happen. This could be in the form of a particular smell, a taste in their mouth, headaches, pins and needles, in fact it could be anything. Different people get different warnings. It is also true to say that the period of time from the occurrence of the warning until the start of the seizure is also different for each individual. Some people just have a few seconds warning before the seizure begins, and others, like our store manager had somewhere between twenty minutes and half an hour. He was lucky, if that's the correct term to use, that he had time to prepare and to put himself in a safe environment. Unfortunately not many people who suffer from this illness have that luxury.

"How long have we got to go?" I looked at my watch, just out of curiosity, and having nothing to do with finishing on time; at least I hoped it didn't seem that way.

"Anytime within the next fifteen minutes," he said.

At this point the stairway door opened and in came the lady who had taken us to the lift. She was carrying a large silver tray with a pot of tea, milk, two mugs and a plate of biscuits.

"Thanks Carol," said the manager.

She set down the tray on one of the cardboard boxes, smiled, and left the way she came without saying a word.

Brian and I spent the next ten minutes drinking tea and munching biscuits. The conversation was mainly about football and the weather. I liked the manager because he was an Evertonian. Not that I'm big on football, it was just that my uncle was a fanatical Everton fan and he had taken me to a few home and away games when I was a kid, so my allegiance was to Everton. Brian just wasn't into football at all.

The manager suddenly fell quiet and his face became bright red. He began to arch his head and back, his body became rigid. This was it; he had started with the seizure.

We stayed with him and looked after him until it was over. From beginning to end, it lasted no more than three minutes.

Eventually he came back to a reasonable conscious level where he could make himself understood, and could understand what we were saying, although he was completely exhausted.

We drained the last of the tea and finished off the biscuits.

"How are you feeling?" I asked.

"Bloody awful."

"Do you want to go to the hospital for a check up?"

He shook his head. "Nothing they can do." You can get away if you want lads; I'll be right as rain in a few minutes."

"Are you sure you'll be ok?" asked Brian.

We knew he would, unless he had some sort of relapse and went into another seizure. But the manager insisted he would be fine. He thanked us for looking after him during the episode. We thanked him for the tea and biscuits.

By the time we got back to station, it was fifteen minutes after finishing time.

"Fancy a pint on the way home?"

"Yes, sounds like good plan" said Brian.

We left in our separate cars and headed towards the Claremont pub in Lower Breck Road. Not only was it on the way home, but it was the regular haunt for the staff at Anfield station. We could catch up on any gossip or rumours that we'd missed, as Hatton Garden was quite isolated from everyone else.

Brian got the first round in and we sat with a few of the staff who had walked in from the station over the road, absorbing the latest gossip on the grapevine. My first day at the Garden had been a good one.

What I heard during the conversations around the table took my interest. Rumour had it, there were a few shift vacancies coming up on the permanent rota at Anfield. I would have to give Charlie a ring tomorrow and suss out the possibilities.

But it wasn't to be. Charlie informed me the next day that there were others ahead of me who were due to go on the permanent rota.

13

Christmas and New Year had come and gone without anything special happening. Beryl was six months pregnant and we were now in serious search mode for a bigger place to rent, we even considered buying, but it would have taken too long to save up a deposit and move into a new house before the baby was born. Beryl had given up work and we only had my wages to pay the bills.

There were plenty of flats to choose from, but we wanted a house with a garden and there weren't many of those in the Anfield district. We decided to apply to the council for a house, we were placed on the council waiting list, but found ourselves low on the priority list. We had to pull out all the stops to get a bigger place as soon as we could.

The phrase, "If you were to write about this, no one would ever believe it," is a statement uttered, I am certain, by many Ambulance staff at one time or another during the course of their careers.

I was back at Hatton Garden station again. It had been six months since I had last worked here and the place hadn't changed. Brian took the phone call from control.

"What have we got?" I asked.

"Someone collapsed in the public toilets in Lime Street Station."

"Male or Female?" Not that it made any difference, as all would reveal itself in the next few minutes.

Brian shrugged. "Didn't say."

Off we went with blue lights flashing and sirens blaring. The first problem was not knowing which entrance to head for, the Control hadn't given us this information.

There are three entrances to Lime Street station. One on Lime Street itself, which was more for pedestrian traffic; one on Lord Nelson Street, which was a smaller side entrance and one on Skelhorne street. This was to be our choice of entrance as it was a vehicular entrance which the post office used to drop the mail that needed to be transported by rail around the country.

We arrived at the railway station within four minutes of getting the call, but we discovered that 'Murphy's Law' was about to take over.

Skelhorne Street was the best entrance as far as the Ambulance was concerned, but Lord Nelson Street would have been closer to the toilets and less of a walk, we chose the wrong one.

I carried the first aid bag and Brian carried the chair and blanket as we walked across the large concourse towards the toilets.

We were met by a uniformed railway employee, with the usual peaked cap and silver buttoned waistcoat. He had been waiting for us at the Lord Nelson Street entrance as when calling for the Ambulance he gave this information to the Control room. For some unknown reason the information wasn't passed on to us.

Three of us headed into the pungent smells and dimly lit entrance of the male public toilets. Typical Victorian décor of green and white ceramic tiles adorned the walls from floor to ceiling

"I'm sorry to call you out for this, but I wasn't sure what to do."

"Someone collapsed, isn't it?" queried Brian.

"In a manner of speaking, you could say that, and I've called the fire brigade as well."

Brian and I looked across to each other.

"The fire brigade?"

"Yes, you'll see why in a minute."

We were escorted down a corridor, past the urinals to a row of about five toilet stalls. There was a second railway employee standing guard outside the last stall in the row. He had a grin on his face from ear to ear as we approached him.

The stall door was closed and I pushed it open, half expecting that I would have a problem with a slumped body behind it. That wasn't the case; it opened easily.

The first thing I saw was a pair of knees and white hairy legs, with trousers dangling around the ankles and a pair of black, shiny lace up shoes. These were not touching the ground, but seemed to be hanging in mid air over the edge of the toilet pan. I leaned a bit further into the stall and could now see a middle aged man, well dressed with shirt and tie. He was of slender build and had his backside lodged firmly down the toilet pan. His arms and elbows were splayed out to stop himself going down any further.

"I can't get out," he blurted. "I'm stuck."

I had a sudden urge to laugh and had to cover my mouth with my hand to stifle it, although unfortunately a snigger did escape.

"It's not bloody funny from where I am I can tell you." He didn't have a Liverpool accent.

"No, I'm sure it's not." I was finding it terribly hard to keep a straight face. "How did this happen?"

"I was desperate to go, you know, for a number two. There was enough time before I caught my train to Euston. There isn't any fold down seat on this toilet. All the others were taken, but I was so desperate. The next thing I know, I'm down here feeling like a complete idiot."

On closer inspection I could see that his backside had slipped below the upper rimmed edge of the pan and his hips were wedged in tight, preventing him from getting out. He was well and truly stuck. The toilet pan was unusually bigger and rounder than normal. Maybe this was a feature of public toilets, I didn't know.

I turned expecting to find Brian behind me so that we could try getting under each arm of the man and pulling, but Brian was not where I had expected him to be.

I popped my head out of the stall and saw him crouched down, arms across his tummy and leaning against the next cubicle door frame, his shoulders bouncing up and down.

"Brian?"

He looked up at me and his eyes were streaming, it seemed strange as there was hardly any noise coming from him.

If I wasn't careful, I would be infected too. It was so difficult not to burst out laughing and join him, but somehow I managed to keep some composure.

Brian wasn't fit for anything so I got the assistance of a railway man and told him what we could try.

"We've already tried that." he said.

"Well let's just try it once more."

In the confined space of the cubicle, we stood as best we could on either side of the so called patient. I hooked my arm under one arm of the man and the railway official took the other arm and we both pulled.

The shouts were unmerciful and must have echoed around the railway station.

"Stop, stop, stop" he screamed.

It was clear that plan of action wasn't going to work.

It was at this point that a herd of boots echoing from the corridor could be heard, heralding the arrival of the water fairies, aka the fire brigade.

Brian, now managing to hold a straight face, explained to the leading fireman what the problem was, the fireman now went to have a look for himself, closely followed by his team.

I felt really sorry for the bloke in the toilet. There must have been five firemen squashed in the stall trying to get a look at him. How embarrassing that must have been.

After a minute or two and a few murmured discussions, the firemen emerged from the stall, each with a grin from ear to ear.

"How about we take a hammer to it? It's only porcelain and should break easily" one of the firemen said

I shook my head. "No, it could cause some serious wounds if any sharp edges cut into him."

There was only one option left. We would have to dismantle the toilet and take him to hospital still in it.

Luckily I'd had some experience as a plumbers mate for a few months when I first left school, so I knew how to dismantle a toilet pan.

I explained to the patient what we were going to do and a look of relief came over his face, but that soon changed as I pulled the chain that was dangling from the cistern overhead.

He gasped as the cold water flushed around him into the pan. "What are you doing?"

"Don't want to have any extra little passengers, do we?" I smiled.

Brian, who had settled a bit by now, had gone to fetch the Ambulance so it was as close as possible to the toilets.

Most toilet pans are screwed into the floor and this one was no different. With the assistance of the fire brigade and their equipment we soon had the pan loose and uncoupled from the cistern.

Brian had now arrived with our trolley and positioned it outside the cubicle. It was a bit awkward getting him out of the cubicle because of the confined space, but finally we managed it. The next problem was, in what position could we put him on the trolley? It turned out to be the most comfortable and least painful position to have him on his hands and knees.

So there he was, on hands and knees, on our stretcher with a huge toilet pan stuck to his backside, I wished I'd had a camera.

We covered him with a blanket and wheeled him to the Ambulance.

At the hospital casualty department, we took him into a cubicle and drew the curtains to save his embarrassment. When the nurse arrived it was a bit like unveiling a statue in front of her.

"Oh my God," she said. We left her to it, our job was done.

Brian and I settled into the comfy arm chairs that adorned the nurses staff room after making ourselves a brew.

On the coffee table there was only one newspaper which was that morning's edition of the Daily Post. The rest was a collection of women's magazines and a copy of the Nursing Times. Brian beat me to the newspaper, so I had to leaf through the Woman's Weekly for my source of entertainment while we waited for our stretcher.

We sat in silence, savouring the brew and smiling to ourselves each time we heard the sporadic groans from the toilet man as the staff attempted to remove the toilet from his bottom. It wasn't too long before a cheer erupted from the cubicle. The patient had gathered quite an audience of nurses and doctors who wanted to witness the problem and how it would be resolved. Lots of KY jelly I had thought. The cheering clearly indicated a success.

We finished our cups of tea and sauntered over to the cubicle. On the floor in the corner the toilet pan, unbroken stood upright. The patient was now lying flat on his tummy while a doctor examined his backside. There was plenty of bruising around his hips, but no serious harm done. He would be physically sore for a while but the damage to his pride and dignity would take longer to heal.

I don't know why, but he thanked us for all we had done for him as we said goodbye.

No sooner had we cleaned up the back of the Ambulance and climbed into the cab than control was calling over the radio.

"Male collapse outside Woolworth's in Church Street."

This time it was my turn to drive.

We rolled out of the hospital grounds with blue lights and sirens and headed towards Church Street, just a two minute drive away depending on the traffic.

As we approached Woolworth's we could see the problem; a man lying face down on the pavement. But there was something not quite right about the scene.

A post office van was parked just a few feet away so we had to pull in behind that. Crowds of people were walking past this man on the floor and not taking any notice of him. Usually there would be a crowd of onlookers.

I came to a halt at the kerbside behind the van and almost where the man was lying. Brian grabbed the first aid bag and opened the cab door to get out. It was a bit unreal as the man turned his head and looked up at him, as if surprised.

"Hi, are you all right?" Brian asked.

"Sure, is there a problem?" was the reply.

It was then I noticed his arms were missing, and the picture became clear.

He was a post office engineer who was working on the wires that were down a small manhole. The only way he could do this job was to lay down on the floor and reach down to access the cables.

It then became obvious that some Good Samaritan must have seen this bloke lying on the floor and mistakenly thought he had collapsed, and, without checking, had called for an Ambulance.

The engineer apologised profusely as he really should have put up the low level windbreak to surround the manhole and a sign to say work was in progress, but he had thought it was just going to be a quick job and he wouldn't be there very long, so he hadn't bothered.

We left the man in peace, still on his belly, and made our way back to station.

It was a nice day and we were in no hurry as we ambled along, taking note of all the short skirts that seemed to throng the City Centre on a nice day. We listened to the babble that came over the radio and nudged each other if either of us spotted a particularly short skirt and long legs.

As we cruised through the city centre streets we started to hear little snippets of unusual talk from the control to other

Ambulances. Things like, "Make sure you're wearing your cap," or "They're at the Southern Hospital." This went on for some time and we wondered what the heck was going on as it didn't make any sense.

Brian couldn't stand it any longer, grabbed the mic and called control to ask what was going on?

They wouldn't tell him over the radio, just said to call them by phone when we got back to station.

Our amble back to station now became a bit of a race as we were eager to find out what the mystery was. However, our curiosity had to wait for a little while longer as we received an emergency call to a male who had taken an overdose, located in a side street off Islington.

From experience, and I could begin to say that word now, the majority of people who take a deliberate overdose of tablets are female. I'm no expert on these matters, but it would seem that the female of the species is more apt to cry for help than the male, meaning that most of these overdose calls are from females who are attention seeking rather than being intent on killing themselves.

It does happen, but it is rare that a male will take an overdose. If a male intends to commit suicide it's usually through brutal means; either hanging himself, standing in front of an inter city train, cutting his wrists or a shot gun in the mouth. This meant that the call we were now speeding to was a bit of a rarity in the male self-harming category.

We turned off Islington and into a narrow cobbled street. It didn't take long to find him, still in the phone box that he had presumably called from. He was sitting on the floor of the booth.

"Oh, shit." Brian's character changed from 'emergency mode' to 'being pissed off' mode.

"What is it?" I didn't understand.

"It's Wondering bloody Walter."

"Wondering Walter?"

"Forty three Shaw Street one day; pissed at the Pier Head on the next. He gets around does our Walter. I should have known it might be him."

"How would you have known that?"

We were parked up at the roadside next to Wondering Walter while the conversation continued inside the ambulance cab.

"We used to get him regular, but not at this time in the afternoon. More like eleven o'clock at night, when we were just about to finish shift," continued Brian.

"So what's his story?"

"If he was pissed, he knew he wouldn't be allowed a bed in Shaw Street, so the crafty old sod would dial 999 and claim he'd taken an overdose of paracetamol. We turn up, he's as pissed as a newt, like he is now, then Bob's your uncle he's got a mattress in the drunk room at the Royal for the night."

We eventually climbed out of the ambulance and ambled across the pavement to stand next to Wondering Walter, and sure enough there was a strong whiff of alcohol about him.

"Afternoon Walter." Brian started the conversation.

Considering Walter was a homeless person, he was surprisingly well dressed in a suit and tie, a little grubby maybe, but not the usual attire of ill fitting overcoat tied around the middle with a length of string.

Walter looked up at him, bloodshot and bleary eyed, and he had difficulty in focusing. "I don't know you."

"But I know you Walter."

"Hmm." Walter nodded and let his head droop.

"What's the problem this time, Walter?" I asked.

He didn't look up this time, but spoke to his feet. "Taken pashishitmol."

"You've taken paracetamol?"

"Thass it yeah, that one"

"How many?"

Walter shrugged his shoulders.

"How long ago?"

Same shrug of shoulders.

"It's not worth the effort, let's just get him on board and take him in" said Brian.

I had to agree. We could have been there for hours and still have got no sense from him.

Brian opened the back doors and I made a start, trying to get Walter to his feet. He wasn't being very co-operative and kept buckling at the knees. Brian came to assist and between us we managed to walk him into the Ambulance. We sat him in the bench seat and pulled down the arm rests on each side to prevent him from flopping sideways.

Brian was attending so he had the happy job of sitting in the back with Walter while I drove to the hospital.

The Royal Hospital was the nearest, so it really should have been the hospital to take Walter to, but Brian and I knew this was the perfect opportunity to take our patient to the Southern Hospital and find out exactly what was going on there.

I notified control that we were taking the patient to the Southern Hospital as we believed he residing in that area of the city. It was an outright lie, but it gave a good reason why we didn't take him to the Royal.

"Roger" said control. "And by the way, make sure you're looking smart and caps worn by the time you get there."

I didn't bother asking why. We'd been hearing this type of chatter going on all afternoon.

I made my way through the city traffic and headed for the Southern Docks, finally turning into Sefton Street where the Southern Hospital was situated. As we approached the hospital Brian was leaning through into the cab, not too bothered about Walter, who was sitting quietly in an alcoholic daze.

As we drew closer we could see a small group of people outside the casualty entrance, facing away from us. They were not hospital staff. Suddenly they all turned to look at us as we approached.

"What the shit is all this about?" I said, more to myself than Brian

"Maybe the boss has people checking out how we're doing our job" replied Brian.

Then a bloke stepped out into the road with a bloody big camera on his shoulder, and it looked like he was filming our approach. The camera was directed straight at us.

"Bloody hell," exclaimed Brian. "What's he doing?"

"Make sure you've got you're cap on," I said over my shoulder.

I pulled to a halt outside the casualty department, which meant stopping at the kerbside. It was an old Victorian building and didn't have any separate egress for an Ambulance.

I climbed out of the cab and was followed to the back of the Ambulance by the cameraman and a microphone on a long pole.

I didn't ask what was going on as I felt that would have seemed un- professional, and in any case, there must have been a good reason for them being there.

Suddenly, and most unusually, a couple of nurses appeared and helped me open the rear doors. This was obviously effect for the filming. Nursing staff never did that unless you had requested them, over the radio, to be standing by for your arrival.

The doors swung open and there was almost an audible disappointment when they saw Walter, chin on his chest, asleep and snoring.

The camera crew and nurses vanished as quickly as they had arrived. Brian and I heaved Walter from his slumbers and frog marched him into the department, where once again we were floodlit and filmed.

After giving the nurse his details and condition and heaving Walter onto the hospital trolley, we discovered what the filming was about. It was to be a documentary for the 'World in Action' programme. 'Blood and Guts Shift' was to be its title, and it would be shown the following week. Obviously our patient wasn't bloodied enough for them. However, we did make it onto the small screen though. Just thirty seconds of Brian and me frog marching Walter into the casualty department. We were famous!

We had finally had a phone installed and It was a Saturday afternoon in February when the phone rang in our flat. I was half expecting it to be work, but it was my father. He said that he had something to tell me and wanted to discuss it, but not over the phone, so I arranged to go and see him later that day.

I dropped Beryl off at her parent's house and drove the short distance to my old house; she didn't feel in the mood to join me.

He looked different. He was clean shaven and looked quite smart wearing a casual grey top and black trousers. These were new clothes. I'd never seen him dressed in them before. His personality seemed different too; he was friendly with less of the authoritative demeanour that he usually emitted.

After the usual pleasantries, we sat in the living room facing each other.

"I have a lady friend." He blurted it out as if he was confessing to a grievous deed.

This now explained why the house was clean and tidy and he wasn't so dishevelled.

"Good." I said, not sure what he wanted or expected me to say.

"You don't mind then?"

"Why should I mind?"

I was shocked, not by the fact that he had a girlfriend, but the fact that he was my father who had been an authoritative figure throughout my life and here he was, almost asking me for permission to have a girlfriend.

"Well, since your mother passed away, I wasn't sure if you would approve of your father having a woman friend."

"Dad." I said, "I'm glad for you. You look much better than the last time I saw you. She must be doing you good"

"I wasn't sure how you would take it."

"I don't mind at all. It's your life; you don't need permission from me."

There was a moment's silence, but I could see he was still a little agitated.

"There's something else you should know."

"Don't tell me she's pregnant." I couldn't resist it. I had to put my hand over my mouth to stop myself from laughing.

"Don't be stupid." He didn't see the funny side.

"What is it then?"

"I'm going to move in with her. She has a flat in Aigburth and we are planning to get married in September"

Once again there were a few moments of silence as I took in the information.

"So what are you going to do about the house?" I eventually asked.

"This is why I wanted to talk to you, to see if you wanted to take over the tenancy?"

I think my mouth might have dropped open at that point. This was a bolt from the blue that I hadn't been expecting. But it was good news when considering that Beryl and I were looking for a bigger place to live.

14

Clanking water pipes traversed the ceiling in all directions. The brick walls were painted a glossy custard cream colour. There was just enough room to fit a small dining table, two dining chairs and two high backed wing armchairs, like the ones they always seem to have in old folk retirement homes.

The small space also housed a small tabletop oven and hob and a small fridge. The phone was on a tiny shelf screwed to the wall with a jotter pad next to it.

This was the crew room at Hatton Garden Ambulance station. No television or even a radio could be installed, as it was impossible to get a signal. The only release from boredom was the old dog eared 'Tit Bit' magazines, an old newspaper or two and a few tatty cowboy paperbacks.

Don't get me wrong, it was a great station to work from. It was a busy place, which meant you weren't always confined to what almost felt like a bunker beneath the health service office block that towered above.

Ironically this was the very same building where, more than four years ago, I had undertaken my medical examination before joining the Ambulance Service.

      Brian and I had read everything that was readable in the room. We had played cards and even played a game of I spy; got fed up with that and then cleaned and polished the Ambulance inside and out until the vehicle was sparkling. That took us through until lunch time. Did I say it was a busy station?

Following lunch we had another few games of cards, after which Brian announced that he was going to have a snooze. "Just making the best of a quiet day" he mused. Tilting his armchair back on two legs and against the wall, he placed his feet onto a dining chair and was ready for the land of nod. "Just think, we're getting paid for this." he said with eyes closed and arms behind his neck.

Even on night shifts I have trouble sleeping, so I wasn't in any mood to join him. I wanted to be out in the real world saving lives, not stuck in an underground room with a car park outside the door.

  I decided to give my car a wash and vacuum it out to pass some time. An hour or so later, my car was looking as good as it could for the age of it.

I had never known it to be this quiet before 'had everyone left the country? When I thought about it, what I was really wishing for was someone to fall suddenly ill or have some kind of accident. Maybe Brian was right, we should make the best of it when it's quiet.

Then the phone rang.

I got to the phone before Brian was fully alert and out of his snooze mode. He was still a bit groggy and struggling to get his arm chair back on four legs.

It was Charlie.

I listened to what he had to say for a few moments, then the excitement kicked in. "Yes." I said and punched the air.

I put the phone down in its cradle and jumped up and down. I punched the air again. "Yes,yes,yes."

"What's up with you?" Have we got a job or what?"

"I've got a place on the rota at Anfield!" I was exhilarated; I had finally reached the top of the ladder as far as being on the road was concerned, a regular partner and regular shifts.

"That's brill mate, well done." Brian was genuinely happy for me.

Getting on to a shift rota was the last hurdle to climb and now I was there, starting on Tuesday night. My first permanent rota shift was to be night shifts.

Ever since graduating from the cadets, I had put up with the hassle and boredom of out patient work, being the lacky, running errands and undertaking relief shifts at different stations and with different partners. That was now all in the past. I felt as though I had come home.

"Who are you working with then?" asked Brian.

"Martin." I said.

There was silence from Brian.

When I thought about it, Brian was almost the opposite personality to Martin, who was soon to be my new and permanent partner. Whereas Brian was a laid back, no rush no fuss type of character and maybe a bit lax in the tidiness department, Martin was the opposite. He was more excitable than most, a stickler for being neat and tidy. Brian was in the same cadet squad as Martin, three years ahead of me, so I supposed he knew him better than I did.

"Have you worked with him before?" enquired Brian

"Yes, a few times, he seems all right."

"Don't you think he's a bit odd like?"

"What do you mean?"

"You know, sort of different."

"You mean the rumour that he's a shirt lifter?"

"Well yes. No smoke without fire and all that."

"That's a load of bollocks; I've worked with him and seen him chatting up nurses."

Martin wasn't the most handsome guy in the pack, but he wasn't ugly either. He was about the same height as me, a little stockier but muscular with it. Always smartly dressed and boots highly polished. He wore glasses with blue tinted lenses which made him look kind of cool.

I had to admit that he didn't socialise very much. He kept himself to himself most of the time and hardly ever frequented the Claremont for a pint after work. He wasn't a recluse by any means; he could be a chatty bloke when he wanted to be and always seemed to be in a pleasant mood. It was just the way he was.

"Well, just keep your back to the wall mate, that's my advice."

I knew Brian meant well, but I felt he was going a little over the top with this. Even if Martin was homosexual it didn't bother me in the least.

"Who's place have you got?" asked Brian, changing the subject.

"According to Charlie, Jimmy has been transferred to Old Swan. It's closer to home for him."

Brian looked at his watch then resumed his previous position, arm chair tilted back and feet on the dining chair. "Half an hour to go, I've never known it happen, a whole shift without a job," he said with his eyes closed.

It was a dangerous statement to make. The phone rang.

I took the message. "Female toilets, in Woolworths, abdo pain."

"Bugger" said Brian. "Why did I open my big mouth."

We climbed into the now gleaming white Ambulance, fired the engine and switched on the blue lights. Sirens came on just as we exited from the underground car park and were directly in line with the fire station on the opposite side of the road.

I was driving and I headed towards Dale Street, turned right and joined the traffic. Cars and buses pulled over to let us through as they heard the sirens approaching them from behind. We headed up Dale Street towards the town hall. The traffic was really heavy. Although we made progress it was painfully slow.

I really had to concentrate to squeeze through small gaps in the traffic, while Brian had the pleasure of smiling and waving at the mini skirted girls on the pavement who would automatically turn to watch an Ambulance with blue lights flashing and siren blaring.

This was all the better for Brian's female watching as we had a slow journey through all the traffic, as opposed to whizzing past pedestrians on a more open road.

"Where's the female toilets in Wooly's?" I shouted over the din of the siren. We both had our windows rolled down and the noise would ricochet back into the cab from the passing buildings.

"Upstairs I think." Brian was waving to a blonde.

I turned into Church Street from Castle Street and it was bus central. Castle Street was a two way street, predominately used by buses and taxi's. It was the main bus route for all buses either heading to or departing from the terminus at the Pier Head. Every twenty yards there was a bus stop and it was guaranteed that a bus would be at each one, taking on board a herd of passengers. This meant that at peak times other buses using Church Street often had to double park to collect their passengers. It was the same from the other direction, on the opposite side of the street passengers were disembarking ready to hit all the stores and shops. The end result was gridlock. We were only about five hundred yards from Woolworths, but it took six or seven minutes to get there, leaving traffic chaos behind us.

Brian jumped out of the cab with the first aid bag and headed towards the row of glass doors that led into the large store. I climbed out of the cab and strolled to the back of the Ambulance and opened the doors. I reached for a blanket from the stretcher then retrieved the carry chair which hung on a couple of hooks secured in place with an elastic luggage strap to the inside of the rear door. There was no great urgency, it was only abdominal pains, not usually life threatening.

I pushed my way through the big glass door and looked around for Brian, blanket in one hand and carry chair in the other. There was a sea of faces all busy with their own agendas, milling around the different counters, shelves and racks. I could have been an alien from outer space and still they wouldn't have noticed me, it was too busy.

Upstairs, Brian had said

I spotted the wide concrete stairs over to the right of the store and headed towards them, pushing through the crowds of shoppers as best I could without causing any injuries with the carry chair.

Eventually I arrived at the bottom of the steps and began to plod my way up. There was a woman at the top looking down at me.

"You'll need your stretcher." she spoke with an elegant voice, not a scouse accent.

"Let's take a look first, shall we," I responded as I continued to plod up the stairs. It was the standard reply to anyone who knew how to do your job better than you did.

"Can't you go a little faster? This is urgent."

She looked like a typical schoolmistress from a private girl's school, or at least how I imagined one to look like. She must have been in her sixties or seventies, it was difficult to tell. She was dressed in a brown tweed skirt that came down to calf level and a tweed jacket to match, a green nylon buttoned up blouse with a string of pearls. Her legs were encased in thick brown stockings and she sported brown sensible shoes with laces. A pair of spectacles hung from a silver chain around her neck.

"Is my mate with the patient?"

"The other Ambulance driver is with her."

"No running." Harry Jones had drilled into us. "Never run to a patient."

I reached the top of the stairs and asked the woman to show the way.

Ambulance driver! I disliked that term. It should be Ambulance man or woman. You didn't get 'Fire engine driver' or 'Police car driver' so why Ambulance driver?

We passed through a doorway and were now on the first floor, women's clothing. The toilets were on the far side of the store.

The woman scurried ahead of me asking people to move out of the way as I came walking through with the chair and blanket but they didn't take any notice of her.

Inside the toilets were a row of four cubicles. Two shop staff in uniform were standing by the middle cubicle.

"They're in here, love," said the prettier of the two. She made way for me to enter the cubicle.

Brian was in the cubicle with the woman. She was sat on the toilet. It seemed as if there was blood everywhere; over the toilet seat, on the floor and down this woman's legs. She was the colour of white marble. She must have been in her early thirties, wore a wedding ring and was quite attractive, considering the state she was in.

She had her left hand up between her legs somewhere and the tail of a bandage dressing dangled down into the toilet pan. Her right hand gripped a hand rail on the wall. Her knuckles were white as she tried to grasp control of herself and the pain. Brian had already attached an oxygen mask to her face.

"This is Susan, and bleeding PV." Brian said.

I kicked myself for dawdling from the Ambulance and up the stairs to this poor woman, she was in serious trouble. Why the hell didn't Control give us the full information? Nothing was said about her bleeding post vaginally. Susan was obviously in shock.

"We need to get her lying flat." I said more to myself than to Brian.

"Yes I know, I've been waiting for you to give me a hand."

Brian gave her some instructions and advised her of what we were going to do.

"Susan, I want you to keep holding that pad to yourself, and we're going to lift you off the toilet an lay you flat on the floor, ok"

Susan nodded; she was helpless and totally reliant on Brian and me.

As gently as we could, we lifted her from the toilet and lay her flat on her back outside of the cubicle. I set up the carry chair and placed it by her feet, then gently raised her legs and placed them onto the chair. She was now flat on her back with legs raised, classic position for someone in shock and fully conscious. Brian placed the blanket over her.

As the driver it was my job to fetch and carry equipment from the Ambulance should the attendant need it. We needed the stretcher for this patient and it was my job to go and get it.

"I should have listened to that woman and brought the trolley instead."

"What woman?" Brian looked at me confused

"The one in a tweed skirt and jacket, she was at the top of the stairs." I looked around in the room, but couldn't see her.

"She said I'd need to get the stretcher, you know, the usual greeting."

Brian shook his head. "Don't know what you're talking about mate."

I shrugged my shoulders, it didn't matter now. I asked one of the staff to get the lift to the ground floor and keep it ready for when I brought the stretcher in. I then left the cubicle and headed for the stairs. There wasn't any sign of the tweed woman anywhere.

I took two steps at a time going down the stairs, then out through the big glass doors to the Ambulance.

The pavement was still busy with crowds of pedestrians. I pushed my way through them like someone trying to swim across a fast flowing river towards the Ambulance. I opened the back doors and pulled out the trolley and wheeled it once more across and through the crowds of people scurrying along the pavement. A kind gentleman must have seen me and held the glass door open so I could get it into the store.

A trolley with four small caster wheels at each corner is a difficult thing to control when pushing it on your own.

The lift was waiting for me at the far end. Once inside the doors were closed, button pressed, we ascended to the first floor.

"I'll keep the lift here" said the staff member, as the doors opened.

I thanked her and wheeled the trolley over to the toilets

Susan wasn't looking much better than she had been just a few minutes ago. I lined the stretcher up next to her ready to lift her on to it.

Brian had packed up all the equipment that had been strewn about the floor from the first aid bag. He once again explained to Susan what we were about to do and she nodded in understanding.

We gently placed her onto the stretcher and put a second blanket over her.

I folded the carry chair and asked the other staff member if she could bring it down to the Ambulance. We were now organised and ready to go.

I was at the feet end and pushing, while Brian was at the head end and pulling. We entered the lift. The staff member closed the doors and pressed the down button.

Brian had ascertained that Susan was three months pregnant and she'd had two previous miscarriages. She wasn't booked into any particular maternity hospital. We decided that we would take her to the LMH (Liverpool Maternity Hospital)

Susan pulled the mask away from her face and looked hard at me. At first I thought she was going to say that she knew me, but instead she asked about the woman in tweed I had mentioned.

"Do you know her?" I asked.

She asked me to describe her, which I did. Then she burst into tears.

Brian, who was facing the exit door, looked around to see what was going on. He looked at me and I shrugged my shoulders. It was understandable that she might burst out crying, having had two previous miscarriages. The staff member handed Susan a tissue which she deftly pulled out from the sleeve of her jumper.

Susan blew her nose and thanked the staff member.

"That was my mum" she said.

"Your mum?"

"You just described my mum."

My first thought was that her mother must have gone ahead to meet us at the hospital, but then how would she know which hospital we were going to? We had only just decided that.

"Where did she disappear to?" I asked her, thinking that she should be with her daughter.

"My mum died two weeks ago." she sobbed.

Two weeks later, after lots of letter writing and form filling, the council had agreed to Beryl and I taking on a joint tenancy for my old house. Everything was going as planned; we would move in the following week and make my old home our new home.

My father had already moved out to live with his new fiancé, and it was just a matter of arranging a removal van to move the furniture from the flat.

It was all going to be straight forward until Beryl had finished speaking to her mother on the phone. I had overheard part of the conversation she was having and she was becoming more excited as her conversation progressed. Finally she put the phone down, she was beaming.

"You'll never guess," she said excitedly

"Guess what?"

"The older couple who live next door to mum and dad."

"What about them?"

"They're emigrating to Australia."

"So?"

"So we could do a house exchange."

Two weeks after that phone call, we moved into the house next to Beryl's parents. I consoled myself with the knowledge that it was a better house and had bigger gardens.

15

I was on a night shift when it happened. It was around two in the morning when Stan the controller called me over to the Control room. He had a message for me.

I had just settled into my arm chair like the rest of the crew, ready for a few hours sleep.

I walked from the garage, over the forecourt and into the control room. The lighting in the control room was dimmed, but I could see sombre faces looking at me.

"I've got some bad news." said Stan.

My heart leapt and my stomach turned over; this was not good.

"What is it? Has something happened?" I could hardly get the words out; I felt myself shaking as I braced myself for bad news.

"It's your missus; she's been taken to Walton Hospital."

My knees almost buckled.

"What's happened?"

"From what I can gather, I think she might be having a miscarriage, I'm really sorry."

Stan told me to go off duty on compassionate leave.

I drove to the hospital like a madman. It was lucky the streets were empty at that time of the morning.

I arrived at the maternity ward and had to ring the night bell before I could get inside. I was still in uniform and the staff nurse who came to open the door looked past me for the Ambulance that I might have arrived in.

I explained who I was and her facial expression changed immediately.

"She's down in theatre right now."

"How is she? How's the baby? Are they going to be alright?"

I was asking questions just like people asked me when they had a sick or injured relative that I was dealing with. I was on that side of the fence right now.

I reluctantly took her advice and went home. I would ring the ward the following morning.

I parked outside our new house and noticed that next door, where her parents lived, the downstairs lights were still on.

I knocked at their door and was greeted by her father. If looks could kill I would have died instantly on that doorstep. I was the one who had got her pregnant and therefore I was responsible for her being in the condition she was in now, or at least that's how it felt.

I told them what the nurse had told me and that I would ring the hospital and let them know what they say.

Her father humphed, and said in no uncertain terms that he would be calling the hospital himself in the morning and wouldn't be relying on me for information.

I said goodnight and walked down the path. The door slammed behind me.

I couldn't go to bed and sleep; instead I drank copious cups of coffee and smoked copious cigarettes, pacing the floor, wondering how they were. It was like a living nightmare not knowing what was happening.

I woke at seven. I must have dozed off on the settee. I was still in my uniform and my mouth felt like the inside of a toilet bowl. I had drunk too much coffee and had too many cigarettes. I lit another cigarette and reached for the phone.

We had lost the baby and Beryl had lost a lot of blood, but she was now stable and they expected she would make a good recovery. It was recommended that she have no visitors today, she was sedated and needed to rest.

I brought Beryl home four days after she had the miscarriage. She was understandably subdued, and was under instructions from the hospital to rest for the next few weeks. I had to return to work, which meant that Beryls mother was in and out of our house every day looking after her.

Looking back, I can see this was the time when the relationship between Beryl and I began to deteriorate.

The permanent rota I had joined had changed slightly since I had last worked at the station.

It now consisted of Kenny and Duggy, Don and Owen and then Martin and myself.

As my name was also Ken, I was christened 'Little Ken' and the other one was 'Big Ken' even though I was a few of inches taller than him.

Big Ken and Duggy were of the old school, but a good crew. Big Ken was the practical joker of our shift, a short stocky man with a hard looking face who had probably seen a few fights in his time, but the same man would do anything for you if he could. He must have been in his early fifties and had seen military service in Korea.

Duggy was probably a little younger than big Ken. He was a quiet, calm and unassuming type of man.

Don and Owen had been cadets, but several years ahead of me and just one year ahead of Martin.

Don must have been in his late twenties and was always smart in his uniform He'd even adjusted the black peak on his cap so it looked regimental, pointing downwards towards his nose. He was the more outspoken of the two and had a continuing battle of wits with Big Ken to see who could pull off the best and most original prank on each other, often accompanied with a water fight using old fairy liquid bottles filled with water.

Owen, by contrast was the quiet studious type and always seemed to have a book in his hands. He looked upon Don and Big Ken's practical jokes as something childish. Don and Owen were destined for greater things and higher ranks in the Ambulance Service.

Martin was a few years older than me, which made me the baby of the rota. I'd worked with all of them at some point or other during my stint on relief shifts.

I got on well with Martin and I admired his experience and compassion towards the patients. He was a caring person, although he did strike me as being a little obsessive with being neat and tidy. Blankets had to be folded in a certain way and the first aid bag had to be stocked just right. The interior of the Ambulance was always spotless, and the chrome shined. Sometimes we might be having a meal or tea break and he would disappear without a word to anyone, then I'd find him cleaning the Ambulance or folding and tidying the blankets in the rear of the vehicle. At first I felt guilty about him doing this, thinking that I should be there helping, but after a while I got used to it and let him carry on. He didn't moan or complain about doing all the cleaning and tidying, in fact he eventually admitted that he enjoyed it, so I didn't argue.

Even after six months on the rota with Martin at Anfield I still had to pinch myself sometimes. I'd actually made it, reached my goal. I loved the job.

I'd just had my long weekend off, Friday to Monday, which came around every month and was always welcome when it did. It allowed me to socialise like other people over a weekend and not have to worry about going into work the following day.

Now it was Tuesday afternoon and the start of the afternoon shifts had arrived, three in the afternoon until eleven at night. Martin and I were due to be crew 2 for this week.
Charlie called me over to the office as I walked through the garage towards the mess room. It was a friendly type of wave, so I knew I wasn't in any trouble.

"Martin has gone sick for few days." Charlie didn't look up from his desk as he spoke and continued completing some paperwork.

"Oh, what's wrong with him?" It wasn't like Martin to be off work, I'd seen him drag himself into work with really bad colds and chest infections. He'd been scolded by the rest of us as we didn't want to catch what he had. He claimed he'd go crazy if he had to stay at home and do nothing, so this was a bit of a surprise.

"Don't know" said Charlie, still getting to grips with the paperwork on his desk

"You're not going to send me to another station are you Charlie?"

"No lad! Peter Whittaker is on his way over from Westminster to team up with you. There was a man short there too, but it seems that he's decided to turn up for work without letting anyone know he was coming back off the sick."

I breathed a sigh of relief. The last thing I wanted was to work somewhere else for the rest of the week.

"Cheers Charlie, you're a pal" I said. He mumbled something about not allowing his station to be an Ambulance short.

Peter was from the cadet squad that came two years after me. He'd gone through the course and had also done his stint on the out patient vehicles, now he was a newbie on relief shifts. I hadn't worked with him before, so was curious as to how it would be.

When on station, if an emergency call came in for our area, the controller would press a button on his console that rang a large and noisy bell that hung in the garage. Its noise was deafening, and some impish controllers would leave their finger on the button for a little longer than was necessary. It was loud enough to wake the corpses in Belmont mortuary just up the road. After the bell had finished ringing, a tanoy would click into life and the controller would call out three times, "crash call, crash call, crash call." This didn't mean there was a traffic accident somewhere; rather it was to let the next crew out know that they were going to an emergency call. After the crash call alert, there would usually be a one word description of what the emergency was, like 'collapse' or 'fall or 'RTA.

The crew would climb into the Ambulance and call the Control on the radio, who would then give further details of the incident. This only happened at Anfield station; all other stations got their calls by telephone.

It was twenty past three when the emergency bell rang out across the garage. Followed by "Crash call" and then "Sudden illness" An emergency to a 'Sudden illness' meant it could be anything.

Don and Owen were first out. They hurried out of the mess room and over to their vehicle. I heard the engine fire into life and drive away from the garage. A minute later we could hear the two tone horns start to sound as they headed away along Lower Breck Road towards West Derby Road, eventually the sound fading into the distance.

"Where's this bloody mate of yours?" Big Ken spoke but didn't take his face out of the Daily Mirror that someone had bought that morning and left lying around.

I had told the rest of the shift that Martin had gone sick and Peter was heading over from Westminster.

"Probably stuck in traffic." I said.

"Well he'd better get a bloody move on, you're next out."

It was as if the Gods had heard him. The emergency bell began to ring and when it finished. *"Crash call, crash call, crash call, a collapse."*

"Oh shit, I knew it; I just knew this would bloody happen." Big Ken threw the paper onto the table in a gesture to enhance his feeling.

"Sorry mate, it's not my fault Martin went sick," I said and grinned as I leaned over to pick up the paper.

"You can wipe that bloody smirk off your face for a start."

I broadened my smile, I knew he didn't mean what he said in a vindictive way, but I didn't want to miss the chance to rub salt into the wound. "Can you bring me a Mars Bar on the way back?"

"Piss off" were the words I heard as he left the mess room.

Ten minutes after Big Ken and Duggy had been called out, Peter arrived at the station. He offered to make a brew, which was a good start.

I could tell he was a little nervous and maybe a little unsure of himself, not having worked with me before. I remembered what it was like for me when I first started working relief shifts. I always had the feeling that I was the outsider, the intruder.

Peter was a couple of years younger than me. He had a youthful, round shaped face and he looked as though he hadn't started to shave yet. His facial skin seemed to be smooth and soft like he might use those skin conditioning creams. Maybe he did, but I wasn't going to ask him.

Over the next hour we had a good chat. I discovered that he lived in Huyton and his dad was a Police detective and he had a girlfriend called Laura.

I quite liked Peter, he wasn't brash in any way and he was interesting to talk to. It seemed our chat was relaxing him a little. He'd been in and out of several jobs before joining the Ambulance Service. His dad had wanted him to join the police, but he wasn't convinced it would have been the right job for him.

It had gone past five o'clock before the other crews began to return to the station. Big Ken and Duggy were first to return, followed shortly after by Don and Owen.

"I'm so glad you decided to join us, eventually." Big Ken's sarcastic remark was directed at Pete as he plonked himself into the armchair, put his feet on the coffee table and reached for the newspaper that he had before being called out.

"I'm sorry, I got here as soon as I could."

Big Ken grunted and flicked over a few pages trying to find where he had left off.

"Take no notice Pete, he's always like a bear with a sore arse," I said

"Anyone want a cuppa?" offered Pete, probably hoping it would help smooth some feathers.

"That's a good idea," said Don. "Count me in," added Owen. "I suppose," said Big Ken.

"Me too!" shouted Duggy from the locker room. Pete looked at me and I nodded, never refusing the offer of a cuppa when it's proffered.

The next few hours were quiet. Don, Owen, Pete and I were playing cards to pass the time and Big Ken was beginning to snore in the armchair. He almost leapt from his slumbers when the emergency bell went off. He looked around to make sure it wasn't for him and Duggy, then returned to his snoozing mode as he saw that we were all still in the mess room.

Don and Owen were out within a minute, two tone horns fading into the distance.

"More tea?" asked Pete. He spoke softly so he didn't wake Big Ken.

"Sure." I said

As he collected the used mugs from the table, Big Ken, still with eyes closed and feet on the coffee table, picked up his mug and waggled it about in the air, his way of saying he would have one too. Maybe there was just a little bit of a message in that waggling of mug for having to go out earlier.

"Yes please." It was the distant voice of Duggy out in the garage.

Pete shook his head. "The pair of you must have ears like shithouse rats."

"It's all in the training son, all in the training," mused Big Ken.

Pete went to collect his mug but didn't get the chance as the emergency bell rang.

Pete put the mugs back onto the table and looked at me as we started for the door.

"Who's attending?"

"I'm afraid you are, sorry."

I wasn't claiming the driver's seat because I could; if Martin had been there it would be his turn to attend today, so I just carried the sequence on as it would have been.

Driving was the better of the two tasks, probably less stressful too. It meant that you didn't have to sit in the back with the drunks, smelly tramps or people vomiting over you when they got the chance. Driving was definitely the better of the two options.

Pete pulled the radio mic out of its holder and spoke to control.

"It's a collapse case, reported as unconscious at the Palace Public House, Westminister." Arthur the controller probably knew who the patient was going to be.

It struck me straight away who this was going to be; my old girl Gladys, probably been too heavy on the gin and not enough on the tonics.

I explained to Pete who she was and my encounters with her in the past. He thought the pregnant woman story was hilarious, which I suppose it was now I look back at it.

There was no need for blue lights and sirens, no big rush for this one. Gladys would be fast asleep, hence the mention of being unconscious.

I had been for Gladys on several occasions now. The routine would be taking her home in the Ambulance, fishing for her door key in her hand bag, helping her into the house then putting her on the sofa and covering her with a blanket to sleep it off. Gladys was a regular, but a lovable one, not like the time wasters we normally got sent to.

I parked at the kerb outside the pub. Pete jumped out and took the first aid bag and portable oxygen bottle, a standard procedure when attending emergency calls, and disappeared through the pub door while I opened the rear doors to the Ambulance and prepared to retrieve the chair and a blanket. In these scenarios it is always prudent to remove the sheets and blankets from the stretcher that you know will soon be used by someone who is worse for wear with alcohol. It would be sods law that if you didn't, the patient would throw up or piss themselves and soil the linen and blankets.

I was just clearing the stretcher when a breathless man appeared at the back doors of the Ambulance.

"Your mate said can you bring the resuscitator, quick like"

My pulse rate increased. Peter had already taken in the oxygen therapy bottle with him, so this meant he needed the minuteman.

The minuteman resuscitator is a PPV, (Positive Pressure Ventilation) machine, which will force oxygen into the lungs of someone who has stopped breathing. This was not looking good for Gladys, that's if it was Gladys. I grabbed the machine and almost leapt from the back of the Ambulance.

My heart sank a little as I saw Gladys lying on the floor and Pete pumping away at her chest.

Pete and I didn't have to say anything to each other; we both knew the procedure and what to do in these circumstances. He continued the chest compressions and I placed the resuscitation mask over her nose and mouth and began ventilating her lungs.

"Come-on Gladys." I meant to say it to myself in my mind, but the words came out as a whisper.

We worked on Gladys for a good twenty minutes, changing over places every five minutes, during which time we didn't get any response.

I was awash with guilt. Memories of Gladys that first day I was on the road, the story of her husband never coming home and the family who had shunned her. What a sad life she had endured and now it was at its end. Then I thought of my own stupid attitude to this call, no blue lights, no sirens, no rushing. Would it have made any difference if we had hurried? Probably not, but then, I would never know now.

There are three occasions when resuscitation should stop. If the patient shows signs of recovery, when the patient is handed over to the hospital staff or when you become physically exhausted. We were rapidly approaching the latter.

"What do you think?" Pete was using the minuteman while I was pounding down on her chest, sweat pouring from my brow. I looked at him, and realised that I had gone a little manic; determined that Gladys would soon start showing signs of life. It was useless, she had gone. What Pete really meant was that we had done enough, we were not going to win this one, and it was time to stop.

Gladys was lying on the floor between the tables and seats; it looked undignified for an elderly woman. The pub customers had moved out of our way to give us room to work. Some stood at the bar drinking their beer and watching our every move. The barman continued to serve people and nobody had bothered to turn down the juke box, Gilbert O'Sullivan was singing 'Alone Again'. She wouldn't be anymore, I thought. She'll be with Bert now.

16

There had been a change in Martin over the past few months, ever since the time he had gone off on the sick. He had been off work for a few weeks and claimed that he had fallen downstairs at home and cracked a few ribs. He was quiet and withdrawn, not saying much to anyone, including me.

Martin had never gone out of his way to find a girlfriend although he was fine chatting to the nurses and had a good laugh with them; but he never seemed to take things any further.

I knew a nurse, Jenny, at Newsham hospital admissions room who quite often went out of her way to talk to Martin, even if she was busy on a ward full of patients. I reckoned that she fancied him, so I decided to play cupid and set it up for them to meet at the pub, a social setting rather than the work environment and with Jenny's full co-operation.

I had insisted that Martin should join me for a pint after work, full knowing that Jenny would be there.

Jenny was a nice person, not the most attractive, but she won hands down with personality and brains, which I considered to be more important than just looks alone.

After lots of insistence and cajoling, Martin agreed to go for just one pint and as planned we bumped into Jenny in the pub.

"Oh what a surprise"!
"Fancy seeing you here"!

They got on like a house on fire as usual so I drifted into the background and left them to it. The next thing I knew, they were an item. I was pleased with my devious plan.
Unfortunately my devious plan fell apart after a few weeks; Jenny and Martin were no longer an item. I felt it was this that was troubling Martin, but he assured me he was not troubled.

It had been a quiet shift until the bell rang at half past two in the morning. It was a maternity call to Oxenholme Crescent in Norris Green. Full term, having contractions and booked into Broad Green hospital.

It was quite a distance to travel from Anfield station to the address, but Gillmoss station, whose area this was, didn't work night shifts, so we were next in line for the Norris Green area. All maternity cases were classed as emergency calls but unless we were told things were desperate, we didn't hurry too much. At that time in the morning there was very little traffic on the roads and it wouldn't take any more than ten or fifteen minutes to get there. Martin was quiet as usual as I drove the Ambulance. Eventually I turned into the crescent and came to a halt outside the house.

Martin was first out the vehicle and scurried up the front path to knock on the door, I had joined him before the door was opened, a good sign, no panicking family.

We were shown upstairs into a bedroom where a woman of about 30, dressed in her nighty and dressing gown, was sitting on the edge of the bed. She smiled as we entered the room.

"I think I have another contraction on the way, can we wait for a minute?" She spoke to Martin as he was the first in the room.

"Sure, no problem."

She asked her husband who had followed us into the bedroom, to go downstairs and get the bag she had packed. This was an organised lady. She held her stomach and grimaced as the contraction started.

"How often are they coming, love?" asked Martin.

Through gritted teeth. "About every three minutes now." She started to rock back and forth a little as the contraction got stronger.

"Waters broke?"

"No."

"Is this your first?" It was obvious that it wasn't her first because of all the toys we had passed on the staircase, but it was the type of question that was meant to flatter, a bit like telling a woman she looked ten years younger than she really was.

Through gritted teeth again. "Third."

I nudged Martin. "I'll go and get the chair and blanket." He nodded in agreement.

I padded down the stairs, clearing some of the toys out of the way; I didn't want any tripping and tumbling of bodies as we carried her down.

I was soon out of the front door and at the Ambulance to open the back doors. It just took a moment to retrieve the chair and blanket and I was soon making my way up the stairs again, this time free of any hazards.

The contraction was beginning to ease when I returned to the bedroom and set up the chair. I placed the blanket over it and invited the woman to sit down. It took a few moments for her to gather the strength to move from the bed and place her self into the chair.

Her husband had now entered the bedroom clutching an overnight bag. Why on earth he had brought it upstairs only to carry it down again was a bit of a puzzle, but I guessed he was a little stressed with the occasion.

Happy that she was secured in the chair, we wheeled her onto the landing and stopped at the first step. I went ahead and down a few stairs to take the feet end of the chair. In unison, Martin and I took the weight of the chair and began the slow rhythmic movement as we descended step by step, her husband following.

Three minutes hadn't yet passed as we were half way down the stairs and another contraction came on quite unexpectedly. We stopped on the staircase until it began to subside and then continued.

Finally we were down the stairs and in the hallway. I opened the front door and turned back to help ease the chair over the doorstep. We were half way down the path heading towards the gate, when something seemed seriously wrong. It didn't register with me at first, but it was Martin who said it.

"Where the fuck is the Ambulance?"

The woman started another contraction; they were now obviously much closer together than three minutes.

"Oh shit," I mumbled, "Someone's nicked the bloody Ambulance." It was an obvious observation, but I said it anyway.

We were now stood on this woman's path at three in the morning with no Ambulance to be seen.

We had to do something. The woman was getting very close to giving birth and to make matters worse her waters had now broken. The baby could come at any time.

We took her back into the house, leaving her in the chair. Martin used their home phone to call the control room and explain what had happened. Eventually he put down the receiver.

"The second crew are on the way, only a couple of minutes away."

The husband looked relieved at this information.

"What about our Ambulance?" I asked

"They're on to the police about it now."

"Who would want to steal an Ambulance?" gasped the woman between contractions.

"There's some nutters out there that would thieve anything if it wasn't nailed down," mused Martin.

Big Ken and Duggy arrived in just a few minutes, the pair of them grinning from ear to ear. They had been told what happened and I wasn't looking forward to when we finally got back to station the ribbing would start.

They were just closing the back doors of their Ambulance after giving us back our chair, when a police car pulled in behind them. We were supposed to wait where we were until the third crew came out to collect us.

The police officer got out of his car and came towards us, a big smile across his face.

"Anyone around here lost an Ambulance?"

Big Ken and Duggy drove away, leaving us with the smiling policeman.

"Okay, okay. We're going to get the piss taken enough when we get back to station without you adding to it," I said.

The grin remained. "We've found it."

"That was bloody quick."

"Have you got the bugger who took it?"

"No, but it's just a few roads away, looks like it's been abandoned."

I squeezed into the back of the police car with the folded chair, while Martin placed himself into the front passenger seat.

"I wouldn't recommend leaving your ignition keys in the vehicle in future" said the policeman as he made a point of taking his ignition keys from his pocket and starting up the patrol car.

Martin just grunted and nodded in agreement. He was the one getting the mild ticking off from the copper because he was in the front sitting next to him. I sunk further back into the seat knowing full well that it was me who deserved the lecture.

The Ambulance had been parked less than a quarter of a mile away and nothing appeared to be missing or damaged. The policeman insisted we wait for the SOCO to arrive and dust it down for prints, which didn't really make much sense as there would be plenty of different finger prints all over the vehicle, but we obliged as it would waste a few hours and bring us closer to the end of the shift.

It was five o'clock before they had finished taking fingerprints, leaving plenty of areas covered in a grey powdery dust. Martin wasn't happy about it; they had spoilt his nice clean Ambulance. Control gave us permission to return to station and give it a clean.

"I'm sorry mate," I said as I drove back to the station.

"What for?"

"Leaving the keys in the ignition and you getting the lecture from the copper."

"Don't worry about it, I wasn't listening anyway."

There was an awkward silence between us as we headed back to the station. I wondered if it was something I had done or said.

"Is something the matter?" I asked, and not for the first time.

Martin turned and stared hard at me. I could see him on the periphery of my vision. I glanced back at him for a moment.

"There is something you're not telling me, isn't there?"

He remained silent for a moment, I could see he was struggling whether to tell me or not.

Then he blurted it out, "I don't do women."

It took a couple of seconds for this to register in my brain, what did he mean? Then it all fell into place. The past rumours, the lack of girlfriends; but what about Jenny, I thought.

"Are you saying you're a queer?"

"Yes, that's what I'm saying"

"But what about Jenny you went out with her for a while didn't you?"

"That was just a front; something to keep up the pretence of being hetro. She is a nice enough person, but it brought it home to me that I shouldn't pretend anymore. As far as I am concerned I am normal and I am who I am."

Not many years had passed since it was illegal to be homosexual. Although the law had changed in the late sixties, the stigma that went with homosexuality hadn't changed much and it was still frowned upon by society. I personally didn't have a problem with it. What two consenting adults get up to in private is their own business.

"Is this what's been bothering you over the last few weeks?"

"Yeah, I need to come out, and I just wasn't sure what to say or how to do it. I just want to stop living a pretence."

"What about your mam and dad, do they know?"

"Mam knows, but dad doesn't. He'd go ballistic if he knew."

"Thanks." I said.

"What for?"

"For trusting me. It can't have been easy to tell me what you just did."

"I still trust you not to breathe a word; not until I am ready to tell the others."

"Cross my heart and hope to die." I said.

"Aren't you disgusted or ashamed of me now that you know?"

"Not a bit" I said.

"Why?"

"I had an inkling you might be anyway, so it's not really a big surprise."

"Bitch!" he said smiling.

"Well you can cut that out for a start." I said.

I was exhausted when I arrived home. It seemed to have been a long night shift, more so than they usually felt. Maybe it was having the Ambulance stolen or Martin finally coming out of the closet that made it feel such a long night.

It was October and the autumn sun was filtering through the closed curtains as I crawled into bed.

Beryl had started work at a local bakery just a few months after the miscarriage, which meant she started early in the mornings, so the house was empty and quiet when I came home after a night shift.

It was now eight months since the miscarriage and Beryl's parents had become even more subdued towards me. There was a kind of invisible wall, an atmosphere of tension. I knew they never would accept me because I wasn't good enough for their daughter, that's how I felt.

There was also a change in Beryl. She had become distant from me. We hardly ever talked and we certainly didn't have sex, she made as many excuses as she could to avoid it.

I tried to understand things from her point of view, but it was difficult when little conversation took place. Maybe the miscarriage had frightened her and she didn't want to risk the same happening again? I just didn't know.

17

In the seventies the word 'gay' had not yet been adopted as the buzz word attributed to homosexuals or lesbians; other descriptive words such as queer, homo, shirt lifter or a few other derisory words were used.

Homosexuality had recently been de-criminalised in 1967 but still remained an enigma amongst society. What people didn't understand they feared, and what they feared they shunned and ridiculed.

From the night Martin had told me about his sexuality, he had visibly brightened up as a person. He was happy and cheerful as he had been when I first began to work with him. I put it down to his knowing that he didn't have to keep up pretence with his work colleague any longer, which must have been like a weight removed from his shoulders.

I didn't know much about homosexuality, It wasn't a subject that I ever gave much thought to.

"I know you're straight," Martin had said that night, and went on to reassure me that I would not catch the 'homo' germ. He smiled as he said it. He went on to explain that a homosexual isn't something that you suddenly turn into, it was always there in a person and that he knew he was different from as young as five years of age. "It's not something you choose, its something that is inside from the beginning. It chooses you," he had said.

To me it was fascinating to hear about and get an insight into a secret world. It was the secrecy, a world of clandestine meetings and social gatherings; they even had a secret language and signs.

It was fast approaching Christmas. Martin and I were sitting in the nurses room at Broadgreen Hospital casualty department having a cup of tea and a chat with the nurses, one of which I had taken a fancy to. Her name was Susan. Trouble was, she was married, just like me, but I had a strong feeling that she fancied me too. It was the way she looked at me, the body language and the attention she paid when I spoke.

It had just gone midnight when the phone rang in the nurse's room; it was Control looking for us and they had an emergency call in the Old Swan area, a collapse in the street.

We downed our tea and departed the room for our Ambulance. Martin was driving.

We soon found the incident on St Oswald Street.

A crowd of people had gathered around someone lying on the pavement, and waves of hands flapped in the air to draw our attention. Martin parked along side the crowd as I jumped out with the first aid bag. Like the parting of the Red Sea, the crowd created a gap so that I could get to the patient.

He must have been in his sixties, lying on his back and eyes closed. I crouched down next to him, squeezed his shoulder and spoke.

"Hello, can you hear me?"

No answer. None of the crowd knew him or had seen what had happened.

I tried again.

"Hello, can you hear me?"

Still no answer, there was a distinct smell of alcohol present though.

It was a little unusual in that he was quite smartly dressed, a dark suit and tie under a smart beige overcoat. He had a short grey beard and moustache that was neatly trimmed. At the other end he was wearing good quality black polished shoes. Not an obvious member of the homeless fraternity.

He was breathing, but it was shallow. His pulse was normal and regular.

I had a quick search of his pockets for any clue as to whom he was and if he carried any medical alert information, there was nothing.

Martin was removing the stretcher from the Ambulance as the crowd started to drift away which gave me the chance to inflict some pain on this guy. I had an inkling that he was having us on and needed to test him out.

I took a grip of his sideburn between my thumb and forefinger then gently pulled upwards. Not a recommended method, but it usually worked. No reaction.

Next was the rubbing of his breast bone with my knuckles, nothing.

Then finally, and quite reliable because there is nothing a person can do about it as the procedure will bring on a reflex action if they are conscious. I gently touched his eyelash with the tip of my little finger. He had his eyes closed so wouldn't have seen it coming, and there it was, the tell tale sign that he was having us on, his eye blinked with the touch.

There is a more radical way of determining if someone is feigning unconsciousness, which I never used, but I know some did. It was to insert an OP airway. This was a shaped piece of rigid plastic tubing that would be inserted into the mouth and positioned over the tongue towards the back of the throat. In genuinely unconscious patients it would prevent the tongue from falling to the back of the throat and blocking the airway. Once in place, it looked very much like the person was sucking on a baby's dummy. However, trying to insert this on someone who isn't unconscious will bring on a sudden bout of balking, gagging and coughing, a drastic measure that did sort the wheat from the chaff, but not a recommended procedure.

To this day I will never understand why people pretend to be unconscious when they are not. It beggars belief that they think they can fool Ambulance crews and Hospital staff. But so many people do it, particularly when alcohol is involved. However, it does provide the opportunity for a little fun.

We loaded our 'pretend' unconscious patient onto the trolley and wheeled him to the back of the Ambulance. The crowd had fully dispersed so we could raise our voices a little more in order that our patient could clearly hear.

"He's obviously dead, Martin."

"Yes" Martin said. "I can see that from here."

We loaded the trolley into the ambulance, not taking any particular care on how rough we were.

"I suppose we should show the old timer some dignity." I said.

I threw a blanket over him and covered his face with it. There wasn't any response from him but we hadn't expected any.

Martin aimlessly drove around the local streets for a few minutes to give the impression we were on our way to the hospital, plus it killed time and kept us unavailable for any call that might come into the control room and be passed on to us. Eventually we would head towards Broadgreen hospital, but for now we were just having a joy ride.

"What day is it?" I shouted from the back of the Ambulance to Martin in the cab.

"Friday, well Saturday morning now," he shouted back.

"That's handy; they do the post mortems through the night on Fridays." I shouted back.

"That's true. We'll go straight to the mortuary with this one then."

This was a conversation Martin and I had manufactured on several occasions for just these circumstances. Sometimes it was difficult to keep our sniggering under control, particularly as the patient began to realise what was going to happen and began to respond.

What they tended to do was make slight movements at first or low grunting sounds in the hope that we would notice and dash them to the casualty department instead. Of course, we didn't take any notice of these discrete movements or sounds, we just continued the conversation.

"There should be a few empty fridges to put him in then."

"I don't think we'll be putting him in a fridge" shouted Martin from the cab.

"Why is that?"

"They like the fresh ones on the slab first, rather than the frozen ones from the fridge."

A little moaning sound drifted from beneath the blanket.

"Do you reckon they'll cut open this old timer as soon as we get him on the slab then?"

"Definitely, without a doubt."

Slight movement beneath the blanket.

"Shall we stay and watch? I like to see them cut off the top of the skull and take out the brain."

"Na, the best bit is when they slit open the chest; slice the rib cage and cut out the heart."

Movement and low groaning from beneath the blanket.

Martin was now driving through the hospital gates and heading towards the casualty department.

"I'm not too keen on that part, makes me feel a bit sick."

"The only problem with that procedure is all the blood and body fluids sloshing around on the slab and on the floor; you have to be careful not to step in it"

More movement and louder groaning sounds.

Martin brought the Ambulance to a halt outside the casualty department and switched off the engine. He leaned through into the saloon.

"We'll have to leave him on his own for a few minutes while we both go in and explain the circumstances."

"Yes, it's not as if he's going anywhere, is it?"

Martin climbed down from the cab and I made my exit through the rear doors. We didn't stand nearby, but waited around the corner out of sight, trying our hardest not to make a sound from sniggering.

    Sure enough, we heard movement from the Ambulance and the rear door burst open. For a bloke well into his sixties and the worse for wear with alcohol, he was certainly nimble enough to leap from the Ambulance and run like hell from the hospital grounds. Maybe our conversation had sobered him up a little.

We returned back to the staff room in the casualty department. It was time for another cup of tea with the nurses.

    For the past few weeks, we had taken all opportunities to stay away from the station as much as possible. Martin had bravely, and I should add proudly, 'come out of the closet' and told the rest of the shift. It hadn't taken long to go around the whole of the service that Martin was a poof and proud of it.

Charlie, our shift leader was ok with the news, but sadly it wasn't well received by the rest of the shift; in fact there was a malevolent air that cast a cloud of tension around the station. Martin was ostracised and shunned. No one would sit near him or even talk to him in case they were tarred with the same brush or caught the queer germ.

At first he brushed this off with a shrug; he didn't see it as his problem. As the weeks passed, the tension became practically unbearable and it began to get to him. It was for this reason that we now stayed away from the station as much as possible. We hung around casualty departments more than we used to do. Cups of tea and coffee would last longer.

I reluctantly agreed to his suggestion that we volunteer to be first out on the shift, which invariably meant that we would be kept busier than the others and see less of the station. Going back to station for meal breaks was like walking on a thin tight rope that was ready to snap.

Martin didn't smoke, but I did. We were having a coffee with the nurses at Broadgreen cas, and I just mentioned that I was going outside to have a cigarette.

I was standing close to the ashtray that was fixed to the wall near to the entrance doors. It was a quiet night for a Friday in the casualty department; then again it was only half past one in the morning so plenty of time yet.

"Hello, just thought I would join you in our bad habit."

It was Sue. She pulled a cigarette from a packet, lit it and blew the smoke through pursed lips up into the air.

"I didn't know you smoked," I said.

"Only after sex." Her eyes had a knowing smile to them.

"So you've just had sex then?" I smiled back.

"No, but I've been known to have a cigarette before sex, as well as after."

I could feel biological things happening to me. Was I getting an invite?

"Where could you go round here at this time of night to have sex?" I said.

I was thinking the back of the Ambulance would be a possibility. I'd heard rumours that others had done it in an Ambulance.

She stubbed the cigarette out into the ash tray and took hold of my hand.

"This is a hospital, plenty of beds around here."

I barely had time to flick away my cigarette as she almost dragged me back into the building. However, I wasn't exactly kicking and screaming in protest.

She led me down a side corridor then across the main corridor that led into another small corridor. The hospital was as quiet as a church at that time of the morning. She came to a stop outside the day ward, took out a key and opened the door. Inside were six empty beds.

There was frenzy as she unbuttoned my shirt and unzipped my trousers, I in turn was reaching around her back to unzip her uniform, but had forgotten to unfasten her blue belt that circled her waist. In the end it was trousers and knickers around ankles and nurse uniform up to the waist, and that was how we were when the night porter walked in. The lights in the ward were off, but the beam from the porter's torch hit us full on.

"What's all the noise?"

It must have taken a few seconds to register in the porter's brain what he was actually seeing. The torch beam shone at us like a searchlight and we had frozen like rabbits in a headlight.

Then realisation must have set in. "Oops," he said, and quickly closed the door.

We giggled as we carried on were we had left off.

Making sure we were properly attired, we went back to the nurse's room to find Martin and the other nurses still chatting. I was wondering if this would be a regular occurrence, when the phone rang. It was Control.

A nurse handed the phone to Martin who was sitting next to her. Martin listened for a moment then replied. "Ok, we're on our way." He gave the phone back to the nurse and stood.

"It looks like we might be bringing you girls some business."

"What have we got?" I asked

"A traffic accident just down the road in Thomas Lane; one car hit a wall and rolled over."

"Very nice," said one of the nurses.

"Not sure how many are in it though," I heard Martin say to them as I was heading out to the Ambulance.

Thomas Lane was just a stones throw from Broadgreen Hospital and it only took us two minutes to get there.

Sure enough, as we approached we could see the dark shadow of a car on its roof, partly on the pavement and partly on the road. It must have taken out a street lamp too because all the other street lamps were in darkness.

Martin parked the Ambulance in such a way that it would protect the scene from other traffic that may be behind us, I jumped out of the cab with first aid bag and torch in hand.

The Police or Fire service hadn't yet arrived but no doubt they would in due course. We were on our own except for the dark figure of a man who was talking through the broken windscreen and re-assuring the young lad inside the car.

I heard the man telling the lad that it would be alright, the Ambulance was here now and the crew would take care of him. There was something about his voice that seemed familiar.

I got down and shone the torch inside the car. It was pitch black without the street lighting and the yellow and fading beam was just sufficient to light the interior. I reminded myself to get the batteries changed when we got back to station as I had done dozens of times but always forgotten to do so.

The patient must have been in his teens or very early twenties. He was conscious and talking without any problems so I knew his airway was fine. There were minor cuts and contusions to his face but nothing life threatening. His main complaint was the pain in his right leg, and he told me he was the driver.

I turned to the man who had been talking to him, the torch still shining into the car.

"Are you a passenger in this vehicle?" I couldn't see his face properly because of the darkness.

"No, no" he said. "I just live over there, and he pointed to a cottage that was just visible through the trees in the darkness. "I had just got home when I heard the crash and came out to see if there was anything I could do."

"Bloody hell!" I exclaimed.

I said it out loud without meaning to. I had just realised I was talking to Ken Dodd. No wonder the voice had sounded familiar. I knew where his house was, I think everybody in Knotty Ash did, but I hadn't expected to see him at the scene.

I had seen Ken Dodd on stage a couple of times, but this was a side of him that showed how caring a person he was, apart from being a very funny comedian.

He asked if there was anything he could do to help, but I told him that we would be fine, we could manage.

I thanked him for holding the fort until we arrived.

He smiled and gave a nod, and then he remembered something.

"There was another one in the car but he was out and away over that field like a shot." He pointed to a field that was just beyond a low sandstone brick wall.

"All right." I said. "We'll let the police know when they get here. There can't be too much wrong with him if he's running."

He nodded, patted me on the shoulder and walked back to his house.

We eventually extracted the driver and took him back to Broadgreen hospital. He had a broken leg, but nothing more serious than that. We hung around the hospital for a while and managed to get another coffee while we told the nurses about the call we had just been to and bumping into Ken Dodd.

We remained at the hospital as long as we could, but eventually had to go back to station. I wasn't looking forward to that for Martin's sake.

Luckily the station was in darkness when we got back and everyone had found a place to sleep. Martin opted to snooze in the rear of our own vehicle and out of the way from the others, while I found an arm chair in the mess room and dozed until it was the end of the shift.

18

I never saw Martin again after that night when Ken Dodd was at the traffic accident. He just didn't turn up for duty ever again.

I heard from Charlie that Martin had telephoned the boss and resigned there and then, no notice worked.

I could understand the reason why, he had been ridiculed and shunned by other staff since he had announced that he was homosexual. I had felt sorry for him and had tried to defend him in his absence, but it remained the case that most of the staff were homophobes and no amount of cajoling was going to change things.

The boss had interviewed several shift staff in the days after Martin had resigned. Although they all kept tight lipped about it, it was obvious they had been named by Martin as being the bullies and the cause of his resignation.

It was six months later when I heard Martin had managed to enrol on to a nurse training course. I was glad for him; I thought he would make an excellent nurse.

After working with a variety of relief shift staff for six months, I was glad to discover that Peter Whittaker was to get Martin's post as permanent shift crew with me.

Pete had been on relief shifts for some time now and had therefore gathered some considerable experience, which was good for me as I didn't feel as though I had to keep an eye on him or supervise him like a new recruit, so I was looking forward to having a permanent colleague again.

There had been some changes to our shift crews, in that Don and Owen had been promoted to leading Ambulance man status and had moved away to other stations. John and another Peter had taken their places. This meant that big Ken and Duggy were now known as the geriatric crew, being much older than the rest of us.

The gloomy cloud which had seemed to hang over the shift for the past six months because of Martin's resignation now seemed to be lifting. There was a happier atmosphere returning and it was good to feel as though things were getting back to normal again.

It was a Tuesday afternoon shift when Pete and I first found out that we were to have an observer on the Ambulance with us. This had come as some surprise as Charlie introduced us to Barry, a police cadet. Part of Barry's training in the police force was to observe things from the Ambulance perspective. This was a new concept which no one had advised us about. However, it did mean that Pete and I were scoring brownie points with the boss, as he wouldn't have dreamed of putting Barry with a crew who he didn't think could give a decent representation of Liverpool Ambulance service, or at least that's what we liked to think.

Barry had been a police cadet for six months and he had another six to go. He was scheduled to be with us for a month. He had been out with other police officers on the beat as part of his training, but had never come across anything where an Ambulance had been involved.

Barry was quite apprehensive about some of the things he might see while he was seconded to the Ambulance service. He had been fed all kinds of stories by police officers that he might have to help out at serious traffic accidents by collecting bits of body parts and putting them in plastic bags; delivering babies in the back of an Ambulance, or scraping people up from the pavement that had jumped out of a block of flats. It was all clearly designed to frighten the lad, and it had worked.

Barry was clearly convinced that all these kind of things did happen every day and he would have to witness some gruesome incidents in the coming month.

We did our best to reassure him and ease his apprehension, telling him that what he was most likely to see were little old ladies who had fallen and fractured their wrist or had had a stroke or heart attack, and kids with cut legs and hands. It was rare that we had calls to the sort of things that he had been warned about.

Our reassurances seemed to have some affect on Barry, as the first few calls that afternoon were indeed to a child with a cut leg, then a little old lady who had fallen and strained her ankle, all very easy and simple things to deal with.

We were on our way back to station after delivering an elderly man to the Royal casualty department with what appeared to be a bad chest infection when we were called on the radio. There was an incident at the junction of Mill lane and Pighue lane (pronounced Piggy) and the police were in attendance, but they were unable to state what the nature of the call was.

Barry was quite pleased to be going on a call that involved the police; this would be interesting for him.

From our location there was no real direct route to the incident so we had to thread our way across the city using side roads and cutting across major road junctions, it took us a good ten minutes to get there.

We arrived at the relevant road junction to find nothing obvious, except two police cars with revolving blue lights that were a few hundred yards further up Mill lane, parked on the railway bridge. We moved forwards towards them.

"Where's the accident?" asked Barry as he peered between Pete and I through the windscreen from the back of the Ambulance.

There were no damaged cars, no bodies lying in the road, nothing that was looking like an accident.

It took a couple of seconds to take in the scene, then it dawned on Pete and I what the problem was likely to be.

"Oh dear," said Pete.

"What is it?" asked Barry.

"I think we may have a jumper," I replied.

"A jumper?"

"From the bridge," answered Pete.

What's below the bridge?"

"A railway line."

Barry went visibly pale as the information settled into his brain.

We parked up behind the police cars which were void of any occupants. Pete and I stepped from the cab and Barry fumbled with the handle on the rear doors before opening them. We walked over to the metal constructed bridge and peered over the side.

There was a train which had come to a stop directly beneath us. We could see the dark grey roof of the carriages snaking away into the distance and it was difficult from that angle to decide which end was the front and which was the back. However, it was on the left hand track so it must have been heading East towards Broadgreen and we were looking towards the front of the train.

A lone policeman was walking alongside the train towards the front.

I gave Pete a nudge. "Get on the radio and tell Control the situation and have them contact the railway people to close down the track to other trains. We don't want any choo choo's hurtling through here just now."

Pete went back to the Ambulance and Barry asked, "What do we do now?"

"We do nothing until it's confirmed that all rail traffic as been halted on this line."

"But what about the 'jumper"?

"I don't think he'll be putting in any complaints about the delay."

After a couple of minutes Pete came back to join us.

"Seems the police beat us to it, they've already been on to railway Control and all rail traffic on this line as been suspended."

I had been to a similar incident in the past. A man had been standing next to the intercity line near Speke and had just stepped in front of the train. It was a messy job, so I had some idea of what we were about to encounter. This train had been between stations and would have been going at some speed. Not that it mattered; the sheer weight of a train hitting a human body will usually cause a fatal outcome.

I crossed the road and looked over the other side of the bridge towards the rear of the train. There were about the same amount of carriages stretching away westwards. There was another policemen walking along the track towards the back of the train.

"I don't think it was a jumper," I said. "The train would be much further down the track before it came to a stop if he'd jumped from the bridge."

"So what do we do?" there was a little tension in Barry's voice.

"We go down and take a look," said Pete.

"You don't have to come if you don't feel up to it, you know." I was trying to give Barry a way out of confronting his demons of blood and gore, because if he came he was almost certainly going to see it.

He thought about my offer for a moment. "I'd better go; I can't show I'm squeamish to those other policemen down there."

With that agreed, we climbed over the brick wall that marked where the bridge began, then clambered down the steep grassy embankment to the track side. The embankment was steeper than it looked from the road, difficult to get down and it was going to be even more difficult to get back up again.

We agreed that Pete would head towards the front of the train while Barry and I would head towards the rear, checking beneath the carriages as we went.

It's amazing how tall trains are when you're up close and personal on the rail track. Passenger faces were looking down out of the windows as we passed each carriage, curiosity on their faces, probably wondering what was going on, or maybe they now had some idea when they saw Ambulance men traipsing along side the train and looking underneath as they went.

We finally reached the rear of the train and met up with the policeman. There hadn't been anything to find beneath the carriages. The policeman nodded and looked at Barry.

"I'm seconded with the Ambulance service for a month." Barry answered the question before the policeman asked it.

"When did they start doing that?"

"I'm the first. Sort of a trial run."

"So, what's the story?" I asked the policeman, changing the subject.

"The driver reported hitting something, he wasn't sure if it was an animal or a person."

"How can you not know that?" asked Barry.

The policeman shrugged. "Don't know, my colleague is having a word with the driver now to get the story."

"I take it you haven't found any bits of body back here then?" Stupid question I instantly thought. He would have told us if he had.

"Nope, haven't found anything, animal, mineral or human."

Barry saw him first; it was Pete at the front of the train waving his arms in the air like a demented marionette on strings.

"Pete's waving at us."

"Maybe they have some more info?" said the policeman.

The three of us set off towards the front of the train. Just before we reached the engine Pete came towards us.

"Train driver says he hit a bloke about a mile back up the track."

"I thought he wasn't sure" muttered the policeman.

"He wasn't at first, but now we have proof positive."

"How?" asked Barry.

"He's still on the front of the engine."

We all moved off to take a look, then Pete took hold of Barry's shoulder.

"It's not very pretty Barry, are you sure you want to see this?"

Barry's apprehension was almost palpable. He turned pale and swallowed. I could see his dilemma. Here he was in front of two police officers, aspiring to be like them in the future. He didn't want to show his fear of what he might see.

The police officer who we had been with at the rear of the train turned towards him.

"Don't look if you don't want to son, there's no shame in it."

Barry took a deep breath. "I have to do this." The policeman shrugged and we walked the last few yards to the front.

Barry stood rigid for a few moments, his eyes as wide as saucers, and then he started to retch. He moved away to the side of the track and threw up.

I have to admit that it was quite a disturbing sight.

There was a male, maybe in his thirties. He was facing us, which meant he must have had his back to the train when it hit him.

A large metal coupling hook that was fixed to the front of the engine was protruding through his chest wall and had punched out most of the contents, which dangled down the front of his raggedly torn shirt. His neck was obviously broken as his head was thrown far back and resting between his shoulder blades. He must have been wearing a pair of denim jeans, most of which had been ripped away, along with most of his left leg from above the knee. His left arm was nowhere to be seen either. The front of the engine was covered in blood which was beginning to congeal.

Barry was at the side of the track but out of view from the passengers, bent forward with his hands on his knees, bringing up the last dregs of what remained in his stomach. He had just seen something that no one should ever have to see, but that is the nature of the job. I had to admire his spirit as when he had finished throwing up he came back to take another look. This time he was able to handle the image that I knew would be with him for the rest of his life, and me too.

"So what happens now?" Barry said as he held his stomach. "Do we have to take him down off there and take him to the hospital?"

"Na." I shook my head. "Scene of crime will probably want photo's, plus the missing bits will need to be searched for."

"The railway police are on the way, they'll take charge of the scene" said the policeman who had been at the rear of the train.

"How's the driver, Pete?" I had seen Pete climbing up into the cab while we were at the far end of the carriages.

"He's fine, just a little shaken"

"Just so long as he doesn't come down from his cab and see this."

"He has no intention of." Pete had probably thought of that while he was with the driver.

Barry was shaking his head. "What on earth possesses someone to do this to themselves?"

"You don't ever get to know what's going through their heads at the time, but it must take some bottle to do it though." I nodded in agreement with Pete.

"Oh well, there isn't much we can do around here." I put my arm around Barry's shoulder. "Shall we go back to station and have some steak and kidney pie for dinner?"

Barry shrugged my arm away.

"Piss off." he said.

19

Barry had stayed on our shift for a month and as usual we had him fetching and carrying for us on all the different calls we attended and a little bit of fun was had too. We would have him go into a casualty department to ask the nurses for spare bags of fallopian tubes or packets of sphincters. The nurses were used to this sort of request because we did it with our own cadets too. Often the answer was 'sorry we're out of stock' or they would send him back to ask the crew what size did we want? Barry was none the wiser; we never told him the truth.

Barry went back to his police training after we had a good night out at the Wooky Hollow, a cabaret club which was conveniently placed just a hundred yards away from the station. We had a few beers and watched the 'Swinging Blue Jeans'
I wouldn't see Barry again until a few years had passed, and it was to be under different circumstances.

1973 rolled into 1974 and Liverpool Ambulance became part of the National Health Service, and was no longer a local borough council department.

Merseyside Metropolitan Ambulance had evolved and encompassed a much wider area. The service had now taken over Bootle Ambulance service, Southport Ambulance service, and parts of Lancashire Ambulance service including Crosby, St

Helens and Kirkby, and across the River Mersey with Birkenhead Ambulance service and Wirral which had been part of Cheshire Ambulance service.

All these areas were controlled by one centralised new control room at Lower Breck road, which allowed for some transfer of staff and new promotions.

Charlie had been promoted to a rank 5 controller in the new control room. Big Ken had been promoted to a rank 7 and went into the new control room also, but not on Charlie's rota. Duggy applied for and got a promotion to a rank 7 relief station officer and was now based at Old Swan Ambulance station.

I was promoted to Leading Ambulance man, which meant I was in charge of our shift now that Charlie wasn't around.

I was getting on well with Pete, probably more so than I had with Martin.

Pete was laid back and didn't stress as Martin had, which meant I didn't feel on edge like I sometimes did with Martin.

We now had two new members of the shift to replace Big Ken and Duggy; Gary and Tony. They had come through the cadet system as had the rest of us. In a matter of just a few of years, the shift members had completely changed and now I was the only original member left, and at twenty five, the oldest.

They were good crews and we all got on well with each other. I wasn't going to have many problems being their leading Ambulance man.

We all soon got into the routine of what we called our 'Friday Fun' night. This had now become a ritual when we finished afternoon shifts on a Friday at 11pm. Uniform tunics and ties would be taken off and civvy coats and jumpers would replace them. The Wooky Hollow was our destination.

Over a period of time and regular attendance, we had got to know the bouncers on the door and they would let us in for free for the last hour of the current act, which was then followed with a disco until two in the morning.

The Wooky, as we affectionately called it, was quite well known at the time and attracted some well known names and bands. The only act I would have wanted my money back for, that is if I had paid, was the one hit wonder known as Tiny Tim and that awful record he brought out called 'Tip Toe through the Tulips.'

The man couldn't sing to save his life, in fact I did feel embarrassed for him, he, but he was a good laugh with that strange high pitched voice he employed for each and every song he sang.

It was a Friday evening when we were sitting in the mess room watching the telly. The other two crews were out, which just left Pete and I on station.

We were looking forward to seeing Tom O'Connor at the Wooky when our shift finished. It was around half past nine with just a couple of hours to go before we all finished the shift and could relax over a few pints, and who knows, maybe get lucky with a girl or two during the disco.

I needed to stretch my legs and told Pete I was going outside. I walked through the garage passing all the parked Ambulances and outside to the forecourt. I lit a cigarette and then I heard it.

A boom sound. Not very close by, but not too far away from the station to hear it. It wasn't like a car backfiring. This was a deep boom sound, like someone hitting a large kettle drum, that lasted for a second or two and echoed off the surrounding buildings. My first thoughts were of a gas explosion somewhere, maybe at the docks?

Pete emerged from the mess room.

"Did you hear that?"

"Yes, sounded like some sort of explosion."

Maybe a gas boiler somewhere?" he said. "Just so long as it doesn't involve us in any way." Pete looked at his watch. "We're off duty in an hour or so".

The emergency bell in the garage hammered into life.

"Shit, just our bloody luck."

Pete was the driver for the shift. He climbed into the cab and fired the engine while I grabbed the radio mic and called control.

Stan the controller's voice came back at us.

" We have a report of an explosion on Everton Road, near to the Orange club. No further details as yet."

Everton Road was about three miles away from our location. It was the area that gave Everton FC its name when the original football club was established in that area over a hundred years ago. The football club had long since moved to the Walton area of Liverpool.

It was a fairly busy road with a mixture of terraced housing, shops and other small business premises. The Orange club was the Grand Order of the Orange lodge.

Just as we were about to exit, a police car whipped past the Station entrance with blue lights and sirens blazing and heading in the direction we would be taking. We set off in pursuit. We followed the police car along the full length of West Derby Road, which would take us to the junction with Everton Road and the incident.

We were half expecting to see the front of a demolished house, or worse still, a fully demolished house or shop. We encountered neither.

Directly opposite the Orange club was the smouldering wreckage of what looked to have been a mini van. In an instant, reality struck; we were attending a car bomb explosion.

It was the mid seventies and the IRA was active all over the place. Not so long ago, Don and Owen had been called to a jewellers shop in Anfield where a security guard had been shot dead during a robbery. That incident had been reported in the news as being attributed to the IRA.

I had seen car bombs before, but only on the news and pictures in newspapers. Although this one had destroyed the mini, it wasn't like the others where the vehicle had been totally obliterated. The nearby buildings were intact, although many of them were going to need some serious re glazing; glass was everywhere.

The mini was blackened and smouldering; it had lost its doors' windows, bonnet and wheels, a huge hole of torn ragged metal projected up from the roof.

I couldn't see any bodies or body parts anywhere, which was a good start.

People were pouring out of the Orange club, some holding blood stained cloths to their heads and faces,

Pete came to a halt behind the police car we had followed to the scene. I reached for the radio and called control for back up. We would need more than one Ambulance, or so it looked at that time. We grabbed a first aid bag each, climbed from the cab and headed towards the Orange club.

In the distance we could hear sirens which denoted that more Police, Ambulance and Fire Brigade vehicles were on the way; the cavalry. But for now it was just the policeman, Pete and me.

Thankfully, the injuries sustained were only minor ones, and there weren't too many patients. The problem was that we all had to evacuate the area as rumour went around of a secondary device. People were hustled into the Ambulances and those uninjured were shepherded away to a safe distance.

Pete and I took three walking wounded over to the Royal Hospital. We gave the nurses and doctors the low-down on what had happened and gratefully accepted mugs of coffee in return.

The next hour was spent standing by, at a safe distance from the scene, just in case there was a secondary device.

Our shift was due to finish at eleven but we didn't get back to station until well past midnight. The Wooky would have to wait until the next time.

I was tired when I finally arrived home. The house was in darkness and Beryl was either in bed or still out with her friends from work. She'd begun to go out with her work colleagues on a regular basis over the past few months.

I climbed the stairs and crashed into the bed in the spare bedroom a place where I had now been sleeping for a while. Beryl and I didn't sleep together any more.

20

I closed the front door of the house behind me at half past ten at night and drove for the twenty minutes it took to get to work.

Beryl had gone to bed before I had left the house, but that was normal. We were strangers who lived in the same house. It had been like that for a long time now, and I looked forward to being at work more so than being at home, it was less stressful. I had tried on several occasions to discuss what the problem was between us but it always ended in an argument, so now I didn't bother anymore.

Pete was sitting in the faded green armchair, feet up on the coffee table. He had removed his shoes ready to get his head down for a good nights sleep, but was flicking through Jetsave and Skytrain brochures. It was one thirty in the morning and the radio was on low playing 'Stand by your man' by Tammy Wynette.

The other two crews were out on calls. We were third out, a good position to be in when on night shifts, particularly when its brass monkey weather outside; it almost guaranteed a warm restful night.

I brought two mugs of hot tea back from the kitchen and placed one on the table for him, then took the other armchair and sat opposite to enjoy my brew in comfort.

"What's that you're reading?"

"Brochures, flights to the States."

"Going on holiday?"

"I've got a cousin over in Cape Cod, in America, and I'm seriously thinking of going over there, they've invited me over to stay for couple of weeks next summer."

"Wow, I've never been abroad before."

"You don't know what you're missing mate, especially the flying bit."

"You wouldn't get me in a flying tin can."

"You don't know what you're missing, there's nothing like it. I went to Spain a few years ago with my parents and the flight was incredible; I was well and truly hooked by flying."

"Not many people survive crashes though, do they?"

"It's a fact that flying is the safest form of transport. You're more likely to get killed crossing the road than you are from flying."

The emergency bell began to hammer out around the station.

"I'm sure they've got a bloody camera in here and wait until the tea's been made before they ring that bloody bell."

Pete threw the brochure onto the coffee table and I took a last slurp of tea before we scooted out to the garage and climbed into the Ambulance.

I was driving, while Pete grabbed the radio and called control.

"Prescot Road, near to the railway bridge." There was silence for a few moments and then the voice over the radio continued. *"RTA, a vehicle overturned and possible fatalities."*

"Oh shit" I said as I pressed the pedal and accelerated out of the garage and into the street.

These were not the kind of calls anyone wanted, not just because of what you might be faced with, but the emotional feelings it brought too.

The radio clicked into life again.

"Just to advise you that your second crew are on scene and have requested back up."

"Roger," Pete replied.

It was dark, it was cold and it was getting windy; just the sort of night when people should be tucked up in a warm bed and not lying around dead in the street, or inside crashed cars.

We could see quite a few blue flashing lights in the distance as we headed towards the incident. It looked like a blue flashing kaleidoscope.

As we got closer we spotted Gary and Tony's Ambulance parked close to a car that had finished up on its roof. There were six police cars and two fire engines; it felt as though we were late for a party.

Pete spotted Gary about twenty yards from the crashed car. He was moving slowly and staring at the ground, almost as if he had lost something and was desperately searching for it. He had something in his hand.

I pulled our Ambulance to a halt close to the other Ambulance. We couldn't see Tony anywhere, and it struck me as strange that there wasn't anyone milling around the upturned car. It was just lying there like a dead tortoise lying on its back and pressed hard against a brick wall.

Pete went over to have a word with Gary while I made an inspection of the car. I crouched down and shone my torch through the smashed windows. It was empty. However, there was an awful lot of blood splatter around the interior and particularly on the roof lining. Someone had spilt a considerable amount of blood in this vehicle.

I noticed a two way radio system attached to the dashboard; a coiled wire with a handset at the end was dangling out of the driver's window.

There was nothing for me to do here so I started to make my way towards Gary who was now talking with Pete.

Pete was nodding as Gary was speaking, then he pointed to where most of the police officers were standing. Pete waved me over, even though I was walking towards them.

There was a flash of light to my right and I looked over in the direction of the flash. It came from amongst the police officers Gary had pointed to, and then there was another flash. Someone was taking photographs.

Pete left Gary, who had once again begun his slow moving search for something, and started towards me.

"This isn't good at all," said Pete as we got together.

"What's happened"?

Pete described what Gary had told him.

It seems there were two girls in the rear of the car, which we learned was a private taxi cab. They were on their way home from a club in the city when the accident happened. No one knows how it happened yet, but it flipped over and threw the two girls out of the smashed windows as it rolled. They were both still lying in the road.

They were both dead, so Gary and Tony had covered them with blankets. Tony was next to them clutching a body bag and waiting for the police photographer to finish.

"So what's Gary moping around for?"

"He's looking for bits of skull and brain and putting them into a plastic bag."

"What?"

"One of the girls has the top of her head missing and there isn't any brain inside."

"Oh jeez."

"They called us out because they only have one body bag."

Two thoughts hit me. Firstly the emotional side of this, and no doubt the others were feeling it as well. There were two families somewhere right now, probably watching the clock, waiting for their daughters who would never come home again.

There was always a tendency to put your-self in their shoes and imagine the heartbreak and pain they must soon have to endure. It didn't bear thinking about.

Secondly was a memory of my misguided information given to Police Cadet Barry who had fretted about this type of incident.

"Don't worry," I had told him, "nothing like that ever happens." How wrong could I be. It just reinforced the fact that in this job you could expect anything to happen at any time.

"I'll get the body bag," said Pete.

I nodded agreement, and then walked over to Gary.

"What happened to the taxi driver?"

Gary nodded towards the police cars. "He's in a car being interviewed. Not a thing wrong with him. Except for few scrapes, he walked out of it."

"Jammy bastard," I said.

"I heard one of the coppers say that he worked for himself and he wasn't insured.

"There's a two way radio in his car though, I saw it." I said.

"Probably just a fake to make it look like a genuine taxi to the passengers."

"Then the girls must have flagged him down in the city somewhere."

Gary took a quick look at the bag contents. "Must have done."

"Then he's up shit creek isn't he."

"Yes." Gary's mind was somewhere else. He held the bag up and considered its contents.

"I reckon that's about all we're going to find; looks near enough to be the right amount don't you think?"

The bag looked to be a police evidence bag, as we didn't have anything like that on the Ambulances.

It was difficult to see its contents fully as the sides of the bag were blood smeared.

He weighed the bag in his hand. "A few of pounds in weight, probably about right."

"If you say so, Gary."

We walked back to the Ambulance as Pete came out of the rear doors with a thick black plastic body bag. It was still folded neatly into a square shape.

Tony walked over from the crowd.

"They've finished the photographing now, we can ferry the bodies off to the Royal."

"How about if we take one and you take the other?" I said.

Pete gave me a look that said. 'What for? They can take both.'

I don't know what it was that made me decide that, because Gary and Tony were quite capable of taking both bodies to the hospital and then the city mortuary. I suppose it was something inside me that felt it would give the deceased some sort of dignity. It didn't make any sense, I knew, but it felt right. And anyway, I was the LA.

We placed each girl into a separate bag and loaded them into our vehicles, then drove away from the scene in convoy, heading firstly to the Royal hospital to get them certified, then onwards to the city mortuary to leave them on the cold metal tables to await the arrival of the mortician the following morning.

Three of us were having a cigarette outside the city mortuary, Gary didn't smoke.

Not the most salubrious place to stand around and have a natter, but it allowed us to talk through what we had just experienced.

Gary and Tony's radio crackled into life. It was an emergency call to a club in the city centre, an assault, which basically meant somebody has probably been involved in a fight.

"You can take this one for us if you like," quipped Tony.

"No thanks mate, I can hear my bed calling me."

It was half two in the morning, just about right for clubs letting out and fights to begin.

We watched as they pulled away and disappeared around the corner.

"Time for bed I think," said Pete to himself as he called Control and told them we were clear.

"Back to station," came the reply.

We almost made it too, until we were on West Derby road. Control called us up and gave us an emergency to an address just off West Derby road, in the Tuebrook area, about five minutes away.

Control was apologetic as they knew the call out rota we used and that we were the last to be called out on the shift. It seemed that the whole of Liverpool were dialling 999 for Ambulances tonight.

The call was to an attempted suicide by a male.

Pete queried the message. "In what way has he attempted?"

"We're not sure, the caller hung up before we could get that information." said control.

Pete put the handset back in its holder. "Well that's nice init! Could be anything; knife to slit his throat, a gun to blow his brains out. What would happen if we arrived and he had a gun, sees us and decides to have a go, bang, bang, two more for the city."

"Well it won't be sleeping tablets, that's for sure," I said.

We arrived at the address in just over four minutes, to be met by a woman standing and shivering on the kerb out side the house. I parked at the kerb and she came running up to us. She must have been in her fifties, dressed in a white towelling robe, and obviously had curlers in her hair which were covered with a head scarf.

"He's got a razor blade," she said just as I opened the door to get out of the Ambulance.

"Who's got a razor blade?" asked Pete.

"Jimmy. He's our lodger and he's going to top himself."

"Where's Jimmy now?"

"He's upstairs in his room. You've got to stop him!"

Pete and I climbed the stairs towards the bedroom, not sure what we were going to be confronted with.

Although the lights were on it seemed gloomy, synonymous with low wattage bulbs in the fittings. We edged into the bedroom, not sure if we were going to be attacked by the man.

The bedroom was untidy with clothing and newspapers strewn around the floor. The curtains were closed and a small bedside lamp was the only light available. There was a double bed on the far side of the room, with its headboard pushed up against the wall.

The bed was unmade and a man was sitting on its edge. There was a chair with clothing draped over it in the corner by the window.

The man was dressed in shirt and jeans, but with nothing on his feet. Both sleeves of his shirt were rolled up to his elbow. He was probably about forty years of age but looked much older.

"Don't come near me or I'll slash you."

I held both hands up in a gesture that I wasn't going to rush him.

"What's your name?" I asked, even though I knew it was Jimmy. It was an attempt to start up some dialogue with him.

"Just fuck off."

"That's not very nice, jimmy." I could have kicked myself as I let slip that I already knew his name. It got a reaction though, up until now he hadn't taken his gaze away from the floor.

He looked at me with wild eyes.

"Why did you ask my name if you already knew?"

"Just trying to make conversation, Jimmy, that's all"

"Are you trying to be funny or what?"

"No, no I just want to help you."

Pete was standing by the bedroom door as I moved towards the chair in the corner. I removed the clothes, placing them on the floor to join the rest and slowly sat down.

We were between a rock and a hard place with this one. It was definitely a job that called for police assistance because he had a weapon, but if Pete was to leave the room to go and call for assistance, that would mean leaving me on my own with the man. Not a good tactic.

He held the razor blade, the type that has only one sharp edge and a metal strip over the other edge. The blade was in his right hand and he was holding it close to the wrist of his extended left arm.

"No fucker can help me, so why don't you just piss off back to where you came from."

His gaze returned to the floor.

"We can't do that, Jimmy."

There was silence for a few moments.

"I'm going to do it, so don't think about rushing me."

"No one is going to rush you, Jimmy."

"So why don't you bugger off then, just leave me alone will you?"

"Because we can't, not now that we're here."

A voice came from outside the room; it was the woman in curlers.

"Jimmy, for Gods sake will you put that blade down and listen to these men. They're here to help you."

The next few moments seemed to happen in slow motion and it's something I'll never forget. Jimmy shouted. "I'm sorry, Mary."

He pushed the point of the blade deep into his wrist and blood began to trickle, then he drew it up the length of his inner arm to the elbow joint. The wound was deep. His flesh fell apart like a butcher slicing a joint of meat. For a moment there was nothing, and then suddenly blood was spraying over the bed and the floor. Jimmy was looking at the wound and spurting blood as if he was fascinated with what was happening. Pete and I made a move towards him, but he held up the razor as if to say we would be next if we tried.

"Shit," said Pete.

We had been to many calls where people had self-harmed, having cut wrists and throats, and even many stabbed themselves. But never had we been to a call were they had done it in front of us. We usually arrived after the injury was inflicted and we just applied the bandages. This was a whole new experience.

There wasn't anything we could do; we couldn't approach him for fear of sustaining injuries to ourselves.

There was nothing else to do but wait and keep out of the firing line of spurting blood. He would soon grow weak and eventually pass out from shock.

I undid the first aid bag and hurriedly ripped open several large bandages in anticipation. It was only a matter of moments before Jimmy began to grow weak and groggy, but it seemed like an age.

Finally, the blade dropped from between his fingers and he began to slump back onto the bed. We moved quickly towards him now that he was no longer a threat. Our boots slipped and squelched on the floor where all the blood had pooled. Pete and I worked quickly without saying a word between us, wrapping bandages around the wound to pull the skin together and hopefully slow down the bleeding. When Pete had finished his bandage he dug his fingers into Jimmy's shoulder and pressed hard down behind the collar bone. This was a pressure point to stem the flow of blood to the wound.

Jimmy had lost a horrific amount of blood. Even now, with the wound dressed and the bleeding stopped, it was touch and go whether or not he would make it.

His skin was marble white and he was unconscious. His pulse in his neck was barely palpable; I didn't bother trying to take his radial pulse as I probably wouldn't have found it.

We put him on a high concentration of oxygen and struggled down the stairs with him on our carry chair. Soon he was in the back of the Ambulance and we were on our way to Broad Green hospital.

It was at times like this that we wished we had the training to set up drips; Jimmy certainly needed fluids.

We arrived back on station at five in the morning. The other crews were back and fast asleep in the back of ambulances somewhere in the garage.

Pete made us both a mug of tea. We would be finishing the shift in a couple of hours so it wasn't worth getting our heads down; we would just snooze in the armchairs.

"I'll tell you what," said Pete, as he once again flipped through the Skytrain brochure, "Why don't you and me have a day out at Manchester airport on our next long weekend. Watch the planes coming and going."

"Are you serious like?"

"Yes, of course I am. I go by myself now and again. There's a nice pub just at the end of the runway; you can sit in the beer garden with a pint and almost touch the planes as they go past, they're so close. You'll enjoy it"

"You're sad, did you know that?"

"I mean it; couple of pints, and a pub lunch. You can even go on the roof of the terminal building to watch; loads of people do. Come on, it'll be a day out!"

I didn't have anything planned for next Saturday and Beryl wouldn't be bothered whether I was there or not, so what was the harm? She was in her mother's house next door more than she was in our own home.

I gave Pete's suggestion some serious thought. What else would I be doing next Saturday? Nothing was the answer. At least there was a pint or two in the frame if I went.

"Ok then, so long as you don't tell anyone."

21

It was the Saturday of our long weekend off work, which turned out to be a sunny, crisp, winter day with a clear blue sky; a perfect flying day. Pete had been right; it was a nice pub with a huge beer garden at the back, which is where we sat for several hours in the sunshine.

The pub, the Airport Hotel, strangely enough was situated at the Northern end of the runway. From this vantage point, you were so close that you could clearly see the flight crew as they came in to land, or almost touch the wings of the aeroplanes as they taxied out, ready for take- off to exotic far away lands, or at least that's how it felt. It was fascinating to watch and I could see why Pete had a thing for aeroplanes.

I enjoyed the day out, a couple of pints and a pub lunch. I now had the aeroplane 'bug' and the urge to fly somewhere exotic.

Pete had booked a flight to the States on Freddy Laker's Skytrain for a two week holiday in the summer, staying with relatives in Cape Cod. I was so envious.

On the Tuesday it was the start of our afternoon shifts and we were first out for the rest of the week, which meant it would be a busy time for us. True to form, we were called out on the first job of the day.

It was to a RTA at the junction of Queens Drive and Townsend Lane; the very same location I had gone to, all those years ago, on my first day on the road in an Ambulance.

Many things in the service had changed since then and I had gained much more experience.

Richie was our new station officer. There weren't any shift leaders any more, just a leading Ambulance person on each shift. We had newer and more modern radios in the ambulances, and not before time. It was rumoured that extra training was to be introduced so that we could set up drips, give electric shocks certain types of heart attacks and intubate people. Intubation was a method of keeping someone's airway open by placing a long tube through the mouth and down into the windpipe.

Pete was driving today and didn't waste time as we learned that a child had been knocked down by a van.

Road traffic accidents involving two vehicles were rarely serious; however it was a different matter when pedestrians were involved; they always got the brunt of the damage. I was hoping this wasn't going to be the case with this call.

We approached the traffic lights at the location we had been given and could see on the far side of the carriageway that a small crowd had gathered around someone on the ground. Close by was a red post office van which had stopped in the middle of the road.

Pete brought the Ambulance to a stop in such a position that the rear doors were as close as possible to the person on the ground. The crowd moved away to allow us space.

I jumped out with my 'emergency bag', as they had now started to call them. There was a young boy, possibly about nine or ten years old, in a school uniform, lying unconscious, face down. There wasn't any obvious bleeding or broken bones, but his breathing was shallow. This was serious.

The story I got from one of the crowd was that he had run out into the road, and had actually run into the side of the van, not in front of it.

I was about to learn a valuable lesson in communication and the need for clarity of speech when talking to someone who was obviously under a lot of stress.

Pete had brought the portable oxygen from the Ambulance. I inserted an OP airway and then placed the oxygen mask over his face. Pete went to fetch the scoop stretcher which is a metal frame that will split into two parts down its length. You then place one half of the frame along one side of the patient and the other half along the other side. Both parts are then pushed towards each other and will clip together under the patient. You can then lift the patient onto the Ambulance stretcher in the same position as you had found them on the ground.

I was crouched down next to the young lad feeling for a pulse in his wrist, when I became aware of someone crouched down next to me. I turned to see a man studying the child lying on the ground. He was in his late thirties and dressed in overalls. At first I thought it was just a man from the crowd who had a ghoulish appetite for watching traffic accidents, and then the thought struck me.

"You his Dad?" I asked

He stared back at me with horror in his eyes.

"He's what?" he said.

It took a moment or two before it sunk into me what he thought I had just said, so I repeated myself a little more clearly; this time with the word 'are'.

"Are you is dad?"

"Yes," he said, "how is he?"

"He's unconscious." I looked at my watch. From the time we had been given the call, he must have been unconscious for at least ten minutes by now. His pulse was slow and it was strong. The lad had all the signs of a serious head injury.

"Will he be all right?" asked his Dad.

"We'll take him along to Alder Hey; you can come in the Ambulance if you want."

"I've dashed around here in my car; can I follow you?"

"Of course you can, but if we have to go through any red traffic lights. Don't follow us through."

I knew there were at least four sets of major traffic lights that we would have to pass through on the way to hospital.

He nodded in agreement.

We put the lad into the Ambulance and set off for the hospital. It was one of those cases where we needed to be as fast as possible because of the seriousness of the injury, but also as smooth as possible because of the possibility of a spinal injury. Pete did well and had us at the hospital within five minutes. We had advised the hospital what the injuries were over the radio and the nurses were opening the back doors of the vehicle as Pete brought it to a halt outside the casualty department.

I noticed the lad's father parking his car nearby. We did go through three sets of red traffic lights en route; he must have followed us through them to be so close behind. I couldn't blame him, under the circumstances; I would probably have done the same.

We left the lad in the very capable hands of the doctors and nurses, as we had taken him directly to the resuscitation room and handed over all relevant information.

No sooner had we got the stretcher back into the Ambulance, than control began calling us again on the radio. It was for an emergency call in the Old Swan district. An elderly female had collapsed and a GP was in attendance, giving heart massage.

It took us five minutes to get there. There wasn't anyone waiting for us at the door as people usually do, but the front door to the terraced house was open. I pushed inside and shouted "Hello, Ambulance."

A voice came from somewhere upstairs. "Up here."

Pete and I took the stairs two at a time, laden with our resuscitation gear. In a bedroom, not too dissimilar to the one where Jimmy had slit open his arm, we found an old lady lying on the floor wearing a sleeveless nightgown. .

There was a man, who didn't look much younger than the patient, kneeling on the floor next to her and rubbing the woman's left breast in a circular motion. He was wearing a dark green tweed jacket and wore spectacles that hung at the end of his nose. He looked up at me as I entered the bedroom.

"Ah, the cavalry. I'm this lady's doctor and I was called out by her sister who said she had fallen over. When I arrived she was in this position and there was no heart beat or breathing, so I've been giving her heart massage for the last ten minutes." His accent had a hint of Scots in it.

He stood up with difficulty, having to use the bed for leverage and then brushed his hands together as if wiping off some dirt.

I looked at Pete who was just inside the doorway, "Heart massage?"

I knelt down next to the old woman, who must have been in her nineties at least. I couldn't feel a pulse in her neck and there wasn't any breathing. Her pupils were widely dilated and there were the beginnings of pooling in her bare arms. Pooling is a process that happens after death when the blood sinks with gravity to the lowest part of the body. This poor woman had been dead for quite some time.

"What time did you get the original call from her sister, doctor?"

"Lets see, I was in the middle of seeing a patient in the surgery when the call came through, then I came around here after that, so that would make it around four o'clock."

We all looked at our watches; it was now quarter to five. Three quarters of an hour had elapsed since the woman had collapsed.

"I don't think there's much use in attempting resuscitation, doctor," I said.

"She does have a long history of heart attacks and had a couple of wee strokes in the past. She wasn't a well woman." He said.

Pete disappeared from the doorway and I heard him padding down the stairs. He was taking the equipment back to the vehicle.

"I think the only thing we can do is get her back onto the bed, make her look a bit more dignified."

"Yes, maybe that would be best," said the doctor.

"I take it you can issue the death certificate?" If he wasn't prepared to, it would mean we would have to take her to the hospital.

"Yes, I can do that."

"And will you advise her sister?"

"Yes, I'll see to that too."

Pete padded back up the stairs and into the bedroom.

"So her sister didn't actually see her fall; she just heard the noise from downstairs and called the surgery."

"Yes" said the doctor. "Poor woman can't manage the stairs, she's housebound, poor mobility you know, she sleeps downstairs. I suppose we will have to arrange something for her, she was dependant on her sister you see."

Pete and I placed the lady back onto her bed and covered her up; it was the least we could do. Then we left the doctor to sort out the paperwork, went outside and climbed into our vehicle.

Pete drove off and stopped around the corner out of sight from public view while we both had a cigarette.

"Heart massage, he calls that heart massage? Rubbing her left tit in circles!", Pete said, almost laughingly.

"Well, he's old school isn't he? Probably never done CPR in his life."

"Does that mean that we can do that on the young ladies and claim we were only doing heart massage?" Pete gave a lecherous grin.

"Now there's an idea!", I said.

"It's a pity women don't have two hearts, one on each side; can you imagine it?"

"Pete, you're sick."

I took the mic from its holder and called control, explaining that the patient was a DOA and the GP was in attendance. We were now available.

As if we had timed it just right, Control came right back at us.

"Emergency call please, it's an emergency transfer from Alder Hey casualty to Walton neuro. A police escort is being arranged."

Alder Hey is where we had taken that young lad from the traffic accident. We wondered if it was going to be the same patient.

When we arrived outside the casualty department, three police motorcycles were already there and waiting, engines purring.

Hospital transfers with police escorts are not for the feint hearted. It's probably one of the most exhilarating experiences of driving that a person could ever have. If you were the driver, that is. The Highway Code and road traffic laws were thrown out of the window and speed was the word, with a hell of a lot of trust in the police bikers doing the escorting.

However, if you were the attendant, it was one of the most terrifying experiences known to mankind.

It was the same young lad that we had brought in earlier. He had sustained a serious head injury and required immediate neuro surgery at the specialist neurosurgical unit at Walton hospital.

As luck would have it, Walton hospital was more or less a straight run along Queens Drive, a major two lane dual carriageway that skirted around the South Eastern side of Liverpool; a busy road especially at the time of day we were about to make the journey. There were several intersections controlled by traffic lights that would have to be blocked by the police as we approached them.

The patient was intubated and his breathing was being supported by a portable ventilator. I had brought the trolley into the resus room and jacked it up to the same level as the hospital trolley that the lad was lying on. Pete had already discussed the route we would take with the police, so we were now ready to go.

An anaesthetist and two nurses would be travelling in the Ambulance with us, which meant no seat for me in the back. I would have to stand and hold on for dear life as we hurtled across the city.

We were told that speed was of the essence and not so much a smooth journey. A theatre and surgeons at Walton hospital were waiting for us.

Within two minutes we had departed the hospital grounds and were heading towards the dual carriageway.

Two police motorcyclists had blocked the traffic on both sides of the duel carriageway as we emerged from the side road and took a hard right turn.

There wasn't much I could do in the back of the Ambulance. The anaesthetist and nurses were looking after the patient.

I stooped down a little, holding onto the frame of the stretcher and I could now look through the rectangular opening that connected the cab into the saloon and watch our progress through the windscreen.

It was about a six mile journey between the hospitals and this wasn't going to take long. When I checked the speedometer we had reached 70mph and were still accelerating.

Two police motorcycles zipped past and ahead of us and began waving to traffic that occupied the outside lane to move over to the nearside lane, the intention being that we would have a clear run in the outside lane.

It was like a parting of the waters as all the traffic ahead moved over and left a clear path for us to follow. The speedometer was now at 80mph. Our truck was flat out in a 40mph speed limit area.

A cacophony of Blue lights, headlights and sirens blared as we sped towards the first of the traffic light controlled junctions.

The two motorcycles were way ahead of us now and were stopping the crossing traffic at the junction. The lights were on red as we sped through at 80mph, leaving the two stationary police motorcycles behind. The third police motorcycle that had been close on our tail now zipped past us at an alarming rate, to once again part the 'waters' ahead whilst a second motorcycle passed us from the rear to join him. The third remained at our tail. The same sequence of manoeuvres continued through a total of five sets of traffic lights at busy junctions.

My knuckles were white as I hung onto the stretcher frame, I knew it would only take one road user to do something stupid and we could all have been wiped out in an instant.

Eventually we came to the slip road that would allow us to leave the dual carriageway. There was an incline that took us down to a large roundabout beneath the flyover of the road from which we had just emerged; we needed to turn right at this roundabout.

Pete took it easy going around the roundabout; the rear of an Ambulance is not the best place to be when negotiating sharp bends at considerable speed.

It was often the case that if any equipment was not strapped, tied or stowed in a secure cupboard when taking a sharp bend, then you would end up with an unholy mess in the back of the vehicle. The same law of physics could be applied to people too.

The intensity of the speed and police escort was coming to an end; we were now just a few hundred yards from the hospital gates.

Staff were waiting for us at the entrance to the neurological building, and the young lad was quickly transferred over to them and rushed away to theatre.

The Ambulance had been reversed close to the building's doors. This meant that while the rear doors of the Ambulance were open, the public could see next to nothing inside of the Ambulance. It also meant that the three police motorcycle riders, along with Pete and I, could drink our plastic cups of tea from the WRVS and have a cigarette without the worry of being reported by a zealous member of the public. Anyway, after those sorts of rides nerves needed calming, and what better than a brew and a smoke.

22

It was the first call we got on Peter's return to work from his holiday in the United States. I listened to him in awe as he told me about the flight on Laker Airways Skytrain. I was so envious.

Over the tanoy. *"Emergency call, RTA. Lower House Lane and Storrington Avenue. Car into a lampost."*

We were first out and wasted no time in hitting the road. The location was a good six or seven miles away in the area usually patrolled by the Gillmoss Ambulance. We presumed they were on another call somewhere.

Lower House Lane and Storrington Avenue was a busy dual carriageway junction, controlled by traffic lights. The infamous Western Approaches pub sat on the corner of this junction, well frequented by the Ambulance service to attend fights, both inside and outside. There was also a fire station not more than a hundred yards further up Storrington Avenue.

Pete and I were convinced that the accident victims would be getting at least some first aid from the firemen, who would only need to roll out of bed and saunter over to the scene. As we approached, we could see that wasn't the case.

We had been to many traffic accidents over the years and always, there would be a milling crowd and most of the time someone would be administering first aid.

This time it was surreal. The junction was empty with no traffic anywhere to be seen. The traffic lights were changing colours with no traffic to obey them.

On the far side of the avenue a handful of pedestrians had stopped walking and just stood and stared in the direction of the accident.

A couple of men stood watching from the pub doorway, cigarettes and pints of beer in hand. The sound of the crash must have brought them out.

We were still a hundred yards away from the accident; Pete slowed the Ambulance to take the corner, turning right into Storrington Avenue.

A concrete lamp post was leaning precariously at a dangerous angle over the pavement. At the base of the post, and at least twenty feet to side, were the two halves of a mini Traveller. The rear wooden-piped passenger exterior of the vehicle was still in the upright position, propped up at one end by its rear wheels. The front half of the vehicle was facing away from us and we could see the back of the driver and passenger seats quite clearly, but no-one was sitting in them. There seemed to be bodies everywhere, strewn across the road.

The Mini had turned right at the traffic lights, probably travelling much too fast, and had skidded side-on into the lamp post, cutting the vehicle in half. Each half of the vehicle must have spun violently, discharging its occupants as it did so.

There were four people lying in the road who must have been there since the time we got the call but no member of the public, or anyone from the fire station, had approached them. It was almost like an explosion had just taken place scattering metal, plastic and bodies in all directions and people had not yet reacted to what was in front of them, although it must have been a good ten minutes since we first had the call.

Pete brought the Ambulance to a halt and reached for the radio to call for back up whilst I jumped out and was suddenly hit with the sounds of the injured screaming out in pain. Which was good news, If someone is screaming it means they have a healthy pair of lungs which tells me they're not dead.

They were all young lads, not much older than early teens, which begged the question, was this a stolen vehicle? Not that it mattered to me; I wasn't here to judge, but to treat.

The accident required triage, which is the procedure if you are overwhelmed by the amount of casualties you are initially confronted with.

I went to the one who had been flung the furthest from the vehicle. He was lying face down and screaming about his leg, which I could understand as his left leg was bent hideously forward from the knee joint. He had a few minor cuts and abrasions to his face, probably from coming into contact with the road surface as he was thrown out, but nothing else that was immediately obvious. In between bursts of profanities about his leg, he also wanted his Mam.

I moved on to the next young lad in the road. He was sat upright holding his arm and just sobbing. He had a two inch long gash to his forehead which had now stopped bleeding as the blood congealed down the side of his face.

"Does your arm hurt?" I asked.

He just nodded and carried on sobbing.

"Have you got any pain anywhere else?"

He shook his head. Maybe he didn't yet feel the wound on his forehead.

"Have you been unconscious?"

He shook his head again.

"Can you remember everything that happened?"

He nodded.

"Is it just your arm?"

He nodded.

Pete, by this time, had surveyed the other two young lads and I needed to know who we were going to deal with first. I padded over to him as he was examining a leg wound.

"This one's probably a broken ankle and shoulder and a few cuts-n- bruises. "The other", he nodded in the direction of a lad lying on his side' "has been unconscious but is quite lucid now, just feels sick."

We had now completed our triage and were about to decide who we would deal with first.

We made our decision. "I think the lad over there who's screaming for his Mam, he's got a nasty fracture at his knee joint; his leg is so far disjointed forward that he could probably pick is nose with his big toe."

There was a whistle from the pub doorway and we both looked over. One of the men in the group that had been watching, a pint in one hand and a cigarette in the other, was pointing to an area somewhere behind us.

"There's another one in the grass behind you;" he shouted.

We both turned to look into the patch of waste ground that had become overgrown with weeds and shrubs. From where we stood, we couldn't see anything.

In the distance we could hear the sirens from the re-enforcements that had been requested.

I told Pete I'd check out the grass and he could grab a few blankets and fold them over the other lads who were still moaning and crying. I headed for the waste ground.

I was only about six feet away before I could see a limp and pale young face lying on his back. He was quite still and as I got closer, not breathing. I knelt down beside him. There was no chest movement, nor could I feel or hear any breathing.

The lad couldn't have been more than ten or eleven years old. My mind took me back a few years to the young lad who had been knocked down by the post office van. He was about the same age, but at least that lad had been breathing when I had arrived.

I started CPR and shouted to Pete who was dishing out the blankets.

"Need the Oxy, I'm doing CPR."

I knew Pete would understand what I meant, which was, 'Drop what you are doing and let's concentrate on this one now.'

I felt pangs of guilt; I hadn't fully carried out what my training in these situations had said I should do. It was a part of the triage process in accidents like this to establish how many were in the vehicle and do a head count. If it wasn't possible to establish the number, then check the surrounding area. I hadn't done that and valuable minutes had been lost before starting CPR.

Then it struck me, it had been the scene itself. It had been surreal. No traffic noise, no birdsong, no crowds of people except for those few who had stopped to watch from a distance as if they were watching some sort of theatrical drama unfolding. It was still and quiet except for the crying and moaning. I still couldn't hear any birds.

The sirens from the re-enforcements turned out to be a fire engine, no wonder there hadn't been anyone from the fire station to help.

Pete gave the leading fireman a quick run down of who had what injuries and dispatched them to render first aid.

I continued CPR as I began to think about this young lad's parents. Right at that very moment they were blissfully unaware of what had happened to their son. Their lives had suddenly changed and they didn't know it yet.

Whether or not this young lad had been some sort of delinquent, as it was possible he might have been in a car that was almost certainly stolen, didn't alter the fact that it was a young life ebbing away in front of me and he was someone's son or brother. I wondered which school he went to.

Two Ambulances arrived at the scene, while Pete and I continued CPR in the grass. We left them to liaise with the firemen.

I was doing the chest compressions while Pete used the bag and mask to inflate his lungs. This was now connected to the portable oxygen.

The scene was now a hive of activity, three Ambulances, a fire engine and four police cars. Totally different from when we had first arrived.

We had been performing CPR for a good ten minutes and were not getting any response. The sweat was pouring off me. Giving chest compressions is an exhausting task after just a few minutes. We knew we were fighting a losing battle. There must have been severe internal injuries.

We decided it was time to make a move. I continued CPR as Pete went to fetch our trolley. He awkwardly bounced it across the pavement and through the grass and weeds. Ambulance trolleys are notoriously difficult enough to handle by yourself, particularly over rough terrain, the swivel castor wheels have a mind of their own.

We loaded the lad onto the trolley and continued CPR as best we could while we bounced across the rough ground towards the Ambulance. We had to postpone CPR for a few moments while we lifted the trolley into the back of the ambulance but once inside with the trolley secured, I continued CPR while Pete closed the back doors. I wedged myself into the side of the trolley as securely as I could as I knew it was going to be a fast and rough ride into Walton Hospital.

Doing CPR in the rear of an Ambulance while it is speeding around corners and through traffic, is probably one of the most difficult things to do. You can use both hands to give cardiac compressions on a straight road, but once the corners and bends come into play, you have to hold on with one hand and give chest compressions with the other. I did my best.

I knew Pete would radio ahead and alert the hospital that we were on our way in with a cardiac arrest.

Two nurses flung open the rear doors as Pete backed into the Ambulance bay outside the Casualty department. One of them jumped in the back of the Ambulance and thankfully took over from me, I was almost exhausted.

Pete unlatched the trolley and we pulled it out of the Ambulance and made a dash for the resuscitation room where a crowd of nurses and doctors were waiting to receive our patient, the nurse still bouncing up and down on the lad's chest.

Dripping with sweat, I gave a quick breathless description of what had happened and what we had done.

Pete and I stood back from our trolley and let the hospital staff take over. We would come back and collect our trolley a little later but for now it was time for a brew, a cigarette and the adrenaline to come down.

We sat outside the building and tried to relax.

Moments later we saw the Gillmoss Ambulance turn in through the hospital gates, followed by a police car. They were bringing one of the lesser injured from the accident. Their vehicle reversed into place next to ours and we watched as Snitch and Snatch unloaded the trolley with the patient who had been unconscious, and wheel him inside the casualty department.

The casualty waiting room at Walton Hospital was quite spacious and bright with large plate glass windows allowing lots of daylight into the room. Pale blue plastic seats were secured to the floor in neat little rows that faced in the direction of the entrance. On the opposite wall, in the corner was the WRVS counter selling tea and coffee, and next to that was the long reception counter. This arrangement allowed the waiting public to see all the comings and goings as Ambulance crews wheeled patients into the department through the entrance doors. Today it was almost half full.

Snitch and Snatch emerged from the sliding glass doors, trolley now empty of its passenger, and loaded it back into the Ambulance. They waved but didn't stop to talk. They must have been on a mission to get back to station for Corrie Street or something.

Pete and I finished the dregs of coffee left in our paper cups, stubbed out cigarettes in the container of sand near the doors and went inside to retrieve our trolley. I could feel all the eyes in the waiting room watching our every step as we passed them for a brief moment and then we disappeared from view along the corridor to the Resuscitation room.

A lone nurse was busy clearing up the mess that inevitably assembles around the hospital trolley when a patient is undergoing emergency resuscitation. Plastic wrappers from drips, tubes, syringes, needles and a host of other none sterile equipment lay scattered on the floor. Our trolley was in the far corner of the room, cast aside and out of the way once they had transferred him onto their own trolley.

The lad was still on the hospital trolley. A sheet as white as the painted wall was now covering his body. There was an eerie silence in the room, an emptiness, a strange feeling of calm as though something was over.

I tried to brush the thought of his parents away. Did they know yet? I couldn't allow myself to dwell on that, it was the sure fire way of screwing up your emotions.

We pushed our trolley out of the room and down the corridor, past the waiting room and towards the exit. We stood back a little as the glass doors automatically opened inwards. We headed out towards the Ambulance, and that was when I heard a woman's voice shouting after us, "Excuse me."

Pete and I turned to see a woman scurrying towards us from the waiting room. She was about forty years old, shoulder length dark hair and a little shorter than me.

We waited for her to reach us before putting the trolley back into the Ambulance.

"God, I hope she's not a relative of that lad" I said to Pete between clenched teeth.

She came up close to us and stood for a moment without saying anything and studied me in particular.

"It is you, I thought it was."

"I'm sorry?" I said. I didn't have a clue what she talking about.

She didn't say anything, just beamed a smile and then threw her arms around my neck and hugged me.

She held me for quite some time without saying anything. I looked over her shoulder to Pete and raised my eyebrows in surprise.

He was smirking a dirty smirk; I knew how his mind worked.

She pulled away and composed herself.

"You saved me son's life."

"Did I?"

"He was knocked down by a post office van on Queens Drive."

I remembered it, and it was so uncanny that I had just been thinking about that job while dealing with the one we just dealt with.

"Right, yes I remember, how is he?"

"He's fine now thanks to you."

"Good I'm glad to hear it, but I don't think it was me who saved is life, more like the hospital"

Yes it was you. The doctors told me that if it hadn't been for the Ambulance crew he probably wouldn't have survived."

My mind raced back to what I had done at the scene of that accident. It was just maintaining his airway and high concentration of oxygen. It was probably the oxygen that did it. The brain can swell after a serious head injury, almost certainly resulting in a fatal outcome, but high concentrations of oxygen given soon enough can help minimise the swelling.

"Anyway, I just wanted to thank you after all this time."

"You're welcome love." I didn't know what to say.

She smiled, turned and walked back to the waiting room.

"I thought you had clicked there for a minute, mate." Pete was still grinning.

"Yes, so did I, I do like a mature woman like."

Driving back to station I was full of mixed emotions. I was elated by the woman's thanks but felt it strange that the latest victim had reminded me of her son.

It felt weird that she had found me on this day of all days. Half of me was pleased for her; while the other half was sad at losing some other mother's son.

I guessed it was the nature of the job.

23

It was sunny, it was Friday and it was early evening. Pete and I were working our last afternoon shift of the week, the Wooky would be given a miss at the end of the shift, we were looking forward to our long weekend off and the adventure that waited for the next day. Thankfully it was a quiet, shift during which we spent most of the time watching the television and dozing.

I got home around midnight. Beryl was out with some of the girls she worked with on a 'girls night out' and she hadn't yet arrived home. The television stations had closed down for the night, so I turned on the radio to break the silence in the house.

I had changed out of my uniform and had just sat down on the sofa, ready to read the paper before going to bed, when the front door rattled open and Beryl came staggering into the house. She was well inebriated.

I couldn't get much sense out of her other than she had had the best time. She dropped her bag, took off her coat and kicked off her shoes before sitting down in the arm chair in the corner of the room. Even sitting down she was swaying a little. I thought it looked quite funny, I hadn't seen her like that for a long time.

I tried to talk to her but only got grunting replies. Then suddenly, it was as if everything turned into slow motion. Her eyes were closed as she sat on the edge of the chair; she was sporting a grin as if remembering something and her swaying increased. She leaned forward, but unable to maintain her balance, she slipped from the chair, onto her knees.

The momentum of her body brought her head down and she crashed into the side of the fire grate.

It all happened so fast. Although I made the surge towards her, to try and catch her, I was too late. She now lay crumpled on the floor.

She was still giggling to herself as I helped her up and back into the armchair. Sitting her well back so the fall couldn't be repeated, I examined her face where she had smacked it against the fire grate. There were no cuts and she seemed to be in some sort of inebriated anesthetised state, I was happy no serious harm had been done.

I stood in front of her and pulled her up into a standing position by her hands, then crouched down a little and let her flop over my shoulder to carry her upstairs to bed. Although she was still fully clothed, I placed her on top of the bed and her onto her side. She was fast asleep.

We had it planned to travel down to London on the train, do a bit of sight seeing and then fly back from Heathrow to Liverpool. I could hardly think of anything else since we had agreed to do it. Not having flown before, I was both apprehensive and excited at the same time. We would get the train from Lime Street, arriving at Euston around eleven in the morning, then make our way down

Tottenham Court Road and maybe have a look around the Soho area, just to see what all the fuss was about. Then find a café for some lunch, and carry on to Leicester Square and catch the Piccadilly tube out to Hounslow West and then over to Heathrow.

The plan was to find somewhere and watch the coming and going of aircraft, preferably from a pub beer garden if we could locate one, until we took an evening flight back to Liverpool.

I checked on Beryl before leaving the house. She was still fast asleep and would probably wake with one hell of a hangover.

It was a little overcast as I drove to Pete's house at six in the morning, but it was promised by the weather man to be a warm summer's day. The plan was to leave my car at Liverpool airport, catch a taxi to Lime Street station and get the 8.55am train to Euston, do our bit of sightseeing and find a pub near to Heathrow for a few pints before catching the 7pm flight back to Liverpool.

We arrived at Euston around eleven in the morning. Too early for a visit to a pub, so we ambled down Tottenham Court Road in the direction of Leicester Square. The day had turned out to be warm and sunny just as the weather man had promised, just a few puffy white clouds dotted around the clear blue sky.

Eventually we made it to Leicester Square and took the tube on the Piccadilly line to Hounslow West. This was all new territory for us, but we eventually found a pub called, as I remember, 'The Green Man.' Or something like that. It was set in a leafy suburb and had almost as good a beer garden as the Airport Hotel in Manchester.

Our flight wasn't until 7pm, so we had several hours to spend watching aeroplanes. The pub seemed to be directly under the approach flight path to Heathrow, and we sat mesmerised as aircraft after aircraft flew above us. The aircraft, wheels down, were almost skimming the rooftops. The problem was that the aircraft would only be in view for a few moments as they flew over, then they would disappear behind the rooftops, but the frequency of them flying past outweighed that disappointment.

We enjoyed a few pints and had something to eat before moving on to the airport itself.

On arrival we clambered up the stairs to the rooftop garden on the Queens building, where we had a panoramic view over the airport and the runways. It was fascinating to watch all kinds of aircraft from all kinds of countries, coming and going. It was certainly a busy airport, much more so than Manchester.

The time came to complete the day's adventure and experience the highlight of it. Pete and I made our way to the domestic terminal where we would catch our flight back to Liverpool.

I was eagerly looking forward to my first ever flight. It was a strange combination of fear and excitement. First time flyers will recognise the emotions instantly.

We arrived in the departure lounge and bought two overly priced coffees as we waited for our flight to be called, which eventually it was. I was a little disappointed that we didn't get to walk down one of those tunnels that lead straight to the aircraft door; instead we sat on a bus that took us out on to the apron somewhere.

The bus stopped close to the rear of a British Airways BAC one eleven jet, this was our aircraft. I had seen these many times before at Manchester. They're only tiny when compared to a Jumbo jet, but it didn't matter to me, I was about to fly for the first time.

There were only about forty passengers including ourselves. We decanted from the bus and into the aircraft via an integral stairway that dropped down from the rear end of the aircraft, between the two jet engines that were slung at the back of the fuselage.

Pete and I had pre booked our seats and had chosen a window seat each. It wouldn't have been much fun if I wasn't able to see out of the window on my first flight. Even with forty passengers the aircraft seemed empty, no one sat next to me so I had the row of three seats to myself.

I watched the seat belt demonstration given by a stewardess and a steward, then we were taxiing out to the main runway and I had a good view from my window. It took some time but eventually we were lined up for take off. My heart must have been beating ten to the dozen. There was no turning back now, no way out; I had to go through with this.

The engines roared and within moments I was pushed back into my seat with the gathering speed of the aircraft down the runway. The ground was rushing past and the plane rumbled as it gathered even more speed. Suddenly I had the feeling I was being transported upwards in a fast elevator, the rumbling stopped and the aircraft was smooth. The ground began to drop away and people, vehicles and buildings began to shrink in size. I was airborne for the first time and was absolutely enthralled by the experience.

The flight lasted about forty minutes and I had my head permanently turned to look out of the window all the way, save for once when the steward brought the trolley down the aisle and I asked for a coffee.

It was a nice clear evening as we soared above little wisps of clouds which allowed a view of the ground far below. I enjoyed the thrill of the flight, every minute of it, even the landing at Liverpool. I had well and truly been bitten by this flying business. It was then that a thought crossed my mind.

Beryl was in her mother's house as usual when I arrived home from London; it wasn't until later in the evening that she returned to our house, sporting an impressive black eye.

"Wow, that's a whopper." I said jokingly as she walked in.

"You seem to think its funny, do you?"

"What do you mean?"

"What did you do to me last night?"

"What you mean?" I was confused with her attitude and question

"You hit me didn't you?"

"I beg your pardon, what did you say?" I knew exactly what she had said and what she was accusing me of; I just couldn't believe what I was hearing.

"You hit me because I came home late and was a little bit drunk."

"You don't remember what happened then"? I was hurt, very hurt to have been accused of hitting her.

"You tell me."

"You were so pissed you fell off the chair and cracked your face against the fire grate, that's what happened."

She was quiet for a moment; maybe her memory of the incident was coming back?

She shook her head as if she didn't believe me.

"I'm sleeping next door tonight."

Now I was feeling angry.

"Suit yourself; you can live there for all I care."

She said nothing and stormed out of the house. I spent most of the rest of that weekend in the pub. By Monday most of Beryl's clothes and personal things had been removed from the house. It seemed that I was now living alone.

Pete and I were back at work on Tuesday morning at 7am. Our conversation was of not much else but our day out in London and the flight home. It had cost us a bit, but had been well worth the expense.

Like a toothache, the incident with Beryl kept on gnawing away at me; I was angry and hurt at the same time.

We were second out on our shift, so didn't get our first call until half past seven. It was to a house in the Sheil Park area, something to do with a hand injury, Control didn't have much information.

We arrived on this leafy, tree lined street in a well to do area. Large detached Victorian houses were set back from the pavement.

The house we were looking for had two cars parked on the driveway, a new BMW and Ford Zephyr.

"Not short of a few bob here then." mused Pete as we trudged up the path with me carrying the first aid bag.

Pete rang the bell and we waited. We rang and waited again. I tried the door handle but it was locked.

"False call?" said Pete.

"At this time of the morning?"

We got many malicious false calls, usually made by kids during the evening throughout the week, or anytime at the weekends.

"Come on, we'll have a look round the back" I said.

There was a path which led us down the left side of the house. A six foot high red brick wall marked the boundary with the property next door. At the end of the path was a six foot high, black painted fence which incorporated a latch gate of the same height.

I raised the latch on the gate and pushed but it was bolted on the other side.

"What now?" said Pete.

I dropped the first aid bag on to the floor.

"Cup your hands and give me leg up, I'll climb over and unbolt it."

"Are you sure? It's probably a false call."

"I know, but two cars on the driveway and no answer, says it might not be."

Pete steadied himself with feet apart and cupped his two hands together. I put my right foot on them and launched myself up as

Pete pushed me to the top of the fence. I pulled myself up until I was half over the top of the fence. There was a large grassed garden, secluded by bushes and trees around its perimeter. Large terracotta pots, each with a variety of brightly coloured flowers, were spaced out at intervals around the perimeter. There was a garden table and chairs at the far end. It all looked neat and cared for.

I was about to swing my leg over the top of the fence when I caught movement in my peripheral vision.

It was brown and black. It came at a rate of knots towards the fence and had white snarling teeth. Saliva dripped from its mouth. It growled for a few moments as I froze on the fence and looked down at it. Then the Alsatian dog began to fire rapid barks at me, deep and strong barks. It was ready to launch itself at the intruder who was climbing over the fence and invading its territory ready to rip it's throat out, mine.

I didn't give it a second thought; I dropped back down to join Pete. The dog continued to bark and jump up at the other side of the fence. Pete grinned.

"Remind me not to burgle this place!" I said.

"Hello." said a voice behind us. We both turned to see a man who had appeared at the front of the house.

He was in his thirties with long fair hair down to his shoulders, but styled. He looked a bit like Barry Manilow. He was wearing a dark blue silk shirt; open at the neck, and white tight fitting jeans with white slip on shoes to match.

He steadied himself against the side of the house with one hand, the other being wrapped in a tea towel. He looked pale and just about ready to pass out.

"Did you call for an Ambulance?" asked Pete.

He leaned forward as if to steady him self and nodded.

I picked up the first aid bag and we both approached him.

Pete and I took an arm each and helped him back into the house through the front door.

"What's happened?" I asked. Stupid question really, we could see his hand wrapped in the tea towel.

"I've cut me bloody hand love, well me fingers actually."

Pete's right eyebrow rose as he looked at me. I got his meaning straight away, this guy was homosexual.

We led him down a corridor into the kitchen and sat him down. It was a large kitchen with a farmhouse table in the centre. French doors looked out to the back garden, where the animal was now prowling.

"I was opening a can of dog food for 'Tinker' and caught my stupid fingers on the lid didn't I it just sliced right through them."

"Is that 'Tinker' outside?"

"Yes."

"Can he get into the house?" The rules say that we must make sure the area is safe before we attempt giving any treatment to patients. This was a prime example. If Tinker could have got into the house we wouldn't have been seen for dust.

"No."

"Good" said Pete.

"Ok, let's start with your name?" I said.

"Bill."

Bill leaned over the table and grasped a packet of cigarettes. He took one out and lit it with what looked like a gold Ronson lighter. He held the cigarette between his thumb and index finger and sucked in the smoke. It reminded me of an old black and white war movie where a German baddy was interrogating a captured prisoner and was smoking a cigarette in a similar fashion.

"Sorry, do you mind if I smoke?" he asked.

"Not all, Bill. It's your house after all" said Pete.

"Ok, I need to take a look at your fingers, can I unwrap the towel?" I said to Bill through the haze of cigarette smoke.

"Oh, must you? I can't stand the sight of blood, especially my own, I'll pass out."

"Just look the other way."

"I know, I know love, but I can just imagine it when you take it off."

"Well we do need to see what the damage is."

"If you must then, but be prepared, I might pass out. Oh God, I wish my fella was here."

"You're fella?"

"Yes, he left for work earlier; we've got a large order to get out to day."

I began to unravel the towel and Bill sharply turned the other way as he realised what I was doing. My best bet was to keep him talking and keep his mind off what was happening.

"You have a business then?"

There was very little blood showing as I unravelled the towel, I was expecting a lot of congealed blood that might have soaked into the material. I did notice his nails were neatly manicured though.

"Yes, we have a unit in Aintree."

I pulled the towel away from his fingers. The towel had stuck to a small amount of congealed blood, and he flinched a little.

"Oh my God, I'm going to pass out."

"You'll be fine, just put your head between your legs," said Pete.

"If only dear, if only I could."

"You know what I mean, just lean forward and put your head down."

"So what is it you do in Aintree?" I continued, trying to keep his mind off things and me from laughing.

"We import garden furniture and sell it on to garden centres."

"Like those plant pots you have in the Garden?" I had caught sight of several large clay pots in the back garden before Tinker had shown me his teeth.

"Yes, how bad are my fingers? Will I need an operation?"

He had two minor incisions across his index and middle finger from the can lid, something a couple of plasters would fix.

"I'm happy to tell you, Bill, that you'll not require any hospital treatment to day. It's nothing a couple of plasters can't put right."

"What do you mean?"

"I mean you're going to live, isn't that wonderful news?"

"But all that blood!"

"I've lost more blood cutting myself shaving."

"So you're not going to take me to hospital then?"

"No Bill" I said, "you don't need to go."

"But what if I pass out again?"

"Just lay down on the couch or in bed for while and you'll be fine."

"Are you sure?" Bill was dubious about my advice but we eventually convinced him he would be fine.

"Have you got any plasters? We don't have them on the Ambulance."

He pointed to a kitchen dresser and Pete walked over to rummage through the drawers. After a few moments Pete returned with a tin of Elastoplasts. I removed two of them and fixed them around each finger.

"There, all done" I said. "Good as new."

Bill took a furtive look at his fingers, and then sat upright.

"Are you sure I'll be ok? I know am a bit of a wimp, I am sorry."

"You'll be fine mate, just lay down if you feel a bit dizzy or if you feel that you're going to pass out, all right"

Bill nodded. "Ok, thanks. I'm really sorry to have dragged you out for this, what you must think of an old poof like me?"

I hoisted the first aid bag over my shoulder.

"We'll be on our way then, Bill. Take care now."

Pete and I walked across the room heading for the hallway and the front door, when Bill called after us.

"Do you think it wise to call my fella and ask him to come home?"

"That's entirely up to you, Bill, whatever makes you happy, mate."

There was just a moment of silence, and then we heard him, almost as if he was talking to himself.

"I'll call Benjamin now, he should be in the office by now"

It wasn't until we closed the front door behind us that Pete and I realised at the same time.

"Benjamin?" I said.

Pete snorted, trying to hold in a laugh.

"Bill and Ben, eh." I said as I climbed into the cab.

Joviality was short lived when Control started to call us on the radio. I took the mic and answered.

"When will you be clear?" asked Arthur, the controller.

I told him that we were clear now; the patient didn't need to go to hospital.

Arthur gave us another emergency call just a few streets away from where we were. An elderly female found on the floor.

We arrived at the address within two minutes of taking the call. It was a small two up two down terraced house, the front door leading directly onto the pavement. We could see the door was open as we pulled up.

As usual I took the first aid bag and climbed out of the cab. I gave a cursory knock at the door and wondered into the house finding myself instantly in the living room. It was empty.

"Hello" I shouted "Ambulance."

I heard someone reply from upstairs. I walked the length of the living room to the staircase which was on my right.

"In here" a woman's voice shouted as I reached the landing.

I entered the bedroom to find a woman kneeling next to what at first appeared to be a bundle of bedding. On closer inspection I could see it was an elderly lady lying on the floor with the bed clothes pulled over her.

"Hello, what's happened here then?" I asked as I approached.

"This is Agnes" said the kneeling woman, "and I'm her home help, I found her lying here on the floor when I arrived about ten minutes ago."

Agnes gave me a toothless grin as I looked at her to get a general observation of her condition.

Agnes was probably well into her eighties. Her face was weathered and wrinkled and she looked frail. From what I could see of her, which was just her head and neck, the rest being covered with blankets, she must have only been about seven stone in weight.

"Hello, Agnes." I tended to raise my voice when speaking to elderly people, as nine times out of ten they are stone deaf.

Her voice was croaky and her lips were dry and crusty. She lost her grin and looked seriously at me.

"I'm sorry you've been called out," she said and started coughing.

"Don't you worry about that, Nan. Can you tell me if you have any pain anywhere?"

"Eh?"

"Any pain?" I said, a bit louder.

"No, I don't think so."

Pete walked into the room. I turned to him and asked him to fetch the chair, blanket and oxygen; and then turned back to Agnes.

"What happened, Nan?"

"I was getting up to go to the lavatory and I must have lost my balance a bit and then the next thing I know I'm laying on the floor, I just couldn't get up"

"Ok, I see, do you ever get dizzy spells?"

"Oh yes, I have blood pressure, you see."

I smiled at her. "I'm glad to hear that." Better than having none was my train of thought.

"And when did this happen, Nan?"

I could see the thoughts whizzing through her brain, then she gave me a sorrowful look.

"I had to do it here; I couldn't wait any longer, I'm very sorry."

"Ok Agnes, don't worry about that just now, but can you remember when it was when you got out of bed."

She thought for a moment. "Was it this morning?"

"I don't know, Nan. I wasn't here."

Agnes thought hard "Or was it yesterday?"

I generally hated talking about a patient in front of them as it felt as if I was being condescending, but if needs must.

"Do you know when she was last seen? Were you here yesterday morning?" I asked the kneeling woman.

"She only has two days home help, Tuesday's and Thursday's. I saw her last Thursday and she seemed fine then."

"Does any family come around?"

"She has a younger sister, but she lives down in Wales somewhere."

I turned back to Agnes.

"How are you feeling right now, Agnes?"

"Eh?"

"I said, how are you feeling right now?" I had to raise my voice

"I could do with a cup of tea, I feel a bit thirsty."

"We'll get you a cuppa sorted out soon. Do you have any pain? I asked again.

"No, I don't think so, I just feel a bit stiff."

I nodded. "Can you move your legs?"

I watched as she slowly shuffled her legs underneath the blankets.

"Yes" she said.

It was obvious that Agnes was dehydrated, and each time she coughed I could hear the mucus bubbling in her chest. She could have been lying on her bedroom floor for three or four days, we had no way of knowing.

"Are you hungry, Nan?"

"A piece of toast would be nice," she said with a gummy smile.

The poor old girl was probably thinking I was going to make her a nice cup of tea and a round of toast. I was more worried about her chest and dehydration. Also it wasn't uncommon for an elderly person to fall out of bed and fracture a hip and not realise it.

"I'll tell you what we'll do, Nan. I'll let you have just a sip of water and then we'll take you to hospital, let them have a look at you, then you can have as many cups of tea and rounds of toast as you like."

"I'm really sorry to put you through all this trouble son," she said

I gently cupped her face in my hands, not for any diagnostic purposes, more of an affectionate response, but her face was cold. "It's no trouble at all, Nan. I just wish they were all as nice as you." I was rewarded with another gummy smile.

Pete arrived with the chair and we gently placed her on to it, wrapped her in a blanket and fixed the oxygen mask to her face. She gave me another toothless grin now that she was off the floor and sitting up in our chair. "I'm ninety two, you know."

"Well blinkin eck!", I shouted. "You don't look a day over eighty" She took it as a compliment.

The home help lady said she would lock the house up and leave the key with the next door neighbour until Agnes returned from hospital.

We took her into the Royal Cas and explained to the nurse what had happened. I knew she would get fussed over when they learned what she had been through.

The next day we arrived at the Royal Cas with another patient, and that's when we discovered that Agnes had passed away through the night, from pneumonia.

24

Beryl had been sleeping at her parents' house for over six months. I would occasionally arrive home from work during the day or when I had finished a night shift and find her in the house where she was either looking for something, doing some washing or on the phone to someone.

We would usually acknowledge each other with a grunt or two and she would depart the house within a few minutes of my arrival. Quite often, if I was on a day shift, I would see her through the front window going out from her parents' house, dressed for a night out. I would later learn that these were not 'girls nights out' with her work colleagues.

Apart from Police cadets, we often had other people accompanying us on the Ambulance, more as observers than giving hands on assistance at the scene of accidents or medical emergencies we attended except that is, for Dr John, as we called him.

John was in his early thirties and a consultant of A&E medicine. He had fair hair, a rugged rugby type build and short stubby fingers. He was about the same height as Pete, which is five foot ten.

Dr John had a great interest in the pre hospital treatment given to patients and was an avid supporter of advanced ambulance aid, which in years to come would culminate in the Paramedic qualification.

He would frequently, and in his own time, ride with a crew and help out where he could, often giving much needed advanced treatment; much more than we, as Ambulance crews were qualified to do.

One such occasion was to a call in the Tuebrook area of the city. We were tasked to attend a block of flats where it was reported a man had fallen down some steps.

The only complication to this call, as far as we were concerned, was that we were given the wrong location to the entrance of these flats which delayed our actual arrival.

Eventually we found the patient in a nearby block on the third floor landing. We were told by his wife, who was with him, that he had misplaced a step on the concrete stairway and tumbled down the next twenty or so steps.

The patient was in his sixties and lying in a crumpled mess at the bottom of the landing. He was unconscious and his breathing was of a rasping snoring sound. This indicated that his airway was compromised. His face was flushed and his pulse was slow but strong, indications of a severe head injury, with one dilated pupil.

Pete and I let John take charge of the situation. We knew this was a serious injury and needed to be dealt with quickly.

Pete placed an oxygen mask over the patients face and fed him oxygen from the portable bottle. Pete and John stayed with the patient as I went down the stairs and out to the Ambulance to get the scoop stretcher as he would need to be carried down the stairs on this piece of equipment rather than the carry chair.

Pete had secured a neck collar and eventually we had him secured to the scoop, and carried him down the steps to the Ambulance. The patient wasn't any lightweight and it was a real struggle to carry him that distance. Finally, sweat pouring; we got him onto the trolley in the rear of the Ambulance. It was at this point that the patient did stop breathing, but thankfully he still had a heartbeat. He'd gone into respiratory arrest.

John began to squeeze the ventilation bag, inflating his lungs with every squeeze. Time was fast running out for this patient, He obviously had a serious head injury, a subdural haematoma, which meant he had some serious bleeding going on inside his skull.

We raced as fast as we could to Broadgreen hospital, warning them of our impending arrival.

We arrived and off loaded him into the resus room. John decided that he would stay with the patient at the hospital rather than returning to station with us in the Ambulance.

Pete and I didn't get back to Broadgreen hospital until a few days later, which was when we asked about the patient. We were told that he was taken straight to theatre and had a burr hole procedure. This is quite simply drilling a hole into the skull, which will then release the pressure that had built up from the bleeding inside, and it had been a success. The patient was now on a ward and sitting up.

I like to think that Pete and I played a small part in that success, and hoped that more advanced training for Ambulance staff would be introduced into the Ambulance service.

John was a big supporter of advanced training for Ambulance crews and would, in later times, provide training and lectures for that purpose.

Unlike some of his peers whom we had come across over the years, John was a gentleman. He never seemed to have a bad word for anyone. He was friendly to all the Ambulance staff and never had a 'holier than thou' attitude, unlike some that I could mention.

What I liked about john, was, he liked a pint of beer and would often end up in the pub with us at the end of a shift. He was one of the lads.

We had many people who came to observe with us on a shift, nurses, midwives, police cadets and of course, Dr John. On most occasions when people came to observe with us, we would have a pretty boring shift; just the usual tummy pains, back pains or chest infections. Nothing of any significance, nothing to get the adrenaline flowing.

Tony, a mate of mine from school who had joined the army at the same time as I had joined the Ambulance Service, had occasional leave from the army. We got together at least once a year when he was home and we would go down to the local pub were we lived, catching up on what each other had been getting up to.

He told me how much he liked being in the army, which was a complete turn of attitude. There had been no one more of a hippy and anti establishment in our group of peers than Tony. In fact it had been a surprise to us all when he had joined up.

He still looked the same, except for a notable lack of hair, which used to be down to his shoulders, but had been replaced by the mandatory regimental crop. He had a willowy six foot frame, thin sculptured face and brown eyes that could penetrate into the soul.

Back then, I had no comprehension of the different types of regiments which existed in the army, to me it was just a case of a soldier being a soldier, nothing more than that.

He told me that he had now joined a regiment called the Special Air Service. He gave me some idea of the tough selection process that he had gone through. The arduous treks in the Brecon Beacons that sounded horrendous to me. The HALO (High Altitude Low Opening) parachute jumps at night, relying solely on an automatic opening device.

I was fascinated by his stories and what he had gone through. Apparently many applied to be in this regiment, but not many got through the selection and training. There was one aspect of the training he told me, that I never forgot, and I could see how Tony had passed this part of the test. Tony was always good at keeping his promise. If he said he was going to do something; then he always did.

He told me that at the beginning of the selection process he was given a number to remember, a number that he must never divulge to anyone at any time or for any reason.

Apparently it was part of the training process to go through a mock interrogation scenario.

He and a few of the other trainees were dragged from their beds in the early hours of the morning and taken blindfolded, in a landrover, to a remote location. It was the job of the interrogators to extract this number from each of the trainees. The interrogation wasn't pleasant by any means; it was made as realistic as possible. However, they all came through it without giving away the numbers they had originally been given.

It wasn't until the end of the selection process that individual trainees were called in front of their commanding officer to be told if they had passed or not.

When the time came for Tony to be called in, he was congratulated and told he had passed the selection process. He was also told by the officer that he did well in retaining information during interrogation, but he must now give him the number he had been given at the start of the selection process in order to fully complete the course.

Tony had promised never to divulge that number, and he kept to his promise. He refused to give it to the officer. He was made to feel very uncomfortable about this by the officer, and was threatened with being thrown out of the regiment. Tony stuck to his guns, which was just as well. Had he given the officer that number, he would have failed selection. Apparently it was at this point in the selection process that many hopefuls fell down on.

Part of Tony's training included spells in Hospital casualty departments, learning how to treat wounds, suture and put drips into veins and CPR. This was in case they ever had to treat a colleague out in the field. I was interested in this as I knew we, in the Ambulance Service, would probably be doing this sort of training in the near future.

I asked Tony if he would like to observe on the Ambulance for an afternoon shift which I would be starting the following week. I did warn him that it was sods law we might not get anything of interest, but he was keen to join us. How wrong was I going to be! Tony would turn out to be a trauma magnet.

The following week I picked Tony up in my car and we drove into work to start at three in the afternoon. He was suitably kitted out with an old dark blue Ambulance overcoat that was far too small for him, but he needed to be regarded as one of the crew at any incident we attended.

We were the first crew out on the shift, and typically, no sooner had we made the first brew of the afternoon, then we were called out to an urgent call.

We attended a woman who was six months pregnant and bleeding PV (Post Vaginal). In other words she was having a threatened miscarriage. She was booked to be admitted to Mill Road maternity hospital.

Tony came into the house with Pete and me. I made use of Tony and had him bring the carry chair. The three of us trudged up the staircase and into the bedroom where our patient was lying comfortably. I asked her the usual questions including if she had any pain? And was she still bleeding? The answer to these questions was "No."

We placed her into the carry chair then trundled down the stairs and out to the Ambulance, where we then heard Arthur the controller calling us on the radio. I didn't rush to answer him as we had to get our patient settled onto the Ambulance trolley, only then did Pete reach into the cab and answer the call.

Apparently there was an emergency nearby, but it was too late for us to respond, we had loaded our patient.

"Shouldn't bloody give us urgent calls then, should they?" muttered Pete to himself as he replaced the mic back into its holder.

We took the patient into Mill Road maternity hospital and off loaded her into the admission room, then returned to the Ambulance, loaded our trolley back on board and had the mandatory and unofficial cigarette break at the rear of the vehicle.

"I told you it would be 'sods law. We'll probably just be ferrying patients around like that all night," I said.

Tony shrugged. "Que sera sera."

Cigarettes finished, we called control and headed back to station as instructed. We were about half-way back when control called and gave us another emergency call. It was to a number 18 bus in the Tuebrook area, on which some one had fallen.

We weren't too far away from the incident and arrived within just a few minutes. Tony struggled into the ill fitting coat, which he declined to wear unless we were at an incident. I didn't blame him for that.

On arrival we discovered a man, probably in his forties, lying at the bottom of the rear stairs on a double Decker bus. He was unconscious and had a gaping head wound, which fortunately had stopped bleeding.

From the conductor and other passengers, we discovered that the bus had been stationary at a set of red traffic lights. The man had been upstairs and was about to descend the steps when the bus jerked forward as it moved off when the traffic lights had changed to green. He had tumbled down all the steps.

The man was lying face down on the platform with both legs still on the stairs. All the possible injuries he could have sustained raced through my mind, but I had to stick with the priorities of examination and treatment, which was the tried and tested ABC, Airway, Breathing and Circulation. I explained to Tony what I was doing as I got into a kneeling position and checked if the man was breathing, which he was. Next I took his radial pulse, which was steady and at what seemed to be a normal rate, so far so good.

Now we had to worry about broken bones and any possible internal injuries. At this point I wasn't too concerned about any internal bleeding as his steady pulse and breathing indicated there probably wasn't any. The wound on his head wasn't too much of a concern as the blood had congealed and stopped bleeding. There weren't any obvious signs of broken limbs, which just left the possibility of a fractured spine, particularly in his neck.

Tony and Pete went back to the Ambulance to fetch the trolley, oxygen, spinal collar and scoop stretcher while I stayed with the patient and kept an eye on him.

Still in the same position as we had found him at the bottom of the stairs, I managed to fit the collar around his neck while Pete positioned the scoop stretcher on the bus platform, ready to receive him.

It was only at this point that I realised we had gathered quite an audience. People on the pavement had gathered to watch us work, and those passengers from the downstairs of the bus huddled together and peered over shoulders to get a better view of what we were doing. I always likened the job to show business; not only did you have to treat patients, but you also invariably had an audience to entertain.

I had Tony help me turn the man over onto his back. I inserted an airway to protect his breathing and slapped on the oxygen mask. Now we were ready to slide him onto the scoop stretcher.

Pete and Tony gently lifted the scoop while I held the oxygen bottle, and in unison we moved him onto the waiting trolley at the kerbside. We rolled the trolley towards the Ambulance at which point I felt like stopping and taking a bow as the bus passengers and pavement audience began to clap.

"Well done" someone shouted.

The patient was still unconscious when we arrived at Broadgreen Hospital.

I was glad that I was able to get Tony involved with that job. If nothing else happened that evening, at least his time with us hadn't been in vain.

No sooner had we bought our cursory plastic cups of tea from the WRVS counter in the hospital than control were on the radio asking if we were clear for another emergency.

Times like this explained how Ambulance crews can drink scalding hot drinks in a very short time; it comes with many years of practice. It was to an address in the Kirkdale area, a report of a man unconscious, no further details.

I had decided to let Tony sit in my attendant seat in the front of the Ambulance so he could experience the feeling of both trepidation and excitement as we would go through red lights and constantly break speed limits. Unless you've done it, you won't know the feeling.

The street we were in was lined on both sides with two up two down Victorian terraced houses. Some were derelict and were boarded up; others, although probably lived in, were unkempt and in need of a lick of paint.

We knew instantly the house we were going to by the group of people outside it, who waved to attract our attention.

I clambered out of the back door, Tony and Pete climbed from the cab.

"He's in the kitchen but we can't get in, all the doors are locked," said a woman wearing a full length flowery apron and obligatory curlers that were covered with a head scarf.

"There's a smell of gas too," said another woman.

"I think his wife left him; we've not seen sight nor sound of her for a while," added Mrs Headscarf.

The front room curtains were drawn, so there was no possibility of peeking through the window.

"How do you know he's in the kitchen? Is there a back entrance?" I asked.

"We've tried going around the back but the yard door's bolted," said another woman.

Mrs Headscarf interjected: "Take a look through the letter box, you can see him."

I crouched down, pushed open the flap and looked through the letter box. The front door would open directly into the living room. I could see, at the far end of the living room, an internal door that led into what looked like the kitchen.

I could just see the back of a man who appeared to be sitting and leaning forward onto something, maybe a table. I couldn't get a full view of him; the internal door was partly obscuring my view.

"Jeez." I had to pull away from the letter box flap as the stench of gas was overpowering.

I turned to Pete. "Best get the police here, mate. We're going to have to break in."

I pushed on the door at the top and then at the bottom, remembering how Frank had done it all those years ago. There was a little give with each push, I was checking for any dead bolts. There didn't seem to be any.

It appeared the only lock was the brass Yale door lock, for which no one had a key.

I looked at Tony.

"Fancy putting your size ten to the test?"

"I'd use a sawn off normally for this sort of thing." he smiled.

"Not the best idea," I said, "There's a strong smell of gas in there, but a brass door lock shouldn't create any sparks when you trash it."

"Ok folks, can you all move back." I was confident there wouldn't be any explosions, but just in case?

Tony steadied himself, and then lunged with his right foot at the lock. Wood splintered and the door pushed back into the interior wall with a bang. Gas wafted out into the street, sending the neighbours scattering in all directions for fresh air.

Tony was fast, and was first to go into the house. He'd pulled out his handkerchief, covering his nose and mouth and entered before I could say anything. I took a triangular bandage out of the first aid bag, covered my nose and mouth, and followed him in.

Tony had reached the back door and was unbolting it to allow for better ventilation through the house.

I went to the guy in the kitchen. He was probably in his thirties, wearing just a vest and jeans, no shoes or socks.

What we couldn't see from the letter box and was hidden by the internal door, was a gas cooker. The oven door of which had been opened. It was the type that was hinged at the bottom and opened downwards, creating a kind of shelf, about knee high from the floor. All the taps had been opened to full and remained in that position, although no gas was now escaping from the burners. There must have been a slot meter somewhere and the money had run out.

He had certainly meant to kill himself, but in comfort. He had placed a pile of pillows and cushions onto the open oven door, pulled up a chair and laid his head on the cushions, then just waited for the inevitable.

They guy was as stiff as a board through rigor mortise, and very cold to touch. He had long since left the world of the living.

It was a time of transition between coal gas and natural gas. Although natural gas isn't all that good for you to breathe in, it certainly won't kill you. But coal gas was a deadly substance and this poor bloke was proof of that. It was ironic though as he looked as healthy as anyone would with a bright cherry coloured face and pink skin. Almost as if he had been out in the sun for a little too long. It was an obvious sign of carbon monoxide poisoning.

There was the usual note scribbled on to a sheet of paper on the kitchen table.

It wasn't a very long note, but a sad one to read.

Apparently his wife hadn't left him as the neighbours had thought; she had died in hospital of breast cancer a few months previously. The note was to his brother, telling him that he missed 'Carol' so much that he just couldn't go on any longer and wanted to join her in heaven. I wondered if he was with her now.

I left the note on the table for the police to deal with; they would be along soon enough, knowing that we had needed to make a forced entry.

The stink of gas was now dissipating as a gentle draught blew through the house clearing it away.

"What happens now?" asked Tony.

"We wait for the police to arrive and let them take over."

"Will we be moving the body?"

"No, the police will probably want to photograph him. Then they'll get the police surgeon out to certify death".

The smell of gas had now gone. Pete closed the front door to stop prying neighbours taking sneak looks into the house. He closed the internal door also, and then we lumbered out into the back yard and lit up a cigarette each.

We timed it well and had just finished our cigarettes when the police arrived. Having duly handed over responsibility, we climbed back into the Ambulance. Control returned us to station for our meal break.

We didn't get any more calls after that and just sat watching the telly until the night shift came on duty.

Pete went home, but Tony and I dashed back to our local pub where we knew we could get a few pints, even if it was after closing time.

Little did I know then that I wouldn't see Tony again for a few years and then it would be on the telly. The next time I would see him, he would be telling me about jumping over a balcony at the Iranian embassy in London and being very tempted to wave at a TV camera that was perched on the gantry of a crane and filming him from above the roof tops.

Tony and I walked back from the pub; we stood on a street corner and chatted for a while until it was time to go our separate ways.

It had gone past one in the morning when I got home. I turned the key in the front door and entered what I knew would be an empty house. Junk mail, leaflets and royal mail brushed across the floor as I pushed the door open.

I picked up and carried the items through to the kitchen, my plan was to have a coffee, read the days mail then go to bed.

One letter in the pile was different from the usual bills and reminders; it was from a firm of solicitors.

Beryl was seeking a divorce on the grounds of physical abuse and would be applying for an injunction to have me removed from the house. I was gob-smacked.

Within a week I was packing a couple of cardboard boxes with my personal items. A court order had come through two days after opening that solicitor's letter ordering me out of my own house.

I had a mixture of emotions; angry, sad and hurt, all rolled into one. I had approached a solicitor of my own and he had delayed the injunction for a short period, claiming that the court would be making me homeless. The court had then ordered the local council to find me accommodation, and now I was packing my things to move to a high rise flat in the Croxteth area.

I was angry that Beryl had claimed I had abused her physically; she had used the incident of when she slipped from the chair and hit her head on the fire grate as evidence of my abuse. I was sad because after seven years of marriage all my personal possessions would fit into just two cardboard boxes.

I was hurt because without my parents we wouldn't have had the tenancy of the house in the first place, I felt betrayed and used. Not just by Beryl, but by her family too. I had a strong feeling they were the instigators of what I was now going through.

I moved into the one bed roomed flat on the top floor of a high rise block, Sceptre towers. I had left all the furniture with Beryl; I didn't want any of it reminding me of what used to be.

It took several weeks to get my new home into some semblance of comfort. Friends and family had rallied around and provided some furniture and basic items so I could live something near to normal.

Weeks past and I was a spectator to the battle of words in letters that went to and fro between solicitors. Eventually a compromise was reached; we would be divorced on the grounds of the marriage irretrievably breaking down. I had insisted on this with my solicitor, I didn't want the name tag of a wife beater hanging around my neck. That sort of thing would stick on a file somewhere forever more, but most of all because it wasn't true. In exchange I agreed to sign the full tenancy of the house over to Beryl.

Tony, who had observed on the Ambulance, had a younger brother. It was just by chance that I bumped into him one night in the pub. It was several months after I had moved into the flat and it was getting close to Christmas. I hadn't seen him for some years and we began to chat about the ways of the world, how his older brother was doing and had he heard from him lately? Inevitably the subject turned to Beryl and I splitting up, and it was then I discovered that his friend, who I vaguely knew, had been seeing Beryl for some time before we had separated. She had been having an affair with him for months, and now he had moved into the house with her. He thought I knew all this and was apologetic to break the news.

I now understood why she had become distant and why she was out with the girls from work several times a week. I should have seen the pattern.

25

I was nursing a slight hangover from a few drinks the previous night. My bachelor lifestyle was catching up with me. I hadn't seen or heard anything from Beryl or her solicitors for several months. The decree Nisi had arrived through the post five weeks ago, so it was just a matter of time before the decree absolute arrived. I was over it now; it was water under the bridge.

It was eight o'clock on a sunny summer morning in July. Pete and I had been on duty for an hour and we hadn't turned a wheel. We were third out and there was still another crew on station to respond before we did.

I was in an armchair in the mess room, feet on the coffee table, eyes closed and with a copy of last night's Liverpool Echo draped over my face and chest.

I had taken some paracetamol before leaving my flat and they were just about kicking in, but

I was eagerly waiting for Kay, the cleaner, to arrive. She started at eight and would begin making the bacon butties I needed, and more coffee.

Kay had arrived as she always did, promptly on the hour. She got started on cooking the breakfast with the obligatory fag hanging from the corner of her mouth, she reminded me of Hilda Ogden.

The menu consisted of toast, eggs, bacon and beans. We could have any of these, in any combination. I usually plumped for the bacon on toast.

This was Kay's little business on the side. Her actual official job was cleaner. However, she bought the food and cooked it, and we paid her a very reasonable price. It was a system that worked very well for all of us. Even the boss would pay a visit to the mess kitchen on occasions and walk away with some culinary delight.

Gary and Tony were the next crew out, I wasn't in such a hurry to be served, so I let them have their orders cooked first. Gary opted for scrambled egg on toast, while Tony had fried eggs and bacon on fried bread. It was no wonder he was a little thick around the middle.

As if ordained by a higher authority, as soon as Gary and Tony sat down to eat, the emergency bell rang.

"Shit!" they both said in unison.

Gary stood and took a hasty gulp from his mug of tea, ready to make a move, but Tony continued to sit and eat.

"Come on then," Gary said to him.

"I'm not fucking wasting this, it'll be cold by the time we get back" Crumbs of egg and toast flew from his mouth as he tried to speak.

"But it's a crash call, mate."

"I know it's a fucking crash call. It's probably fuck all too."

"Hey," shouted Kay from the kitchen, "less of that fucking language, please."

I was standing in the kitchen doorway now, about to order my bacon on toast. Tony looked at me from where he sat. He didn't have to say anything, I knew what he wanted.

"Come on, Tony I'm starving." I said.

"Next time round, we'll go out for you."

I knew how he felt as there's almost nothing worse than having to go out on a job and leave your meal behind, particularly when you know it won't be edible when you get back.

Pete was out in the garage somewhere, so he didn't know of the little crisis that was unfolding in the mess room.

I wasn't feeling in the best of conditions and I really needed something to eat to bring up my sugar levels because of last night's drinking, but then again, I could understand Tony's frustration.

"You owe us big style, then?"

" Definitely, no problems" said Tony.

I asked Kay to make me two rounds of toast and leave them in the oven for when I got back, I didn't mind cold toast. I paid her 10p, it was 5p a round.

I found Pete in the garage and explained what had happened; he just shook his head and climbed into the cab.

Control told us that the job was to a collapse in Falkland Street, off London Road. Between TJ Hughes and Boots the chemist. I was driving and Pete had taken the message. He looked at his watch.

"Shit, ten to nine. Another ten minutes and Hatton Garden would've been on duty and got this job."

Headlights on and blue lights flashing, we turned out of the garage and headed towards the city centre. Traffic was heavy at this time of the morning and it was a struggle to weave past and through the vehicles on West Derby Road. We were approaching the traffic lights at the junction of Rocky Lane and Shiel Road. I had the two tones on, but the lights now turned to red and were against us.

I managed to squeeze past the front of the traffic queue that had built up as the lights had changed to red, and slowly nosed my way out into the cross flow of traffic. I had everything switched on that could be switched on to warn other drivers that we were there and would like to cross through the flow of traffic, pretty please!

I could see a car travelling from my right had spotted me and came to a stop to let me through. The traffic behind him followed suit. I checked the traffic from my left and they were still whizzing through the junction, as they had a green light.

A police car coming from the left had spotted me trying to get through. He slowed and came to a stop and lit up his blue light to warn the traffic behind him. My way through the cross flow of traffic was now clear. I accelerated just in time to hear Pete shout "Oh fuck!"

I didn't see it as the junction was now behind us, I didn't hear it because the two tone horns were blearing away.

I caught sight in my rear view mirror of the two cars now in the middle of the road junction, one of them was the police car, blue lights still flashing, but with a blue Volkswagen Beetle buried deep into its rear end. Oops!

We couldn't stop; we were already on our way to an emergency. Our intended patient could have stopped breathing or be in cardiac arrest and we had no way of knowing until we got there.

Pete grabbed the radio mic and called control to tell them what had happened, and then suggested that an Ambulance may be required. I smiled at the thought, and Pete punched the air. Tony still wouldn't get his eggs and bacon on toast. What goes around comes around, eh?

It was still a fight to get through the traffic into the city but eventually we made it to Falkland Street. We couldn't see anything obvious as we turned into the street from London Road. It was a narrow and quiet cobbled street, just a narrow cut through to Islington. No shops, houses or entrances, just gable ends to the T J Hughes department store on our left and Boots the chemist on our right. Pete spotted something that looked like a bundle of rags in a narrow recess. I parked the Ambulance and we walked over to see what we had.

It was a dosser. He looked as though he had three overcoats on and maybe a couple of pairs of trousers, although one pair could have been stuffed with newspaper to give that impression. We weren't going to investigate to find out.

He was in a half sitting up position with his legs out in front of him. His coats were pulled together and tied around the middle with a piece of string. He was totally sparked out in this recess, still clinging to an empty bottle of Australian white. Black straggly unwashed hair trailed out from beneath a navy blue beanie hat which had been pulled down over his ears.

He had probably been there all night. Good job it wasn't winter time, he'd be dead now instead of being in deep alcoholic slumber. Some good Samaritan had probably spotted him as they walked past and decided to let the Ambulance service deal with it.

"Hey!" I nudged him with my boot. He groaned, turned away from me and drew up his knees.

"Oi" I tried again.

"Piss off." Or at least that's what it sounded like.

"Come on, we can't leave you here."

No answer.

I crouched down to shake his shoulder. He was facing away from me so I didn't anticipate what was about to happen. I shook his shoulder. "Come on, we'll take you over to the Royal, you'll get a cuppa there."

It all happened so fast. First there was a growling sound, then a short scream. He swung his body around to face me. His arm was outstretched and it held the empty bottle that he had been clinging onto.

Had I been in a different position, a little further away from him, I would have taken the full force of the swinging bottle on the side of my head. Luckily I was too close into him and his arm crashed into my right arm. He lost grip of the bottle and it flew across the street, smashing into a thousand shards.

He grunted, wrapped his coats tighter around himself, turned his back to me and slumped back into a sleeping position. I was annoyed, I could have sent the boot in and I was very tempted, but sanity prevailed. I was still infuriated with him though.

" You little gobshite, I was trying to help you."

Another grunt.

I turned to Pete who was grinning. He was seeing the funny side of it, which oddly enough calmed me down a little. I suppose it was a bit funny if you were a spectator. I had to admit to myself that the guy probably had mental health problems too. But that didn't give him the right to attack people who were trying to help him.

I sauntered back to the Ambulance and grabbed the radio mic and called Control. Once they had responded, I explained what had happened and requested they ask the police to attend as the bloke was D&I (Drunk and Incapable) and advised that we would stay on scene until they arrived.

The police van arrived about ten minutes later and hauled him off to the main Bridewell in Dale Street, where he would be locked up until he sobered up. Then he would be released with a caution. I could have mentioned the assault, but I didn't bother; too much paperwork involved.

When the dosser had been taken away, Pete called Control, who sent us back to station.

Tony had been correct; the job had been 'fuck all.' Not an Ambulance job at all.

When we arrived back on station all the other crews were out, which was a pain because it meant that we were vulnerable to going out again.

Pete made two mugs of tea and I went to the oven in search of my cold toast. I was desperate to eat something, and it tasted wonderful, especially washed down with piping hot tea.

Pete went into the mess room and I heard him chuckling to himself. I followed him through the doorway, and there on the table was a plate with unfinished remnants of cold bacon and eggs. I smiled.

I was feeling much better having had something to eat and drink, but it wasn't long before the emergency bell went again. So much for being third out and having an easy shift!

The call was to an address in the Kensington area, a collapsed patient with a GP in attendance.

The morning rush hour traffic had thinned out by now and I was able to get up a reasonable speed in the Ambulance. We arrived outside the house in just five minutes. Pete jumped out of the cab with the first aid bag and headed inside through the open front door with me following hot on his heels.

We were directed upstairs by a woman in the living room who stood nervously wringing a handkerchief around her fingers. It was a small house, just a two up two down terrace. I followed Pete upstairs and into a bedroom that looked over the street at the front of the house.

There was an elderly lady in a full length flannelette nightgown lying on her back on the floor next to the bed, with an equally elderly man kneeling next to her. He had both hands cupped over the woman's left breast and making circular movements.

He was dressed in an old fashioned brown tweed suit, complete with matching waistcoat and fob chain hanging from a waistcoat pocket. He wore wire rimmed spectacles that had slipped towards the end of his nose, a stethoscope lay curled on the bed. We had met this man before.

"Ah, gentlemen, so glad you're here to help me out with this one," he said, with a Scottish lilt in his voice.

"You're her GP aren't you," I said

"Yes, that's right."

"What's happened this time"?

"She wasn't feeling too well, apparently. Her daughter, that's her downstairs, rang the surgery so I said I would pop around and take a look at her after surgery had finished. I was just about to examine her chest when she collapsed to the floor here. Thought I had better do some cardiac massage under the circumstances."

Pete looked at me and I returned the look, both our mouths must have dropped open. The GP's idea of cardiac massage was to place both hands, palm down on the woman's left breast and gently massage it in a circular motion, exactly as he had done it last time.

Pete knelt down next to the aged doctor.

"Ok doctor, I'll take over now."

"I do appreciate that, I've been doing it for the last twenty minutes. It does tire one out somewhat."

"Twenty minutes"? I said.

The doctor struggled to get up off his knees and I had to give him a hand.

"Oh dear, knees are not so good these days," he said.

"How come we weren't called sooner"? I asked.

"No telephone in the house. The daughter had to find a public one. Took her twenty minutes to find one that wasn't vandalised."

Pete was pounding on the old lady's chest and I started with the bag and mask, but we knew it was fruitless; she had been in cardiac arrest far too long. The GP's unconventional method of cardiac massage would have been totally useless. This old ladies heart had not beat for more than twenty minutes now, far too much time had passed for any hope of success.

"She's not a very well old dear."

"You can say that again!" I heard Pete whisper through gritted teeth as he was bouncing up and down on her chest.

"Has had three heart attacks in the past," the GP continued saying as he collected his stethoscope and placed it into a battered Gladstone bag that I hadn't noticed until now.

He seemed to straighten his back as though it was giving him trouble, but was not concerned about the poor woman lying on the floor.

"I'll have a word with the daughter on my way out, and leave things in your professional hands. You're more used to this kind of thing than I am."

Pete and I knew there wasn't a chance of this lady making any sort of recovery. If the GP left the house now it would mean we would have to cart the old dear out of the house and down to the Royal to be certified, an undignified end to her life.

"Ok Pete, lets call it quits." I said loud enough for the GP to hear, and then I turned to the GP.

"We're going to need you to certify this lady, doctor."

The GP had a look of surprise on his face.

"You're not taking her to hospital then?"

"No doctor, there's nothing that can be done for this lady now."

"I think I would like you to take her to hospital just the same."

"It's not an Ambulance job to be moving dead bodies to hospitals."

"And since when have you been qualified to pronounce death?"

His pompous attitude was getting to me now. At first I thought he was just a kindly old GP who had forgotten the rudimentary basics of CPR, as I had thought the last time we met, but now he was turning into a pompous old shit.

"I've seen enough dead bodies to know when to resuscitate and when to stop."

"I don't think I like your attitude," he said starkly.

"I'm sorry you think that, but we still need you to certify."

"I most certainly will not, and what's more I will be reporting you to your superiors. As far as I am concerned this lady has received constant heart massage since she collapsed, then you arrive here and within three minutes you give up"

I was beginning to feel a bit shaky. I was treading on thin ice here, but I wasn't going to let this smart arse get the better of me.
"Well that isn't quite correct doctor; this lady hasn't had any cardiac massage for at least twenty five minutes. The twenty minutes it took for you to call the Ambulance and five minutes for us to get here."
"I was giving her heart massage."
"No doctor, you were giving her breast massage."
"I beg you pardon!"
"What you were doing when we arrived was just massaging this lady's left breast. This lady has had no resuscitation at all, not until we arrived."

His face turned puce; I hoped he wasn't going to have a stroke, but he knew that I was right. His CPR skills were not as they should be, probably due to too many long years of sitting in an office dealing out prescriptions and sick notes.
He turned away from me. "I'll speak to the daughter."
"And we'll put this lady back on her bed," I said as he headed out of the door.

Pete and I put the lady back onto her bed and covered her up. It was more of a dignified way to leave this life than be hauled down to a mortuary like a sack of spuds.

We gathered our equipment together. "Do you think he'll report us?" asked Pete.

I shrugged my shoulders. I was shaking inside. Had I just overstepped the line? But I knew I was right.

We ambled down the stairs which led directly into the living room. The doctor was sitting on the settee writing something in a leather bound note book. He ignored us.

The daughter was still shaking and twiddling with the handkerchief in her hands; I stepped over to her and placed a hand on her shoulder.

"I'm sorry."

She nodded and gave a thin smile in acceptance, and then we left.

I climbed back into the Ambulance, my hands shaking. I hadn't meant to confront the doctor the way I had, but he was just so much of an arse that I couldn't hold it back.

I asked Pete not to clear with Control just yet, and then drove the Ambulance around the corner into a quiet side street, parked and sparked up a cigarette to calm my nerves.

We went back to our station and managed to get lunch without any disturbance. We had a quiet afternoon just waiting to be called into the boss's office, but the call never came. The other two crews managed to handle the calls between them, that is, until an hour before the shift finished.

Our last emergency call for the day was in the Clubmoore area, a leafy lined road with rows of semi detached houses, front gardens set back from the pavement.

Control didn't give us any information as to what the problem was, so we were hoping for a nice simple job that would get us finished on time.

As we pulled up outside the garden gate, the front door was open and we saw a schoolgirl in uniform. She must have been about ten or eleven years old. She was sitting on the doorstep, head in hands and crying.

Pete and I walked down the garden path towards her.

"What's the matter, love?" asked Pete as he leaned over and touched her shoulder.

"It's my dad," she sobbed. She was crying the sort of cry when you can't quite catch your breath and have jerky inspirations.

"Is he inside?" I asked.

She nodded, still with jerky sobbing sounds.

We began to move past her to enter the house. "Upstairs" she managed to bleat out between sobs. Once again I was following Pete up the stairs. It seemed like a nice clean house, tidy and well kept.

We reached the landing and turned a corner. We were suddenly confronted with this man. He was leaning forward on his tip toes, bent at the knees and his arms were dangling downwards like a gorilla's might do, his chin almost resting on his left shoulder.

There was a length of three ply cable coming from somewhere, through the attic trap door in the ceiling. One end must have been tied to a rafter; the other end was around his neck.

His mouth was open and his tongue was black and swollen. His eyes were wide open and bulging and he looked as if he was staring at something on the floor. There was a kicked over dining chair a few feet away.

The cable around his neck was extremely tight, hardly visible as it had dug deep into his neck. Rigor mortis was present indicating that he'd been like this for some time.

If there had been any chance of resuscitation, we would have cut him down immediately and made an effort, but as it was, we would need to leave him as he was until the police arrived.

The balls of his feet were touching the floor and his knees were bent because the cable that he used had begun to stretch under his weight. There was no doubt that, when he had first kicked the chair away, his feet wouldn't have been anywhere near the floor.

We both came back down the stairs. I sat next to the school girl on the step while Pete went to ask control to send the police.

"Was it you that found him?" I asked.

She nodded.

"I'm sorry," I said, knowing full well that my words wouldn't make a blind bit of difference as to how she was feeling.

"Do you have a mam, brothers, sisters?"

"Mam," she said, and then she stared at me. Her face was serious and her eyes were red from crying.

"Is he dead?"

I couldn't find any words for her, this was so tragic. No kid should ever have to see what she had just seen upstairs.

"I'm afraid so love."

Then I got the shock of my life.

Still staring at me she said, "Good, the dirty bastard won't be able to touch me ever again."

26

Night shifts have their good and bad times. They tend to be quieter as the night rolls into early morning, usually around two or three o'clock; which allows for some sleep time, although this is not always the case.

Another good thing is when the clocks go forward, making it a shorter shift. However, this is balanced out when the clocks go back an hour, making it a longer shift. It's the luck of the draw as to what shift you are on at the time.

There is one night shift that comes around every year, and if you happen to be working that night shift, then certain preparations need to be made. That shift is New Year's Eve.

New Year's Eve is to Ambulances what Bonfire night is to fire engines; exceptionally busy.

I don't know why it happens, just one of life's little mysteries I suppose, but once that clock strikes midnight, all hell lets loose.

Job after job, all night long it's a shift that calls for flasks of tea and wrapped up sandwiches to be carried with you on the Ambulance. It is taken for granted that you won't see your station again until it's time to go home.

It was the last day of 1978, New Year's Eve. Pete and I were on the night shift and fully expecting to be run off our feet.

The new control room had been completed and was now controlling the Ambulances in the entire Merseyside area, not just Liverpool.

Charlie, our old shift leader, had been promoted to a rank 5 controller. He would be the one in charge of us and dishing out the work through the night. I knew Pete and I would be busy, but we were just one of many Ambulances. Charlie would have to contend with all the vehicles in the region. I didn't envy him one little bit.

Charlie had Tommy and George working with him in the control room. Tommy had been an ambulance man on the road, but had now been promoted to a rank 6 controller. I had been crewed up with Tommy a couple of times in the past and got on quite well with him. George was a rank 7 controller and had been moved from the St Helens control room when it had shut down and the new control room in Liverpool had come on line. I didn't know George all that well, but he had seemed a nice enough bloke when I had spoken to him on the phone. There was another rank 7 vacant position on Charlie's shift and I was mulling over the idea of applying for it.

It was just gone eleven as I checked the Ambulance kit, while Pete made the mugs of tea. Strangely enough, the hour between eleven and midnight was always quiet and gave the opportunity to get your Ambulance sorted before the rush at midnight.

Two extra crews had been brought in on overtime, which made five crews in total on the night shift at Anfield station.

Pete and I were third in line to respond from the station, and we actually made it to five minutes past midnight before we were called out on our first job.

The jobs were all predictable ones; cut heads, sprained ankles, broken noses, several fights, one stab wound and lots of drunken collapses.

It was half past two in the morning when Pete and I decided that enough was enough; we hadn't stopped or had any kind of break in the last two and a half hours. We were outside the Royal casualty department and had decided to take an unofficial break.

I drove the Ambulance down the ramp from the casualty entrance and further into the hospital grounds. I found a narrow gap between buildings into which we could reverse and not be seen, particularly by any other crews. The chattering two way radio was switched off, flasks of tea were opened and butty's unwrapped. Pete and I didn't talk; we just savoured the peace and quiet we had found. However, I did swap a cheese butty for one of Pete's corned beef butty's.

After twenty minutes or so, and suitably refreshed, I switched the radio back on. There wasn't much radio traffic going on, just one Ambulance speaking to Control in Birkenhead and another in Kirkby. Other than that it was uncannily quiet. We wondered if we had missed something while we had the radio switched off.

I took the radio mic and called Charlie in the control room telling, him we were clear at the Royal. We were half expecting him to ask where we had been and tell us that he had been calling us for the past twenty minutes, but instead we just got told to return to station for our meal break. Maybe he was just waiting for us to get back and give us a bollocking for going missing?

I drove out of the hospital and past the casualty department expecting to see a line of queuing Ambulances, but there were none.

We headed back to station as instructed. The streets were eerily empty of traffic. Just one or two pedestrian stragglers were weaving their way home from finished celebrations.

I turned onto West Derby Road and headed towards the traffic lights with the junction of Sheil Road, the very same junction where a police car had once stopped to let us cross through a red light, but had been unfortunate enough to be rammed by a car travelling behind. This time we were travelling in the opposite direction and with no traffic in sight.

Normally on night shift when the roads are empty, we wouldn't bother to stop for a red traffic light, but just gently ease through them making sure nothing was coming the other way. We weren't in any rush to get back to station as we had already taken our meal break and weren't desperately needing sustenance.

The traffic lights at the junction were just turning onto red as we approached so I slowed down ready to stop if I had to.

On our left was a row of shops, one of them being a hairdresser salon. We came to a halt at the red traffic lights directly outside the hairdresser's. A party inside was in full swing. The place was lit up like a Christmas tree, still with Christmas lights. Muted music was playing and drifting into the street.

Pete and I sat in the cab waiting for the lights to change when the shop door opened, spilling out music and an attractive blond. She lit a cigarette, took a drag and then spotted us looking at her. She smiled and waved, even though we were only a couple of feet away.

"Happy New Year," she shouted.

Pete rolled his window down; he was in the attendant seat and nearest the kerb.

"Same to you love."

"Have you had a busy night then?"

"Afraid so."

Two more girls and a bloke almost fell out of the door with the same intention as the first, to have a cigarette.

"All right lads," said the brunette.

"All right love," said Pete.

Without any warning, the brunette came to the cab window, leaned in and gave Pete a kiss on the lips, then broke away.

"That's to cheer you up because you have to work on New Years Eve," she said.

This wasn't fair. Pete was having all the fun because he was closest to them, and all that I could do was look past him from the driver's seat.

The traffic lights began to change, but I didn't drive off.

"Are you going to an emergency now, like?" asked the blond. Her right elbow was tucked into her right waistline, her forearm hanging outwards, the cigarette between her fingers. Her left arm crossed her body just beneath her boobs.

"No, we're just going back to the station for break."

"Why don't you come in and have drink?"

"Yes, too many women in there, I'm outnumbered." said the bloke in an effeminate tone, holding his cigarette, mimicking the same stance as the blond.

Pete looked back at me and his eyes said 'shall we'?

I shrugged my shoulders

"Yes, come on in and have a drink," said the brunette.

We didn't need too much encouragement. I turned the volume up on the radio just in case we were called and we might hear it over the music, popped the switch for the hazard lights, and then climbed out of the cab.

The only drink they had left was Babycham and we were given a bottle each. Mull of Kintyre was playing.

The place was a mess; streamers and the remnants of party poppers were all over the floor. The wash basins along the far wall were piled up with empty cans and bottles.

Plastic tumblers sat on every conceivable surface that would hold them. I didn't envy the person who had to clean this place up.

The shop was full of seriously attractive women. They were all pissed of course, but happy pissed, and it made a nice change from the piss heads we normally came into contact with.

We stayed for about twenty minutes before deciding that we were pushing our luck about taking so long to get back to station.

We thanked them for their hospitality, had a few goodbye kisses from two blonds, one brunette and a red head and made our way back to station.

The plan was to sneak in the back entrance from Belmont Road. We wouldn't tell Charlie we were back on station. If asked we would blame each other saying that each of us thought the other had told control.

It was half past three when we finally got back onto station. We were amazed to see all the other crews were back in too. This was highly unusual; it must have been the quietest New Year's Eve shift that I had ever worked. Better still, it meant that we would now be last out on a call if got busy again. Pete and I slept in the back of our Ambulance and woke just in time for the day shift to take over. No one ever asked where we had got to through the night.

Days off duty were categorised as 'free days' and 'rest days' so if I had two days off, the first day would be a free day and the second was a rest day. This would define the rate of pay we would get if we worked overtime on any of our days off. If I worked a 'free day' I would be paid time and a half, if I worked a 'rest' day I would be paid double time. So when overtime was offered, we tended to jump at the chance, particularly if it was for a full shift on a rest day, which meant being paid for sixteen hours instead of eight.

Pete and I were asked if we wanted to do a night shift on our rest day at Quarry Street station. It wasn't so much an Ambulance station, more a corrugated tin shed next to the training school.

We jumped at the chance with extra money being the incentive. Besides that, it was a quiet station so we wouldn't be working too hard for the money. It was quite possible that we wouldn't get called out at all.

When I arrived at Quarry Street, it brought back pleasant memories of my cadet years. It had been ten years since I had first walked through the front door of the building. This time though, the main training school part of the building was in darkness and I entered through a side door near to the Ambulance garage, which took me into the crew mess room.

Pete had arrived before me and had the kettle on for a cup of tea. The television was on and there was a roaring coal fire burning in the fire place. It was a very cosy atmosphere inside, considering the cold night outside.

There was a door in the mess room that led out into the foyer of the building and then into the training school area, but this was normally kept closed to stop prying cadets from coming in and disturbing a dozing ambulance crew.

After completing our vehicle and equipment checks, we settled into the arm chairs in front of the fire. There wasn't anything interesting on the television, so it was switched off and replaced by radio Luxemburg.

I felt this was probably the best time to tell Pete that I had decided to apply for the vacant rank 7 post in control, on Charlie's shift. My ultimate plan was to eventually get further promotion to a rank 6 Station Officer.

I didn't want to stay in control for too long, as I had no intention of spending the rest of my service being cooped up in a control room. I'd done enough of that as a cadet.

After telling him, I got the impression that Pete was a little disappointed with my decision as it would mean he would have to work with a new colleague, or worse still, work with a succession of relief staff.

It was generally known that if you got on with your crew mate, the job became a lot easier, just as it had been for Pete and I.

I just felt a new environment, a new position, a different job to what I was doing now might change things, plus it would mean better pay.

Two hours had passed since we started our shift and it was now one in the morning and we still hadn't turned a wheel. This was money for old rope! The armchairs were comfortable, the fire in the hearth was now a warm red glow and we both must have dozed off to sleep.

We both woke and sat up with a start. I didn't know how long we had been asleep, but the sound of a slamming door had brought us quickly to our senses.

"What the fuck was that?" said Pete. I was about to say the same thing.

There are three floors in the Quarry Street building with several rooms on each floor, and it just sounded as if someone had slammed a door on the top floor. In the stillness of the night, the noise reverberated throughout the building.

Only a few seconds had passed when there was an almighty crashing sound coming from the top room of the building, followed almost instantly by the sound of other doors being opened and then slammed shut, but it was the speed at which they were being slammed and the fact that they were getting closer by the second, almost as if someone had started at the top of the building and had run down the stairs, slamming doors on the way. But the speed at which this was happening wasn't humanly possible.

Pete and I stared at each other, eyes wide open, trying to make sense out of what was happening. No words were spoken as we both leaped out of our chairs and headed for the door and outside. By the time we reached the door, the sounds had reached the foyer area of the building. Neither of us looked back.

I suspect that Pete was the same, but my heart was pounding and I was shaking as we got into the Ambulance and high tailed it up the street. We parked up a few hundred yards away and sparked up a cigarette each. We were still shaking.

"What the hell happened there?" I said, my hand continuing to shake as I drew on the cigarette.

"Fuck knows," said Pete. "I'm not going back in there again though."

After five minutes or so we had managed to calm down, but the problem now was we would have to tell control over the radio why we were not on station and wouldn't be for the rest of the shift.

I checked my watch which told me it was four o'clock and just three hours to go before the end of the shift. I plucked up the courage to call control on the radio and tried to explain that there had been some strange goings on in the building and that we would be remaining in the vehicle for the rest of the shift.

There was a few minutes silence before the control called us back.

"Was it the slamming of doors?" asked Stan the controller.

Pete and I looked at each other; it seemed we were not the first ones to experience this.

I told the controller that it was, and then we turned the heater up and spent the rest of the night in the Ambulance.

27

In May 1979 I applied for and got promotion as a rank 7 officer in the control room.

I was working with Charlie, my old shift leader, together with Tommy and George. They were pleasant enough to work with, but I knew after just a few weeks in my new position that I wanted to be back on the road. I'd made a poor decision.

I felt cramped and stifled in the control room, I didn't like working as a glorified telephone operator, because basically that was what the entire job was about. It was just like being back in the cadets again, only this time I had a silver pip on my epaulette. The increase in pay didn't really compensate for the thrill of being on the road.

I pleaded with the chief officer, almost begged, to go back on the road to my old shift, but I was denied, the rule being that I couldn't, in effect demote myself back to Ambulance crew.
It seemed that I had burned my bridges, there was no going back.

Two life changing things happened to me in 1979. I left the Ambulance service to join British Midland Airways as an air steward. I had been toying with the idea of applying to the airline ever since Pete and I had made that trip to London and taken a flight back to Liverpool. But that's all it had remained at that time, an idea. However, when I found myself feeling imprisoned in the control room, I turned the idea into reality.

I was excited about starting in my new job, it was a new future, but saddened at the thought of leaving all my work colleagues behind, they had become like family over the years.

On my last day in the Ambulance service, a group of us had gone to the Queens pub on Queens Drive to have a few farewell drinks. Even Charlie came, who I had never seen step inside a pub since I had known him. He presented me with a pewter tankard as a leaving memento and apologised that he hadn't had the time to get it engraved.

I did have a fondness for Charlie; he was a kind, gentle and honourable man, who had looked after me in my early days with the service. I would miss him. Sadly I was never to see him again. He passed away a few years later.

Pete was at the pub too. He was one of the first to know that I had secured the job at the airline and he had painted a picture on canvas, in oils, of an aircraft in the BMA livery. He presented it to me in the pub. I would not see Pete again until thirty years later.

The second thing that happened to me in 1979, was meeting Yvonne, who I would eventually marry.

I left the Queens pub and drove back to my flat with mixed emotions, sad to leave a job I had loved to do, yet an air of excitement about new beginnings, a future of being paid to fly in aeroplanes to exotic places.

Printed in Great Britain
by Amazon.co.uk, Ltd.,
Marston Gate.